BE

It's truly wonderful that *BE* has arrived to guide, to inspire, to teach; a gift from Shirlee on the essence of what life is all about. As a Master Teacher, Shirlee explains profound truths in simple ways. She understands the keys to the mysteries of the life we are all looking for. With a deep and comprehensive knowledge of Spiritual Laws, as taught by all cultures, Shirlee synthesizes, weaves, and enlightens our paths with timeless wisdom.
— *Barbara J. Morel, High School Teacher*

Sometimes we get to a point where we think there is not much left to learn about our spiritual life—but if we are fortunate—we find that there is a teacher with insights and knowledge that we have yet to explore, a teacher who takes us to the outer realms of the spiritual universe. Shirlee Hall has done that with her new book, *BE*. She enriches our minds, our spirits and our souls, and brings us an inner peace, a knowing, the gift of feeling a oneness with the universe and with God.
— *Mary A. Yelton, President & CEO, Accu-Rate Traffic Service, Inc.*

I have been an elementary school teacher for 34 years and I appreciate a great teacher. The clarity and enlightenment I received from reading Shirlee's first book, *Circle of Light,* changed my life completely. Her new book has greatly inspired me, and given me more reasons to strive to live a life of love and forgiveness. The words help me to keep my eyes on God's presence, and let spirit transform me so my mind is opened to endless possibilities. This new book is a great gift to humanity.
— *Peggy McCaffray*

Shirlee is a beautiful and loving light who has come to generously and selflessly share her wisdom for our inner healing. Her message teaches us that we are all healers who can help each other, although in order to heal others, we need to heal ourselves. This healing is in the form of connection to Spirit, the light of love and compassion that we show ourselves as well as others, the inner knowing that we lovingly give to others, and in so doing, we give to ourselves. Hearing Shirlee teach is like a coming home to an inner knowing, that is reawakened by Truth.
— *Diane Therese Miller, M.Ed., L.Ac., Health & Healing Wellness Center*

Shirlee speaks to your heart from her heart. She is a remarkable woman

who demonstrates truth and Light. In the last fifteen years that I have known her, I have read her other inspiring works and attended many classes. She is an awesome being who 'walks the talk'. She has always taught Purity, Truth, Unconditional Love and the Path to Self Discovery of our true identity as individualized Spirit. In her latest book, the reader will journey the path of self discovery and empowerment.
— *Dawn Lamprecht, R.N.*

I have known Shirlee Hall for the past thirty years, and have acted as a volunteer administrator in her spiritual organization, The Circle of Light. I have witnessed many spiritual healings of the physical, mental, emotional and spiritual bodies of members of her organization, and the innumerable healings she has personally performed. Shirlee is indeed a messenger of God to bring the truth to people of their own spiritual reality, the divine connection we all have as children of God. This long awaited book is here for our awakening that the time is now for all Souls to become aware of their purpose on Earth, and what to do about it.
— *Ed Kent, A.R.E. Study Group Leader (retired)*

Shirlee has an amazing talent for healing and solving spiritual problems. This latest work will be of great value to the healing of ourselves and our planet.
— *Jack Kuncl, Musician*

Shirlee Hall's teachings come from a desire to know the Truth behind the illusion we call life. She has always taught me to question life and to search for my answers deep within my God Self. 'Seek and you shall find.' Shirlee has done this in this book.
— *Dawn Mucha, Licensed Massage Therapist*

Shirlee draws you in with her contagious love and pure joy. She demonstrates that life is full of miracles when you put God above all else, and realize there are no short cuts. She helps you realize that you can go further than you had ever thought possible.
— *Jan Dresbach Leahy, Engineering Recruiter*

Shirlee has been my Spiritual Teacher since 1971. Her father introduced us and my life changed. Shirlee's teachings on Soul Progression and

other aspects of Higher Truth explain every mystery. The world has been longing for this book.
— *Kristin Knudsen, Social Activist*

Shirlee Hall generously initiated me into the Ancient Wisdom teachings way back in the early 1970s. She has always been a dedicated teacher and messenger of Divine Spirit. Her wealth of knowledge and personal experiences go back to her childhood. Myself along with many others have been inspired by her to listen to and be guided by our inner Divinity. Never wavering from her mission, Shirlee is devoted to bringing God into the lives of everyone she encounters, with love and compassion. My work as a Spiritual Astrologer has been influenced by my knowing and loving her.
— *Dave Gunning*

Ms. Hall is that rare person who combines creativity, literary talent and spiritual awareness from a heart-centered perspective. She has been an outstanding teacher for me.
— *Caroline A. Loose, Ph.D., Director, Infinity Healing Center*

When I was in my sixties and living in Wisconsin, I would drive to Chicago to participate in one of Shirlee's workshops or she would come to my area. Now that I am in my eighties and living in Alabama, she helps me through the Internet. Shirlee seems like an angel sent here to help us in our evolution.
— *Dolores Steib, Seeker of Truth*

Shirlee has been a light, and a treasured friend through the many years I have known her. In today's world, people look for a quick fix and easy solutions, but nothing of true spiritual value comes overnight, unless you have commitment and devotion to God. Shirlee has shown us steps to enlightenment, but won't hold our hand. It's our work to do, and she still loves us when we screw up. Everyone has their own pace, on the same path. That is what she has taught me, and why I love her.
— *Nelson Patterson*

Finally a book that brings us closer to the spiritual knowledge we need and desire and presents it in words that we can understand and relate to,

this is Shirlee's gift to us in her new book, BE. She has made my understanding and studies with Native Americans even more powerful and I am so honored to call her a friend.
— *Irma Petrovich*

I always enjoy Shirlee Hall's lectures and presentations because she is focused on helping others connect with their own divinity. She offers practical suggestions and advice in overcoming the obstacles one faces on the path to higher self awareness. She encourages others to reach higher and employs a lighthearted and compassionate approach in all she does. Shirlee is a wonderful teacher and a source of great wisdom for humanity.
— *Dixie Arnold, Human Resources Specialist*

I was brought to a meeting where Shirlee was speaking 21 years ago, where she openly expressed her inner longing for God. I heard and felt the passion, the love, and understood the yearning completely. I had never heard anyone talk like that before, especially in public. That meeting changed me. That passion for God is a bond that remains between us to this day. Through her writings, this longing can be passed to others, to help in their transformation.
— *Judi Joergens*

My mother's love, devotion and passion for God are unsurpassed and have been a marvel to witness. I invite readers to share her intimacy with the Divine through her book, Be: Embracing the Mystery.
— *Rhonda Johnson Ellis*

Shirlee is such a beautiful and pure soul. Her words and efforts have helped so many heal. Her style is simple, yet effective. She certainly helped me find the Light when I was much younger and searching.
— *Steve Krejcik, Coptic Minister*

BE
Embracing the Mystery

Shirlee Hall

Foreword by Reverend Richard Billings

Be: Embracing the Mystery. Copyright © 2007 Shirlee Hall. Printed and bound in the United States of America. All rights reserved. No part of this book may be reproduced or transmitted in any form or by any means, electronic or mechanical, including photocopying, recording, or by an information storage and retrieval system without permission in writing from the publisher, except by a reviewer who may quote brief passages in a review. Published by RealityIs Books, an imprint of RealityIsBooks.com, Inc., 309 E. Rand Road, Unit 313, Arlington Heights, IL 60004. Tel: 866-534-3366, Email: publish@RealityIsBooks.com.

Although the author and publisher have made every effort to ensure the accuracy and completeness of information contained in this book, no responsibility is assumed for errors, inaccuracies, omissions, or any inconsistency herein. Any slights of people, places, or organizations are unintentional.

First printing 2007
EAN 978-0-9791317-3-8, ISBN 0-9791317-3-1

Cover design by Karl Petrovich

ATTENTION Corporations, Universities, Colleges, and Professional Organizations: Quantity discounts are available on bulk purchases of this book for educational, gift purposes, or as premiums. Special books or book excerpts can also be created to fit specific needs. For information, please contact RealityIs Books, an imprint of RealityIsBooks.com, Inc., 309 E. Rand Road, Unit 313, Arlington Heights, IL 60004. Tel: 866-534-3366, Email: publish@RealityIsBooks.com.

Messenger of the gods.

THIS WORK OF LOVE
IS DEDICATED TO NATURE,
THE SPIRIT OF TRUTH,
AND MY CELESTIAL FRIENDS,
WITHOUT WHOM I COULD NOT
HAVE DONE THIS

Photo by Irma Petrovich at Ludwig II's Castle Nymphenburg in Munich, Germany.

Acknowledgments

During the past twenty-five years I have had the love and assistance of many hundreds of special souls to whom I would like to express my gratitude. These dear friends are an integral part of an expanding circle of light.

My deepest appreciation and gratitude to Judi Joergens, Dawn Lamprecht, Jan Dresbach Leahy, Peggy McCaffray, Edward Kent, Karl Petrovich, and Robert Petrovich who have provided the means to publish this timeless book.

I wish to express my deep love and respect for my late parents, John and Mildred Hall, who lived their truth in love and action.

And finally, I want to express my love and gratitude to my son and his wife, Steven and Jeni Johnson; my daughter, Rhonda Johnson Ellis; and my son, Adam Dunlap, who all understood and supported my aspirations to be of service to humanity.

About the Author

As a direct result of an extraordinary healing experience in 1971, Shirlee Hall's life was dramatically transformed. The gifts of the Spirit became a daily experience. Celestial beings, visions of Light, higher wisdom teachings, a healing power, supranatural phenomena and most important, a conscious communion with God became a living reality. Her first book, Circle of Light, written under the name of Shirlee Dunlap, was a collection of personal revelations.

For twenty-five years, Shirlee lived life as a healing transparency, teacher, author, spiritual consultant and public speaker giving to others what she had received. Her personal goal was self-mastery. One momentous day, she suddenly left a day job, a successful lecture and workshop career, and an active social life to honor and fully uncover the Spirit within.

Shirlee has returned to public life after seven years of personal discipline, intense study, contemplation, profound meditation and prayer to help correct a major identity problem in human consciousness. Her desire is to inspire seekers to remember who they spiritually are and receive directly from God. Through the urgings of those who have experienced her unspeakable joy and inner understanding, this book of love has been written.

Table of Contents

Foreword xvii
Introduction xix

Part I

1. An Invitation 25
2. Invisible Friends 37
3. The Other Side 48
4. The Science of Light 59
5. The Importance of Vibration 70
6. The Higher Self 79
7. Cycles of Brightness 87
8. The Past Colors the Future 97
9. Ancient Schools and Teachers 106
10. A Developed Will 115
11. The Prize 125
12. Seed Thoughts 135
13. Teaching Tools 146
14. The Actor 155

Part II

15. Special Moments 167
16. The Cause Behind Effect 174
17. Steps 183
18. The Eye of God 191
19. Understanding 202
20. Fact or Fiction 212
21. Character 222
22. Love Energy 230
23. The Emptying 238
24. The Filling 250
25. Truth 258
26. Magical Moments 268
27. A Healer 278
28. To Be 291

Afterword 301

Foreword

It is my privilege to support the work and writings of my Spirit Friend, Shirlee Hall, in her revealing work, *BE: Embracing the Mystery*. It is a timeless story of conscious evolution and spiritual awakening.

Time has a way of providing for humanity through enlightened individuals "the mystery hidden for generations and ages." Shirlee has proved her inner Truth in her own life. Infinite mind has blessed her with a powerful intuition and receptive awareness of both the invisible and visible world. This knowing of the connecting link has made it possible for her to live simultaneously in both as One.

Shirlee is a living prayer expressing her Divine nature by being a True Light in the world. Her receptivity has opened the door of illumination and has inaugurated a magnificent unifying ministry of love.

For all those needing support on the spiritual path, this book, by the instruction contained within its pages, offers insight to stay focused as we are stimulated by an inner message. Each and all reading this material are given the rich opportunity to recognize their Divine potential and become a willing instrument for God's goodness to flow into the world for transformation, as we together create "the new heaven and new earth." Thank you, dear friend, for opening the way for us to travel with you in thought and feeling.

Reverend Richard Billings
Unity Church of Oak Park
Oak Park, Illinois, 2007

Introduction

Everyone has a story to tell. The individual story cannot be separated from the collective story. It is all One. This is a valid reason to learn what truth is and then take action for the sake of physical evolution and for the sake of the soul. Through learning from the past and living consciously in the moment, we create a brilliant future. My chronicle has as its foundation a personal connection with the Divine. The connection is alive with holistic thought forms, inspiration, knowledge, transformation and healings that communicate Living Light, the geometries of the soul. The communication is fully experienced within the mind of my higher Self and not subject to any retinal image. The story of all souls is a spiritual liberation where we eventually go beyond the "closed structure" of the physical world.

An important step forward in not suppressing the spirit is to choose to make a commitment to seek our inner Self. I believe, if given a chance, human beings can be magnificent. To evolve, changes are required. Real change begins when we successfully incorporate a high degree of peace, order and harmony within as well as without. Truthful living is experienced when we are willing and ready to leave the self-created abyss of neglect, soul ignorance and disbelief behind. As we struggle between the needs of modern world issues and the needs of the soul, we must be willing to explore truth. Truth is power.

To survive as a race, we must awaken from the sleep of forgetfulness. We can no longer indulge in the leisure of being ordinary. By offering glimpses into my spiritual journey, hopefully you will be inspired with the truth and wonder that is available to every soul. You will be encouraged to think in divine pictures, a non-linear way of thought. The divine language is a linkage between heaven and earth.

It is in our power to regenerate ourselves as well as the Earth. To be successful, we must understand the science of creation and our relationship to the Whole. The Whole is not only that which is seen in our world; it is tangible life in other worlds as well as the invisible worlds of a vast hierarchy of creativity. To joyfully transform the physical into the holy and infuse the holy into the mundane, conscious action is required.

Action is successful when it is supported by the power and knowledge of Light. We receive knowledge and stop violating spirit when we are energized and aligned with the Great Work.

Humanity has been duped mentally, physically and materially. We can no longer afford to wear blindfolds. Hopefully, the words herein will offer a clear perspective of humankind's identity, potential and eventual victory. There are steps we can take now to create a future world of light, love, beauty and truth. We can move forward with confidence and understanding when we are willing to be open to truth by deliberately seeking and daily living it. We are then able to move forward with confidence and understanding.

Let us use free will to create harmony and radiate truth. We are not alone. What we choose affects all life, seen or unseen, known or unknown. As we do not see the Sun in the dark of the night, the many do not see Divine Light in the midst of darkness. The beauty of our journey is the ability to be aware of a loftier reality when we put our mind to it.

Throughout these pages you will read about the importance of making a conscious contact with the energy of the Ineffable Light. The Light has mysterious qualities that produce unaccountable effects. It is a true science that exposes the illusion. It is magic in the sense that it goes beyond the physical or material. Soul faculties must be sufficiently developed to perceive a subtle reality. Workable suggestions are offered to help mold the mind to that point in consciousness where you will joyfully experience the eternal Self. This leap in consciousness will increase personal energy and move you into a permanent intimacy with the One Supreme Indescribable Creator. My intention is to offer hope and give proven suggestions that will enable you to understand and know how to work with the Light using an educated mind that comprehends a higher wisdom and love.

As a higher reality is revealed, you will be eager to make spiritual Light an actuality in your life, if it is not already. As I was writing the above, a recollection of a past practical revelation came to mind. My children and I were staying in a cabin high on a hill at a church summer camp in Wisconsin. A long dirt path led up to our "tree house." There was a sharp drop by the side of the cabin and the treetops from below surrounded us. One night we joined other campers in the valley for a social activity. It was late when the program ended. Without a flashlight and not having my glasses, the return walk to the cabin became a challenge.

As the three of us were struggling up the hill in total darkness, I was thinking how nice it would be if I could actually see where I was going. Immediately, the entire area became lit as if the noonday sun was shining full force. The landscape looked like ethereal waves of light. I clearly saw everything and everyone. Excitedly, I asked the children, "Do you see the Light?" No one had. For one startling moment, the opaque veil of illusion covering limited physical sight was removed and another reality was exposed. An existence of beauty and purity was revealed through an inward flash. The intelligent dimension of Light obliged my wish to see, making the path ahead safely visible with its brilliance.

As you join us on this journey of love, you will be eager to expand God's Light as an actuality in your life. It is our life force. Together, let us be free from collective mesmerism and move past being a slave to spiritual ignorance and being controlled by the physical substance of a passing world. The journey is about our original spiritual blueprint and how to walk trustingly through the inner door and reclaim it. The view offered is through personal experience, interpretation and a continuation of the ancient wisdom science applied in our world today.

The science of Spirit re-energizes and empowers us through lost and rejected knowledge. Before we can move forward, we must accept. This is a call for a renewal of our culture. The task of evolution is our responsibility. It depends on our spiritual reality and sacred unity.

Learn to love truth for its own sake. Allow the soul to express freely and revelation becomes the disclosure of the soul. May the words within lift the veil of forgetfulness offering hope, comfort and truth to the inquiring mind. Great is the soul of man. It believes in itself. It calls the Light its own. Its beauty is immense. The life force within is the selfless love that circulates throughout creation. May God fire your heart with joy and set you free to claim the hidden treasures of your true identity as spirit in form.

— *Shirlee*

Part I

BE

What needs to heal is a sense of separation
Suffering ceases with acceptance of Self
To be is to know Self as all life, regardless of form
To understand is to be one with It
To be one is to be
Truth is simple
This is the Key, the Way and the Word.

S.

Chapter One
An Invitation

I was born remembering what it was like living on the "other side," the side most people refer to as Heaven. The memory of who we really are has provided a personal life where the sacred is a natural experience and the longing to bring the sublime into the objective world has been uppermost in my mind. To remember why we are in the flesh and our purpose on Earth is not an easy mantle to wear. Being aware of multiple realities simultaneously is an ongoing challenge. I am sharing my experiences and explaining to you, the reader, a higher reality as I remember and continue to experience it. It is the same truth given to us throughout the ages by beings that also remembered and lived their truth right here on Earth.

As the blank pages piled in front of me waited for the words of ancient truths, a distinct Voice offered a title for a timeless message. The Voice said, "*BE.*" I knew in that moment, the hour had arrived. The souls of humanity are ready for the ancient wisdom teaching that spoke of union between science and religion, heaven and earth. We have been lost and seek Reality. As you study the words, allow yourself to forget that you are a human and instead realize your great spiritual light. We are the force of Light in form. Now is the opportunity to embrace the mystery and be free at last.

Throughout the book, I intertwine the ancient mysteries regarding God and the universal teachings of Love, Law and Light, angelic beings, and our own divinity and relationship to all life, both seen and unseen, known and unknown. The ultimate truth is the same truth, which the great ones have tried to give us. It is impossible to put it fully into words, but I will do my best. My experiences in the Light are daily. Hopefully, by the time you have finished reading my story, you will be able to feel what can never be fully explained in words. The journey can begin at any age: you are the Light.

Due to mass media awareness and the ability to receive instant world news, attentive people are aware that something is truly amiss on our planet. How do we resolve the imbalances and negative influences prevalent everywhere? How does humankind awaken a limited consciousness regarding spirituality and the purpose of life? What have we forgotten? There is a Higher Intelligence that will help us redeem our inner life through a willingness to reconnect to a subtle energy that is hidden within. We are entering a new cycle, and by aligning consciousness with a field of intelligence of a Higher Order, we can be whole again. This chronicle is about the return of the Light of God to Earth.

To move out of the Age of Darkness, we require truth, understanding and a capacity to really love. Humanity has experienced great difficulty in maintaining itself at a spiritual level. The rise and fall of races, civilizations, countries and souls have brought us into the present cycle, which has at times felt like a downward spiral of illusion and spiritual ignorance. Any sensitive and compassionate person observing the corruption and selfishness of the world consciousness will question the fate of humankind and ask what have we become? What happens to Earth and life belongs to the development of human light.

There are many brilliant minds that have revealed answers to the mysteries of creation. Today as yesterday, there exist souls who are looking for an understanding as to who they are and what they were before the world was made. What is our true face? Are we moving from existence to existence? To be able to build a foundation of truth, we must allow ourselves to be free of dogma and ecclesiastical captivity. We must stop limiting our imagination and finally accept the truth that everything we seek is already in our presence, and not outside our Self.

Who are we? The temporary roles we play are like veils hiding the core of the inner wise being. They may or may not reflect real identity. The roles may cause division. Division stops and unity begins when we explore the truth of spiritual identity and how it can live a grander role that more perfectly reflects the truth of who we are. Imagine a circle. Place a point in the center of the circle. Your real identity is the point in the center. Along the periphery, the outer rim, are the many roles that you play, pretending to be someone else. All roles are temporary and will eventually end.

Throughout these pages suggestions will be offered as to how to distance yourself from the many roles and discard them like garments that do not reflect the "real" you. Eventually, you will stand in purity, free of all hindrances and pretence, and joyfully reconnect with who you were before entering flesh. You will learn what life can be like when you rediscover and live the inner and true identity.

The indwelling spirit is a child of God. It encourages us to weave a pattern of transformation, gnosis and extended life. We are currently living in a period of change when the return of the Light and the revival of cosmic and physical energy will make Its Self known. Resurrection and a cycle in eternity that is golden are ready to unfold. The seals of the cosmic mysteries have been removed in my own journey through exquisite and direct experiences with God. The journey is the same for all returning souls. It is an alchemical process, an intuitive activity. To receive, we must first have the desire to give. When we have true desire, we can recreate ourselves into a likeness of beauty and Light. My offering is an inside view of what to expect when many of the surface roles are no longer in control and the Divine Presence is an active part of life.

Although the focus of this message is on the subject of spiritual identity, it is important to also look at the world situation from more than one view. What happens within manifests in the without. If we are to achieve unity, the two cannot be separated. It is helpful to understand outside influences. Zodiacal cycles are part of the outside influences. We are in the process of leaving the Piscean Age and moving gradually into the Aquarian Age. How does a cyclic change affect life? We are exposed to another form of energy that accompanies the passage of one Age to another.

The collective consciousness appears as if it is shipwrecked. It is a sad truth that man must be shaken to his depths to rise to great heights. In this truth, we have hope eternal. History has shown us that the power of the invisible Spirit penetrates the hard shell hiding the soul and spirit when we are severely challenged. It is our choice to see what we see, feel what we feel, and hear what we hear.

We have four great known races and within them exist many subraces. Every race, civilization and living creature experiences a beginning, its maturity, and eventual decline. Hope is within the truth that beyond the narrow barriers of race and creed, we are all an integral part of the One God. As we strive for knowledge of our origin, evolution and destiny, it becomes obvious that there is a great diversity among men. We come from the same spiritual Source, but our stage or level of mental and spiritual evolution differs.

Humankind as a whole is still in its childhood compared to the deeds of God-realized men and women who have come to Earth like stars in the sky. The magnificent spiritual impulses of the past live hidden in our souls. Man has understood the universal laws imperfectly and thus they are abused. We are free to climb higher by our own efforts. This will only become a reality when we are no longer a slave to unbridled passions and a limited intellect.

We are physically born into the world with vague recollections, mysterious impulses and divine feelings. As humans, we live two distinct lives alternatively. When we are physically awake, the personality is usually the one in control. While the body sleeps, the soul lives its own existence in the invisible worlds of Light. Reading further, you will discover how the two lives can be brought consciously and harmoniously together, enriching the human experience with the Divine.

Real faith is an inner fidelity of the soul to itself. When we actively seek the luminous world of spirit, we unite morality, science and religion. Intuition is developed. It is through the medium of intuition that we receive truth. Rare souls are born blessed. They bring with them gifts of the Spirit resulting from a past as well as a present desire for eternal love, beauty and truth. The ultimate path is to evolve through purification of the body, mind and soul. As a result of a conscious connectedness with God and the development of moral disciplines, an opening occurs where the soul unites with Wisdom and Love. Powers are received and intuition heightened. Normality becomes a journey living in balance between two worlds. Remembering, you find your Self.

If you choose to find balance, light is offered to your heart so you can begin a new journey. Destination is the same for evolving souls, but paths may differ. The spiritual path is not always graced with pink roses, although they may appear in visions as a heavenly gift of love, reminding us of an ever-present magic. Inwardly, the rose blooms as a reminder of the Supreme Creator's power and presence. It is this subtle richness, an intimacy with the Divine, that is our guide, friend, teacher, protector and true love.

A river winds behind my home. The woods nearby are filled with wildlife. Further upstream there is a park, which is basically undetected by humans. A heightened sensitivity is our reward when we spend quality time in nature. Nature quickens spiritual evolution. An Indian proverb says: "Walk softly upon the Earth, for she is sacred." To take time out from the busyness of life and surrender to a softer form of consciousness while tapping into the vast reservoir of the Unknown will bring forth the eternal Being within. In the sacred intimacy, we allow the spirit to be inspired and ascend into a space without boundaries. I am pleased you and I have partnered as we explore the sublime and discover the true savior, the spirit within.

Because mankind is collectively vibrating in a discordant state of imbalance, suffering is the norm. What is at the crux of humanity's suffering is a serious identity problem. If this were not true, humanity would be collectively happy and not be restrained by emotions and fear. Understanding of the meaning of life and our eternal identity is sorely missing in the thinking mind of man. It is time an awakening occurs.

All bodily and psychic suffering is a lack of harmony among the composite elements of a human being. How can there be harmony if people lack understanding? What is it that we must wake up to in order to survive as noble beings instead of a miserable humanity sowing seeds of discontent? My purpose is to offer an overview of Reality as the ancient wisdom teachers lived it, with suggestions as to how all of us can actively bring heaven to earth as our personal experience. The path of spiritual evolution is demanding as well as liberating. To move forward, truth must lead. We begin with knowledge focusing on the ancient teachings. The suggestions have been proven as transforming and life altering. They are similar to the sap of a living tree.

First, we must stop trying to save the illusion. The illusion that I refer to is the state of mind that unenlightened souls have created through spiritual ignorance, forgetfulness and a strong sense of separation from the Divine. Humanity behaves as if it is wearing a straightjacket. How can the Source of life, the Indescribable and Unlimited One, be alive in us if we are not fully awakened and cannot separate the true from the false? This is why it is important that the veils covering the spirit be removed one by one.

In the midst of forgetfulness, there are brave souls who meditate, contemplate, love the Divine, and do their best to serve life. They experience intuitive glimpses into the invisible worlds, both positive and negative. These souls live on trust and faith even though many of their inward glimpses of reality may take years to actually manifest and bear fruit.

In some ways, it can be challenging to handle the nonsense experienced in the human scene if we are no longer deluded. To feel truth requires silence. The common man is not interested in changing his confused and erroneous thinking. Many people are still caught in teachings that have been altered and remain in denial of their own true worth. False identification is corruptive. It is a betrayal of the inner spirit. The consequences of spiritual ignorance are sickness, suffering, and attachment. Darkness, ignorance and harmful choices exist alongside the radiant Light.

Humans lack a sense of the Sacred. To realize holiness, consciousness must be pure. It is within the eternal identity that we find a heightened life, knowledge, love and peace that are real and lasting. When we identify with falsity and lack, we corrupt our spiritual energy. The fault lies in identifying solely with matter, the appearance world. Once a seeker grasps the difference between the ego-personality and the spiritual individuality, he can pull himself out of the abyss of turmoil and utter craziness.

There is a time proven way to heal and elevate consciousness and transform it from a state of imbalance to one of equilibrium. Meditation is one of the answers. It will transform your life. Meditation will help diminish the weaknesses of the personality and increase the power of the spirit individuality. At some point in the journey, the higher Self must be granted the lead over the personality. A high initiation is the subduing and healing of the human personality and the awakening of the spirit within.

When the process of integration begins to materialize, the seeker is blessed in new ways such as hearing guidance from an angelic Voice. The heavenly voice offers love and suggestions. A good example is the message I clearly heard when faced with a past challenging issue. It said, "Change the conditions." Contemplating the suggestion, I was shocked to realize that I had not only been placing conditions on myself, I was also placing conditions on how I perceived and interacted with the Divine. We always have a choice to follow the inner directions of love or to ignore them. The Supreme Creator, the universe, and truth are open ended. We must also be.

As the veils are gradually dropped, the seeker realizes that the higher Self is the final authority. He must learn how to distance himself from projections whether they are good or bad. Accepting blindly what others tell us creates programming that repeatedly places limitations on higher understanding. Disorder is a common result when we allow the personality-ego to take control of thoughts, words and actions. It is also easier to be a laggard and simply go along with the crowd than think and discover what is our own truth. It is never too late to change direction. Thankfully, the mind is one aspect of our identity we can change. A new direction often brings to us a process that creates a radical transformation of our entire being.

If we are not in touch with or expressing the higher invisible Self, human limitations act as veils covering the inner teacher. Due to weakness of character, the personality creates a no win existence. When we begin to see clearly, we realize how ridiculously mesmerized mankind has become. Every human being is an eternal spark of Light, an emanation of the Great Light. Souls remain imprisoned in a flesh form until the true spiritual identity is rediscovered. When we finally accept and awaken to the eternal identity as a spirit temporarily using a physical body, we are in a position where the higher nature will express freely in present time.

From habit, conditioning, and the stereotypes created, the illusion is fed and judged by what is seen and heard. Eventually, the personality will see through the façade. As we awaken to the spiritual Self, it is a typical reaction to feel shaken and horrified by the lie we have been living. It feels like the true Self has been in exile. We have chosen to live as a human; now we begin to explore how to live without limits.

When a soul finally awakens to the depth of truth, it realizes with utter dismay that it has been placing limitations on the important things, the things that make up what are referred to as consciousness, freedom and immortality. Humanity has not allowed the eternal divine spark to surface because of disbelief and restrictive conditions. What is required is a readiness to accept the truth that we are much grander than we think we are. The higher Self must first be firmly recognized and willingly embraced. Its acquaintance is made through will, effort, love and respect.

Acceptance manifests through understanding. Understanding creates a strong foundation on which we build a brighter, balanced and meaningful life. The wisdom teachings stress this truth. If we wish to live the amazing life of spirit in the flesh, we must remember and let ourselves feel love. And in remembering, we fall in love.

BE: Embracing the Mystery

To evolve, humanity will need to finally awaken and live the wisdom truths that illumined masters have freely given to seekers throughout history. Truth must take hold in the mind and feeling nature in order to evolve. The goal is to see clearly through the illusion; it is then that transformation and eventual freedom will manifest. Unnecessary suffering, lack and limitation are an ongoing experience because we try to liberate ourselves through the backdoor method. Stop trying to save the duality illusion, the mess humanity has created through selfishness and fear. Instead, walk through the front door; face the Light with trust and openness. To be a complete and divine human, learn how to integrate the higher with the lower. A reunion must take place with your roots. Proven suggestions are offered to help you celebrate life.

Self-denial on a grand scale is not to recognize or accept who you really are. You are not complete. You are not even fully human. In truth, spiritual identity is an evolving essence that came straight from the One God. It can be likened to an expanding energy field. The eternal Self has both masculine and feminine aspects. All the qualities of God are within the spirit as a seed waiting to be nourished. Inner unity is part of the oneness that connects all life. Why not invite Divine Intelligence into your life and rediscover the fullness and joy of who you really are? Why not be eagerly receptive and open to a lifegiving intimacy with the inner eternal Self? Why allow the sacred Light to be clothed in aging, disease, sorrow, lack, limitation and even death? Why not choose to think deeply as to how you can use intelligence, love and science to liberate the soul?

Firsthand experience is the teacher. What you know and experience intimately as your truth evolves individual consciousness. If you are willing and allow the mind to awaken from the dream of separation from the Supreme Source, you will have the power, through disciplined effort and love, to shake off the self-imposed hindrances and conditions that create endless misery and emptiness. Why should any soul remain chained to ignorance? Since we are the creators of the illusion, we have the power to destroy or neutralize the effects of its manifestation. Yes, the illusion is real in the human sense because we have given it permission to control and enslave us.

You have the inner strength to reclaim spiritual power and awaken to the eternal Divine. Why not make new choices and live as the eternal Self in joy and freedom? It is possible to be free in the midst of chaos. What is required is knowledge. The transformation will begin in earnest when individually you decide it is time to commit and willingly open the front door to God Consciousness. The goal of all spiritual exercises is to assist the soul to evolve and the spirit to express itself freely each day.

What is your truth? Is it the person you see in the mirror with limited understanding and power or is it the sacred invisible presence within waiting patiently to be recognized? Let us together expand inwardly, allowing the beauty of truth to manifest without like a swollen lotus bud. Fall in love with the Divine and you become alive. Be an outcast no more. Step forth for the sheer joy of it! It isn't the lower nature that has the rapturous moments. To accept and stand forth and be who you inwardly are will require change.

How do you change the conditions that bind you to the past? First, it helps to be aware of the great truth that you may be captive to erroneous beliefs. To be able to clearly see the areas where you may cause limitation requires facing issues held in the subconscious and conscious part of the mind. More often than not, we are oblivious to the fetters that bind. You may be so used to a condition that you adapt and assume that the condition is normal.

The ideal is to live an unconditional life where you are not solely dependent on appearances and false judgments. Why not do your own thinking and discover truth through a higher desire and effort? It is not wisdom to assume that everything one hears, reads and witnesses whether it be political, ecclesiastical, social or personal is absolute truth. This holds true for this material; you must prove for yourself what is true.

The majority of people live a way of life which is in contradiction to the scheme of Cosmic Intelligence. Why not put an end to this nonsense and rebel? What you will rebel against is an acceptance of mediocrity, your own weaknesses and laziness. It is time to rebel against the darkness that is damaging a true sense of reality and wake up to the Light that clarifies and heals. Rebel against the lower sense of self and overcome the illusion and reach others through example.

Spiritual maturity on your part will eventually open the door to a greater love and guidance from a Higher Source of Intelligence. You will benefit from developing a strong sense of discernment, belief and determination. The inward journey as Light unfolding will be smoother if you develop these qualities. Discernment looks deeply at everything. It is both intuition and reason working together as a solid team. Discernment is a valuable tool that assists in seeing clearly what has become a personal law in our lives and whether the law requires a drastic change of view. Belief removes doubt. It is our armor. It works hand in hand with a determination to succeed.

As you awaken more fully to reality, consciousness begins the transformation process. People in general have complacent minds and accept whatever they hear, read, or see. Few make a deliberate effort to think for themselves. When you are ready to make the decision to be the true inner Self consciously and physically, you will earnestly practice contemplative thought, prayer and meditation. Reprogram yourself through personal effort to remove all conditions that are working against your own God Realization.

The Tree of Life wisdom, is seeded into our flesh through the presence of our Spirit. Our higher true Self, the God seed within, will give us exactly what we are ready to learn, heal and release. It offers the pure radiance of truth in a way that will resonate as real. An evolving consciousness is sustained by the overcoming of the current personality whom we commonly accept as our identity. Ultimately, we move beyond the conditioning of masculine and feminine limitations. The ideal state of mind is reached when the masculine and feminine aspects blend as one unit of intelligent light.

No longer can any of us be oblivious to the groaning heard all over the world. Humanity is in pain and crying for real love and truth. Good change occurs for all of us when we are willing to open mind and heart to unlimited possibilities and allow the Light of a higher understanding to bless us. Why not develop the habit of receiving knowledge from a spiritual perspective, a loftier view? Surrender the human personality and bring forth the source of all life. Are you willing to look at restrictive patterns and reprogram your life according to Wisdom who beckons? I urge you to stop assuming that the outward disorder is the one and only true reality. It is a temporary school that offers classes in debt payment. Suffering feels like an expanding, consuming fire that for many never ceases.

A seeker is not destined to remain in the flames forever. There is a finer, subtler purification fire. It is the glorified White Fire of the higher celestial realms. As consciousness is elevated, wisdom choices are made. The true flame, Radiant Light, assists the seeker in removing himself from

An Invitation

the muck and mire by opening the mind and heart to infinite possibilities. Are you ready to pursue a deeper friendship with the inner Self? Are you ready to claim a relationship with the Divine and to know and feel what it is like to be wisdom filled and at peace?

By choosing the regenerative drama that takes place within self, we identify with action. We stimulate the necessary virtues and qualities of the higher Self and as a result are given the hidden manna visibly and tangibly that scripture describes. Manna is a state of consciousness that allows the seeker to taste the existence of the Divine. It is inner nourishment. The possibilities are endless. The mind is the bridge that connects the created physical world with the higher celestial creative world of Light.

In ancient days, truth referred to as the "mysteries" remained hidden because the collective consciousness was not ready to receive and understand. Although appearances are frequently bleak, we are collectively evolving towards a state of being where beauty and harmony will be experienced. There is an intelligent and perfect plan. Many years ago, I was blessed with a symbolic vision, which took form as a gigantic puzzle composed of dazzling White Light. The vision hovering in the air generated pure particles of subtle celestial energy. I watched in amazement as the various pieces of spirit luminosity gradually moved together to create a masterpiece representing the order of God's design and our destiny as enlightened beings. There is a higher plan for God's children, although it is rarely seen or understood through the physical senses. It is known as a direct intuitive experience.

I invite you to see both sides of your nature, human and divine. Seed thoughts will be planted. You will learn what it means to live freely as love. You are destined to be genuinely happy. Beauty is the higher nature, the spirit that will light the way. Would you like to know what your higher Self looks like? When you are ready, you will meet it face to face. It will happen in an unexpected moment. The first time I caught a glimpse of my eternal Self, I was sitting alone at the dining room table reading the morning newspaper. I became aware of a presence looking at me. To my surprise, an exquisite female figure stood before me in dazzling white light. She had a crown of diamonds on her head. Everything about her was radiant and glistening with an eternal beauty, even her eyelashes. In awe, I asked, "Who are you?" Divinity answered, "I am you." My ethereal guest was not a guest at all. It was the inner radiant Self revealing her presence to my conscious mind.

The higher Self is the real you. Everyone has one. It is Spirit hidden in form. It is up to you to bring it into the lower nature and live it in passion and love. You must have the desire to be free. Why not expand and enjoy the beauty, luster and divinity of who you really are? St. Paul, in the Epistle to the Corinthians, confirmed this truth in his statement, "There is a natural body and a spiritual body." The words herein will clearly describe the difference between matter and spirit. As we travel together on our journey of light, you will find your depth in the cohesive pattern of the soul's devolution and gradual evolution.

Chapter Two
Invisible Friends

There is an Arabic saying, "If you wish to know God, you must know yourself." As you learn to consciously identify with your divine nature, the greater is the joy of the soul. Once you choose to seek pleasure of a higher order, you breathe to a new rhythm, the door opens and the power and presence of God brings out the perfection and beauty of the sublime life. If there is a physical body, it stands to reason that there is a spiritual one. There cannot be materialization without the energy frequencies which allow for materialization. The physical form is connected to the energy of the higher Self. The typical human works and sees and feels only the common energy because he is caught within his own duality. Those who are psychically and spiritually sensitive experience glimpses of higher worlds and intelligence emanating a Light that goes beyond the conscious parameter.

You have the ability to go beyond conventional time-space. When you do, elevation to a higher vibration and an awareness of Divine Light occurs. In one single moment, you become conscious that you are not alone. You know with a certainty that there is an essence within and without that will enable you to co-participate with other dimensions and intelligences. When you leave the myth and falsity behind and awaken to a higher reality, a quantum leap forward thrusts you into a new consciousness of Light. The gifts of the Holy Spirit are offered. Finally, the joy of working directly with "whole Light beings" and angelic messengers becomes your reality.

Love reigns supreme as the underlying energy of the Living Light. Because of this love, you will learn how to pass from one type of visibility to another. Divine Intelligence partners with this love. The Supreme Intelligence is beyond the nature of description. As a human, one way that you can see representatives of God is through the angels. As inner vision is awakened, the worldview begins to dissolve and you learn to see and

BE: Embracing the Mystery

understand the immensity of intelligent creation. Earth is a dust world creation. Yet, within this field of confused and corrupted thought you will always have an opportunity to align individual energy and intelligence to a higher level of consciousness. One of the most delightful gifts is firsthand experience with invisible beings. You have spirit friends who are ready and willing to help in time of need.

It is important that there is an understanding of a hierarchy of consciousness as well as the wisdom science behind creation. It is equally important that you understand and open your heart to divine love. It is an unconditional and higher love that reveals the mysteries. The two cannot be separated if you are to envision creation as a whole. There is an infinite tapestry that will gradually reveal itself to you, the weaver, through a conscious awareness of both divine wisdom and love. The tapestry is life. In expectation and joy, seek the golden threads revealing the exquisite beauty, symmetry and perfection of the Sacred.

To correctly apply and appreciate the sacred science in human life, learn to view creation from the highest spiritual perspective. Our divine friends, regardless of appearance or vibration, will enhance life in such a way that mediocrity is left behind and a grand adventure, both practical and mystical, is experienced. Your heart will rejoice with thankfulness as generous gifts of protection, guidance, inspiration, comfort and healing are showered upon you. The gifts of the Holy Spirit arrive when you are centered and have fallen in love with God both within and without. When you accept celestial assistance, living comfortably in two worlds at the same time becomes a reality.

The Supreme Being as a concept and as a reality will always remain somewhere beyond mere scientific or theological explanation. Because Infinite Intelligence transcends mere words, I will refer to the Language of Light in describing the melodious music running as a hidden sound within our souls and all creation. God's first emanation was Light. The hierarchy of angels and individual spirits came later. When we think of angels, most of us have an image of exquisite beings that are light, free, beautiful and forever young. When three female angels first appeared to me earlier in life, I was awestruck by their beauty. I couldn't help but think how wonderful it would be to look like them and not show any form of flaw or decay. Our species needs to be educated and go beyond the consciousness of old age, disease and death. Only then will we recapture our original image of perfection.

The ethereal embodiments of goodness and generosity represent our hopes and dreams of immortality and power. We generally think of angels as being strong when we are weak and helping when we cannot help ourselves. The major difference in their consciousness and souls in embodiment is the natural tendency to live God's will in contrast to the fallen angels who desired to create their own throne and dominions in the image of themselves. There are human souls as well who obviously shy away from any true spiritual commitment, let alone seeking God's will.

Celestial beings appear in classical myths and philosophy, in the vision of Shamans, in Hinduism, Buddhism, Taoism, Zoroastrianism and Islam as well as in Judaism and early Christianity. In all traditions, angels serve as messengers of God and are said to hover between heaven and earth. According to many traditions, each person on Earth has at least one guardian angel. Psalm 91:11 states; "For He shall give his angels charge over you in all thy ways." Religious scholars, in general, simply say the number of angels is too great to count. Most modern versions of the Bible carry approximately three hundred references to angels and their duties here on Earth. The Reformation did believers a great disservice because the entire hierarchy of angelic life, the invisible life between earth forms and God, was dismissed.

If you are committed in seeking truth and loving the journey, you will be able at some point on the road toward completeness to establish an intimate relationship with our invisible friends. They are willing companions whose love, light and wisdom enrich our lives immeasurably. Angels desire to share and assist in the area of spiritual growth, helping us move quickly toward the unique spiritual destiny that is designated for the children of God. Their guidance and support is not to be taken lightly; it is something to rejoice in and to give thanks for.

Our heartfelt gratitude is primarily directed to a Supreme Intelligence from whom both angels and individual spirits are emanations. The angels themselves evolve. They, like our spiritual body, are immortals made of Light. Light is the emanation of Divine Love. Angels are friends, not personal servants to whom we can give orders. They serve the All-Knowing Creator.

Angels manifest when Spirit wills. We can't force it, nor should we try. Humans who believe will always have angelic beings as companions.

BE: Embracing the Mystery

We sense their presence and on special occasions actually see them with awakened spiritual senses. In mythology and the sci-fi stories today, the language used to describe this sight is called prescience. A person is able to see everything both physical and nonphysical with his physical eyes opened or closed. It makes no difference if the environment is in total darkness or the lights are turned on. The higher senses are activated as a result of spiritual consciousness and not the surroundings. The inner sight is a divine sight, a dormant talent that may surface for our benefit and knowledge.

As you strengthen a connection with the angels, the greater the help received. People throughout the world have recorded thousands of remarkable encounters. Angels are designated for every type of situation. We are students and our celestial companions are powerful teachers if we pay attention and have the humility to listen. The secret, besides a firm belief in divine intervention, is to establish a working relationship in good times. When you then need help in moments that are not good, reach out and they will come. Guidance may be given through a celestial voice, visions, symbols, dreams and insights, something you read in a book or information coming through another human.

My experience with angels has been primarily with three different types: rescue, healing, and guiding angels. Angelic help is the science of Divine Mind operating. If you keep belief and mind focused and strong, your request for healing will be honored. Requirements include an acceptance and a sense of knowing that you are being heard. No contradictory thought or feeling, only an explicit inner trust that the job is done. Keep vigilant in your belief until you know without a doubt that a healing has taken place.

I particularly appreciate celestial guidance. Seed thoughts are planted into receptive minds. It is then up to us, through contemplative thought, to figure out what to do next. Allow creative imagination and the pure power of intuitive thought to move you forward. Following this pattern will definitely lead beyond ordinariness. When you allow the two to work together, wholeness and maturity is eventually achieved. This is the practice of vertical knowing versus horizontal thinking.

We are all wounded on many levels of our being. The good news is that evolving man and his soul is destined to become complete and whole again. Healing is a partnership with our Creator as well as the intimacy experienced when we co-operate with invisible intelligence. On the human level, we are blessed with caring counselors, skillful and trained healthcare professionals and sensitive ministers who are ready to help restore harmony in our lives. Every type of helper has special gifts for this purpose.

All life forms are involved in the spiritual evolution process. This includes the invisible worlds of Light. Angels and Archangels are a unique form of creation. They may remain unseen for the most part, but with increasing frequency they are allowing themselves to be visible to humanity. Invisible Intelligence takes many forms, not only angelic. It is important at this point to clarify what I mean by invisible beings. They are not necessarily departed relatives, friends, or souls who have lived in physical bodies and are still bound to the material and physical rounds of existence.

Human souls are incarnating lights evolving towards perfection. In contrast, when I speak of angels, I am referring to a different form of intelligence and Light who are normally free from physical rebirth. The Bible mentions that in the beginning of human creation a large group of angels descended into flesh. It is still a possibility that they are with us, because within the Creative Power there are no limitations. In this writing, the focus is on those who vibrate in the worlds of light.

Angels obviously existed before intelligence entered matter, as we know it. They are social creatures with responsibilities and personalities and a sense of purpose and organization. They serve Divine Intelligence and seek to live and grow perfectly in their own realm. Confusion may also arise in the human mind when we mistake another form of celestial assistance, assuming it is the same help bestowed through the angelic kingdom.

Guidance and love may be bestowed upon us by enlightened master beings. In the past, they lived in physical bodies and have already evolved to a state of perfection and unification. The master souls are free from the conditioning of karmic mistakes, vibrate in harmony with the Cosmos and graciously assist humans in rare circumstances. These beings are not angels but are spiritually mature master souls from the great wisdom heights who bless, watch and assist humans who have chosen to live a selfless life. The beings that do the divine work of God experience the Profound in ways that finite mind cannot comprehend.

BE: Embracing the Mystery

Human beings who ask the Supreme Spirit, "What can I do to assist in the Great Work?" are the recipients of ongoing celestial help. When we choose to train and be an initiate in the science of wisdom and completeness, intelligent invisible helpers eagerly support us. The high Master helpers, the ascended celestial souls, have passed through many initiations of spiritual growth and have great compassion and concern for struggling humans who desire to expand light, purify the mind, and increase their vibration. They have walked the narrow path and have won the battle. Celestial Masters are the perfect ones who have attained a sublime conscious oneness with God. Assistance from the perfect ones may occur when an individual has prepared the way through love, belief, efforts and pure intent.

For now, the focus will be on the angelic friends who help us in our time of need. Our intent and success is noticed by the invisible world. Angels genuinely care about us. From the very beginning of the human race, they were appointed as guardians to watch constantly over intelligent life from conception until we leave this world and enter one of subtle dimensions of Light. Part of the assignment is to help a soul evolve, to rescue us when it is not time to be either injured or killed, to comfort when we are depressed and feel alone, to inspire with lofty ideas, and to expedite healing when faith is strong. Angelic help is also available for the subhuman creations.

Struggling souls need love. Angels assist humans physically, emotionally, mentally and spiritually. Their efforts work at the most basic level, healing the deepest anguish of the human heart. When a glorious Presence comforts us, we feel less alone. We are always being watched whether we are aware of this truth or not. One of the most dramatic experiences of my life was the time I was cross-country skiing with my youngest son. It had been snowing all day and the trail was not marked. At the end of the long day our bodies were cold and the location confusing. We had, on a whim, chosen to blaze new trails and as a result, lost our way. Physically we were isolated in an emergency situation and it was fast becoming dark. Without an available flashlight, matches or a whistle, I called on angelic help. All alone, no one in sight, we desperately needed to be rescued.

In a blink of an eye, two figures appeared across a great field of snow motioning us to follow them. Patiently they waited as I fell several times out of sheer exhaustion. The trails were covered with snow and darkness had fallen. The journey back to the ski shack was a long one. As we approached a familiar area, I mentioned this fact to my son. As soon as the words were expressed, the two rescue angels vanished!

Our car was the only one left by the ski shack. No other people had been seen on the trek back to safety and warmth. I called out to the Immensity, "Thank you for saving our lives!" Yes, we would have been terrified by the wild dogs roaming in the area as mentioned in the next day's local paper, as well as suffering and possible death resulting from the intense cold. The next day when I notified authorities as to what had happened, the ski official remarked that we had wandered at least a couple miles off course.

When we co-operate with angels in the area of healing, we must understand that angels also desire for us to be balanced and free. On a soul level, guilt may be lingering from past wrongdoing. Guilt and harsh judgments delay a complete healing. The angels understand and respect this truth and will not act against the soul's plan. A personal timetable or desire is not necessarily the right one according to the energy of the soul. A healing may require a strengthening of character or respect for the body.

Some people are challenged with an affliction or serious problem as an effect of a previous experience where harmful acts haunt the soul memory. Cause will eventually show up in life as effect. There are thousands of reasons for man's suffering. All causes are self-created. God does not punish us; we are the ones who have created disharmony and as a consequence, we subconsciously judge and punish ourselves.

The subtle levels of our being are usually healed first before the outer form is balanced. Healing is meant to teach a valuable lesson. Unpleasant experiences, including imbalances in the body, are a means to connect us more closely with the indwelling Spirit. Understanding this fact, facing it and working with it will accelerate healing. Healing is designed to expand consciousness regarding the endless possibilities available to us as Light living in physical form. We always have a choice to go directly to God, consciously connect with the higher Self, call on healing angels and invisible beings or go to a human specialist. Many of us use all four agencies.

Angels use touch, heat and light, dreams, visions and bursts of energy as their tools. As humans, we can lay our hands on other people and transmit healing magnetic energy from our body to the patient's body.

BE: Embracing the Mystery

Or, we can call on the Divine Presence of the immeasurable Holy Spirit to transmit through us and give healing energy to the one in need. When the angelic light is showered on a patient, words in a form of a command may be stated. I remember a serious moment when one of my children had been ill for days with a high fever, sore throat, and dizziness. He was also hallucinating. He had already seen a doctor and was on medication, but no improvement had occurred. In fact, he was becoming steadily worse.

Alone in my room, asking for help, I was intuitively directed to charge into his darkened room. As I stood above him, a strong voice spoke through me and commanded our son to stand up and be well. This was not my personality or voice. The tone was so authoritative that he immediately stood up. As the child reached out to me, I was amazed by the largeness and strength of his arms. I was not feeling the slim arms of a youth but the great arms of his invisible light body. His inner Self responded to the authoritative tone of the command. Standing, he excitedly told me that all the fever and pain felt as if it was draining downward leaving his body and dropping through the floor. He was totally healed as a result of his obedience and immediately ran downstairs looking for something to eat. Dramatic as the experience was, there have been many similar moments of joy throughout the years. Firsthand experience is a valuable teacher.

We also receive indirect healings in the form of guidance or intuitive thoughts as conscious knowledge that we did not already have. Angels work through other people to help us as well. Inspiration comes through intuitive thought in a form of whispering or a reminder such as making a needed telephone call or writing a special letter or simply knowing what is the right action to take. I frequently hear a whispered word. It is then my responsibility to do research on the word spoken. The word leads to a lesson that is appropriate for further inner growth.

Guardians have been associated with healing since antiquity. They are composed of light either in a recognizable form in a dazzling array of colors or they can be sparkles, flames or beams of light without a familiar human figure. They will, when the situation calls for a manifestation, appear as a human. Their bodies are not subject to sickness and injury. Their knowledge is pure. Their dedication in helping us heal our lives is untiring. Healing comes from God through the angels. We give angels our deepest thanks, but the glory and praise should always be directed to the Creator of All.

Healing is a large part of the spiritual connection. The basis of all healing is forgiveness. We let go of negativity through conscious choice. It is vitally important that we free ourselves from the hurt, anger and the wounds people and events have directed toward us. We have allowed the injuries to remain through lack of a higher knowledge of mental law and spiritual ignorance. Forgiveness is the angelic road that leads to healing. If we do not forgive others and ourselves, we create strong and unhealthy bonds that continue into future experiences.

Most humans exist in an inner state of disorder. What is even worse is that the disorder is accepted as normal. The ideal is to bring order out of disorder. People get so used to being hurt and in pain that they do not realize the depth of healing that is needed. They become too wounded to care. Our angel friends find this situation intolerable. They are perfect messengers, perfect communicators of God's love and grace. They do not like seeing us cut off from our true Source and Light or each other. For this reason, angels are willing and ready to work with us at all times so that we can again trust and let go and understand how imperative it is to ask forgiveness in areas where we have hurt others or ourselves.

Forgiveness is only half of the solution. We must also find a way to balance our previous mistakes. Pray for the right means to create restitution. Angels are delighted whenever we give up our blockages and allow the prison bars to be removed. Use your imagination. Enlightened imagination is a powerful and creative tool.

If you have a person in your life that is a constant irritant, try to visualize the two of you tied together with heavy rope standing on a bare stage. Next, imagine a holy figure of your choice walking towards the two of you with a large scissors in his/her hand. It is time to be free of the restrictions that bind. Watch the holy figure cut through the heavy ropes. Accept the falling pieces as a sign that your unhealthy bond with this other person is being permanently removed. After all ropes have been cut, embrace the other person in love and thanksgiving. You could also include the holy helper in the closing gesture.

If the problem is with your own personality, imagine yourself bound and gagged and the holy being cutting your ropes. Daily repeat the visualization until you experience a release within. Healings occur in the subtle

BE: Embracing the Mystery

worlds of thought before they manifest in form. Be aware that positive change only comes through deep feeling and imagining. It is a heart experience as well as a mind creation.

Forgiveness is vital for your health and harmony. It is an act of will by which you decide to let go of hurt. Deciding to forgive a hurt doesn't mean you condone or minimize it. Rather, it means that you have decided not to retain the hurt and carry it in your energy field or hold it against the individual who was hurtful. Being able to make such a decision begins the healing process because it prevents a wound from remaining raw and open. It also breaks any bondage with the other party.

Time and time again, I have seen how lack of forgiveness in others has prolonged their pain and suffering. The following is a good example. An acquaintance has a daughter with cerebral palsy. The parents brought the daughter to our home for a consultation and healing. She came in a wheelchair and after the session was over actually walked to their car. Weeks later, the father brought her back for another appointment. Her disability had returned. I asked her what she had been thinking about before her condition worsened. She simply hung her head and would not look me in the eye.

The angels came to the rescue with a flash of light accompanied by an intuitive thought. I knew that the young woman felt shame about her past actions. When directly asked what did she feel guilty about, she replied that she is having difficulty in forgiving herself for having sexual relations with her boyfriend. In her mind, she did not deserve a healing or any spiritual help. She was her own judge, jury and prisoner. Feelings of low self esteem, unworthiness, definitely work against harmony and healing. Shame blocks the receiving of good.

It is not easy for everyone to accept God's unconditional love. More people need to change their view of the Creator from a judge to a loving celestial Parent. Forgiveness, regardless of the circumstance, is a great healer because it works to restore harmony and inner peace.

Angels are present although you may not feel or see them. They are authentic beings of intelligent Light whose role is to help when you believe and trust. I urge you to cultivate a taste for the Unseen and be open to God's unexpected ways if you are not already. An awakening awareness of multi-dimensional life is only the beginning of an extraordinary journey of love and fulfillment. There is so much wonder waiting to be discovered and enjoyed. With the growing awareness among people all over the world of a finer vibrating life right here in our midst, I felt it appropriate to honor your soul by recognizing and respecting the celestial friends who are here for you. Throughout your reading you will meet them and marvel at their unlimited talents, beauty, quickness and power. The return journey is about embracing the Presence and Power of God and helping the soul to dance.

Chapter Three
The Other Side

The Celestial Worlds came forth from the Supreme Spirit, the Indescribable All-Knowing Mind. The lower invisible worlds and the physical worlds are products of the elements of the invisible universe. Both are from an identical source, one unseen and the other seen. The lower physical and higher celestial worlds are destined to eventually harmonize with each other. Since birth and death are two gates every single soul who is caught in the electro-magnetic spectrum passes through, the subject of the "Other Side" is always fascinating and sought out by inquisitive minds.

If humanity understood existence as a continuum that goes beyond Earth's energy field, being oblivious to the Living Light would not be an issue. Even while living in physical form, the subtle parts of what you call your self simultaneously exist in finer vibrations. Awareness in more than one dimension is one of the ways that you receive intuitive thoughts, heightened levels of energy, and sense the presence of invisible beings.

The physical body is the outer "skin" covering your lesser force fields known as the etheric, astral/emotional and lower thinking/mind. You also have higher invisible force fields known as the causal mind, soul and spirit. When spirit originally descended into flesh, it was necessary to put on additional layers of dense matter. It is similar to your being naked (spirit) and putting on layers of clothing. Each covering differs in vibration and purpose. All the coverings are one complete package even though most people are unaware of them. The sheaths work as a unit of intelligent light with each finer covering being more subtle in substance than the body it covers, thus making the physical body the densest of the package.

Physical death simply means that the energy package no longer requires the dense physical body and the etheric vital sheath, which maintains the body. The soul will later in the invisible world discard the astral-emotional body and lower mental vehicle and create a new set if it re-enters into another physical embodiment. When the soul is ready to incarnate, it assumes a new zodiac sign and personality, a physical/etheric energy field, an astral/emotional energy field and lower mental energy field. Since it is common for the complete "package" of what we are to forget the past but recollect the spiritual identity, the personality will continue to struggle and suffer on a path toward unity consciousness until it develops a conscious connection with God.

Whether you are in or out of the physical body, you are the one and the same spirit individuality. Some people feel that when they are on the other side, they automatically know everything and are complete and whole. This is not true unless you have achieved God Realization or a very high degree of spiritual awareness prior to physical departure. You are the same in other dimensions, at least in the first stages of assimilating and healing after a physical death. If you have not been taught about the invisible worlds of Light, it can at first be confusing. Heavenly assistance is given to ease any bewilderment. Transformation from one form to another would be a more joyful and meaningful experience if the higher knowledge were already a part of the collective consciousness.

Once the soul assimilates its past life experiences, it begins to remember and integrate the past with the totality of its being. The soul in the invisible world eventually becomes stronger and wiser than the human personality it has recently discarded. The soul has available within it the hidden memory experiences of previous incarnations. Eventually, the most recent incarnation experience is absorbed into consciousness. When the energy is fused, the soul becomes aware of a greater identity and its purpose in working towards reclaiming it.

The glimpse is brief for the soul who has not yet chosen enlightenment. However, the glimpse does provide the necessary impetus to move forward. Souls who have advanced towards the goal of making God a reality and have achieved a high level of understanding and purity may retain some past memory in the next incarnation. Their individual soul history due to personal efforts and growth offer them a much greater freedom and grace than it does to the soul who remains oblivious to its spiritual purpose and destiny.

Many departed souls have appeared to me throughout the years. They ask that I extend comfort to loved ones or friends left behind, relay information, communicate unfinished business, and in rare cases, ask for a healing. Their love and concern continues because they still are functioning from the level of the past personality. Since they are the same consciousness as when they had a physical body, many souls when making contact are concerned regarding material things. Simple requests such as engraving on a tombstone or a missing wallet, apologies or some other subject that remains important linger in their minds. It only proves an earlier statement that consciousness continues as well as the personality after physical death. The only difference between them and us is they have discarded a few of the outer garments that are no longer useful in the invisible world.

Invisible life is free and livelier than the normal human experience. Since tele-thought has power, souls have the option to create and travel instantly. They easily manifest a new reality through desire, thought and creative energy. As humans, we have the same option for otherworldly travel through an out-of-body experience. An out-of-body experience is a temporary excursion where the soul may leave the physical body and easily move consciously or unconsciously in the finer vibratory worlds of Light.

Throughout history, people have reported happenings that are identified as out-of-body experiences or OBEs. They may be a spontaneous or deliberate experience while awake or occur naturally during asleep. People who have the interest and willingness are able to soul travel through imagination, scientific attention and perseverance.

The thinking mind may deliberately choose to venture forth and explore nonphysical realities. The soul of a human remains connected through an invisible cord of light. The rewarding part of soul travel is that a gifted or trained mind, through concentration and proper knowledge, may consciously, with interest and attention, visit departed loved ones in the invisible regions. It is a common experience to visit other realms during the natural process of sleep. This is called lucid dreaming. It is a visitation to another vibratory realm through the gateway of the dream state. The realm most commonly traveled is the astral plane, which is in the immediate energy of the electro-magnetic density field of Earth. Higher evolutionary planes exist beyond this field.

A common weakness in out of body travel while sleeping is the fact that when the astral body returns to the physical body, it automatically passes through layers of mental and emotional energy. The descent may alter and influence the memory of the experience when fully returned to the body. If you are serious and wish to be concise, there are exercises and mind techniques available to help you manage a scientific approach to other realities, past lives, the soul, and life after death. You cannot consciously travel farther than developed consciousness. If your goal is to be free from mental, emotional and physical limitations, you can learn how to dissolve the veils and blockages that have held you back from your true identity as spirit in form. When intent is selfless, visitations and higher teachings may be experienced in twilight space/time between wakefulness and sleep, meditation and contemplation.

The integrity of an out of body experience is easier to control under meditative disciplines. The more accepting you are of the idea that you are not limited, the more likely that a contact can be made, whether awake or having a lucid dream. There are many ways to experience a personal contact with finer energies and reach into another thought dimension. A sense of a presence, a voice, a touch, a fragrance, an intuitive thought, a flash of light, or a quick image of a loved one is typical of communication attempts. The sensations can actually be physical such as tingling, warmth or coolness, and sound. Contact often manifests through movement of objects. If you do not harbor fear and are open to communication, anything is possible.

Physical death is the final out-of-body experience. To accept that there are other dimensions available for growth and enjoyment is rewarding knowledge. There actually is no thing as death only a change in the outer garment. Fully accepting the continuation of consciousness will bring peace of mind and a heightened understanding during physical loss. In direct contrast, the soul in the invisible world is free to be fully alive. He can make his presence known in times of need and also continue his own spiritual growth and creative pursuits. Freedom is a mental state, an issue of choice that exists on Earth as well as in nonphysical environments.

When you lose a loved one, it is natural to grieve. A great deal of the sorrow is grief that you feel over your own loss. There is a sense of deprivation regarding the loss. Continued grief attracts a departed soul like a magnet, downward into the despair. This does not honor the soul. If you continue to indulge in grief, loved ones on the other side are negatively influenced by your sorrow. Sadness is the worst of demons. When grief continues, it becomes a selfish act.

Love and trust the orderliness of God's creation and allow the departed one to go and explore grander parts of self. In letting go of attachment, he will be closer to you than ever before. He will be grateful for your ability to unconditionally love him enough to see that he has a new and higher life to live that is only a thought away. Because you cannot see him, it does not mean that he does not exist. True love requires understanding of how multifaceted we are. It goes beyond physical separation. Love continues whether the individual is here in the body or is living in a finer dimension of thought. When real love exists, you are together regardless of the dimension or the form used.

Many souls who have left their bodies of matter welcome the opportunity to offer comfort, protection, inspiration and healing from a finer level of vibration and power. They willingly join us at the appropriate moment of need. Educate yourself about the eternal identity, the hierarchies of consciousness and higher evolution. Learn about the many levels of invisible helpers, the orders of angels, and the "whole Light beings" and you will have confidence and be comforted regarding the onward journey of friends and loved ones as well as have hope for your unlimited future.

Give yourself time, and when psychologically ready, begin to reverse your thoughts and, if necessary, change your attitude. Be positive and thankful that a loved one or friend is now free of limitation and pain. Offer gratitude and love, forgiveness and blessings. Think or speak freely because you are heard. Dwell on the good and beautiful and you will not only make a departed one happy, you will experience a genuine peace.

Learn to trust in God's orderly universe. There is no such thing as loss. You keep love alive in the heart and mind. In understanding this, you will find peace and know that you are never alone. A loved one simply lives in a greater vibration of safety, health and freedom. Positive contact can be made through a conscious desire and the sending of loving thoughts. Why make a loved one sad because of your grief? This is neither kindness nor love. A physical loss is an opportunity to demonstrate faith, courage and healing. Nothing is over. Life continues. What you can do is pray. Prayers are thoughts of love that will help a soul adjust with ease in the new environment. Also, pray for those who appear as selfish and ungodly who are now on the other side of life. They need prayers more than the souls who have been good and are cherished.

The holidays are difficult. Loved ones do join us when needed. It is common for some to come and participate in the festivities, particularly the first several years after physical death. In truth, there is no death, only a changing of the form, nor are there accidents. God does not reach down and take your loved one. Departure is determined by an individual's soul history and the destiny that has been preplanned for its growth experience. The form that physical death takes is normally a soul choice prior to incarnating. Keep in mind that there are always exceptions.

When those who exist in the finer vibrations visit, they view activities clearly and know your deepest thoughts. Special days are opportunities to demonstrate a faith in the ongoing process of life. Although the departed one may not be seen, offer a gift of love by acknowledging his/her presence. Use sensitive moments to give trustingly from the heart and a contact will occur.

There is a hierarchy of form and consciousness from the lesser to the greater in the kingdoms of nature, including our own physical evolution, as well as an intelligent and invisible evolution thrusting upward past space and time. Intelligence vibrating in the higher Invisible Worlds experiences an ongoing consciousness and evolution, as do all created forms here on Earth. Expansion in the Light is unlimited and in a state of constant change whether visible or invisible. Once you become more familiar with what actually constitutes energy and the various levels of creativity, you will have the necessary understanding that will help you grasp the whole of creation and its purpose. You will accept with a certainty that eventually the physical body will gather Light into its image and give way to a garment of Light. True evolution is spiritual evolution.

Many people question, "What is my loved one doing on the other side?" There is little difference in the finer subtle planes that have a close proximity to Earth than what you are experiencing right here and now in heavy matter. For instance, what a person is in character and consciousness here in the physical dimension is what he is in the nonphysical life. If he believes in a hell and judgement, a hell and judgement environment will manifest as a result of his belief. Whatever is the inner truth at the time of physical departure influences the immediate environment in the next dimension.

It is extremely important for the health of the soul that there be a peaceful departure. The transition is smoother when love and acceptance accompanies the soul. The subtle dimensions are purposefully created and linked together through the power of Mind. If a departed soul feels he must recuperate from his earthly physical illness, he will find himself in an "astral hospital" with other beings lovingly offering the care he feels he needs. Whatever has been the personal belief system will continue into the nonphysical reality.

If personal conditioning and belief is hampering spiritual progression, at some point in spiritual growth invisible help will be offered to the confused newcomer until he is ready to look at new possibilities. Since the will of the individual supports the existing patterns, it is up to the soul whether it will accept help when offered. Guidance is available. It is the same wherever we exist; it is choice that determines progress.

Assistance arrives from different sources. There are also humans who have learned how to consciously go out of the body for the purpose of offering assistance to souls who need temporary help in making the necessary adjustments in a subtle environment. Existing in a finer dimension with unlimited possibilities enables the soul to express itself in fresh and exciting ways. The soul vibrating in a nonphysical reality continues to have access to learning, healing, teaching and greater creativity.

In many ways, it is easier for a soul to be more productive and helpful in the invisible dimensions than here in the visible world of dense matter. Life does not end. The higher view is grander and unlimited. Without a physical body, the soul inhabits a place unbounded by time or space. The common human is oblivious to the amazing finer worlds of thought and is usually unaware of his friend or loved one's presence. This may cause frustration for the departed soul.

It is possible for a gifted human to consciously project the mind to other dimensions of thought. Not too long ago, I decided to mentally locate my earth father who had left his physical body approximately twenty-five years ago. I found him in a spacious room bent over blueprints. The blueprints were from ancient times. When dad was in his physical body, he was involved in a serious study of the pyramids, the Kabbalah, mysticism, the invisible worlds and healing. As I looked closely at his current spiritual environment, I noticed stones with hieroglyphics carved upon their surface placed neatly in rows on a long table. His inquiring mind was deciphering the glyphs with great enthusiasm. Light was streaming across the worktable and he was peaceful. It was satisfying watching him so absorbed in learning and pursuing an interest in something he loved to do while here on Earth.

A human is more likely to experience subtle dimensions when the mind is peaceful and trust has been achieved. Peace is acceptance and gratitude, a sense of unity within God's creation. It is a definite advantage for your own growth to acquire a nonjudgmental openness and a conscious connection with the subtle worlds of Light. When you are privy to a grander view, fear and confusion are absent regarding the Unknown. Collective humanity consciously knows very little about invisible creation. When aware of a higher reality, it is both comforting and exciting to discover that there is ongoing activity and learning available.

The soul identity assumes a finer, healthier, younger and attractive body that will serve its needs in the dimensions of Light. I have never seen anyone who has crossed over look anything other than healthy, youthful and attractive. Although the soul does not normally suffer physical pain in what is referred to as the Heaven worlds, it feels deeply because the next level near Earth is the invisible emotional world. You will meet your loved ones again. Do them and self the greatest favor, honor life by allowing both the departed and yourself to live confidently in love and peace.

It is a great blessing to be involved with the invisible worlds while in the flesh. The following message is a powerful example. My father in his later years went through a triple by-pass surgery. During his recuperation, he experienced the presence of invisible beings that he referred to as the "Little People." Although Dad was a very deep and contemplative man, he had never experienced visions prior to his surgery. He claimed that the invisible Little People, who only he could see, devotedly "worked" on the healing of his incisions while he was lying in his hospital bed.

Later, after returning home to recuperate, Dad had an experience where he felt dizzy as he walked around his room. He slumped back onto his bed. Feeling discouraged and sorry for himself, an unexpected and sudden vision of radiant Light appeared. He was shown a very ragged, poorly dressed, dirty, skinny, pale barefoot young boy. A celestial voice said to him, "This is how you see yourself. Now, we will show you how we view you from our perspective." The first vision vanished and a new scene appeared that was dramatically different. Dad appeared as a well dressed, handsome, clean, healthy and joyous looking young man. The voice continued and said, "This is the real you."

BE: Embracing the Mystery

One of the most dramatic and loving stories I have ever heard is what happened so exquisitely to my mother after Dad physically died. Many soul experiences happen to us when we least expect them. Mother was in the kitchen preparing dinner. The television was on in the den. It was set on her favorite channel. When the news came on, the voices were not familiar. Confused, Mother ran into the den to see what was wrong, and there in the middle of the room stood my father who had died the previous week. If the will is strong and the intention is pure, you can do what appears as impossible regardless of what side of life you vibrate in. Dad, with love and a determined will, manifested a natural recognizable form long enough so his wife could reach out, throw her arms around him, and actually feel his subtle body. She cried out his name and then he disappeared.

Nonphysical beings can easily manipulate matter, as can those who have awakened to the higher currents within the spirit individuality. Manipulating energy through the deliberate change in television stations was a powerful action on his part to get Mother's attention. His demonstration was a remarkable act of love proving the existence of an ongoing life.

There are a variety of methods used by spirits to make contact with humans. Some of them are symbols, numbers, manipulating electricity or matter, dreams, words whispered and vivid mental pictures projected on the screen of the receiver's mind. Creative possibilities are endless. One afternoon, I was psychically privileged to see Dad's presence in his nonphysical body relaxing in a lounge chair. He looked much younger and very healthy. I could actually hear him laughing. The message of relaxation was an obvious one. His posture and demeanor suggested that I needed to take time out for relaxation. They say "a picture is worth a thousand words."

Recently, I attended a memorial for a friend's husband. I deliberately arrived early so there would be an opportunity to visit with the widow and her immediate family before the other guests arrived. Suddenly, an attractive woman joined our circle. The widow and other family members ignored her. She looked very much like the widow and I assumed she was a sister. The woman appeared frustrated. She left as suddenly as she had arrived. Her stay was brief but long enough for me to closely examine her appearance and behavior. Later, when the widow walked me to the car, I inquired regarding the woman and the strong family resemblance. My friend was startled and said that no other woman was standing by us. The more I described the appearance of the frustrated woman and her mannerisms, the more shocked my friend became. I was describing her sister who had died five years previously.

The widow asked if we could meet the following week and whether I would look at a photograph of her sister to verify identification. It was her sister. What was amazing was the fact that the physically deceased sister definitely did not look ethereal. She looked human. When I moved my face and body to show the widow the mannerisms of the deceased sister, my friend said that I was imitating her exactly as she remembered her. Think about this for a moment. The fact that a soul is powerfully alive in a nonphysical realm and can master matter also indicates that if you truly believed in the power of intention and attention, you can create and manipulate matter here in the flesh.

When it is understood that other vibratory realms exist right here in our midst, it makes the soul journey much easier and understandable. There are many dimensions finer and more vivid than the familiar physical-material life. Just because they may not be seen does not mean they do not exist. I will share one more experience of family love that recently occurred to an acquaintance. We correspond by letter and have never physically met. A month ago his sister died. Since he was incarcerated, he could not be with his sister during her last physical hours. Instead, the sister came to him in her subtle astral/emotional body and said goodbye. The sister appeared in golden white light. Their farewell experience was holy and uplifting although it happened in a lucid dream state. When she was ready to ascend, he watched his sister's soul joyfully ascend. This is love expressing as kindness and one more piece of evidence demonstrating God's orderly universe.

Challenge yourself to learn to see with new eyes and understand with a greater clarity the gentleness and love that can easily occur between different life forms throughout the invisible and visible dimensions of thought vibration. It is through the higher part of the mind that you have access to dimensions beyond space and time. Activate and use dormant organs of perception. It is a blessing to spiritually see, hear, feel and have developed an understanding of the higher realities. When we spiritually awaken, we are actually using the higher part of the mind as well as the spiritual senses. It is then that we make contact with the immaterial, divine worlds of the clear Light.

The rhythm of the universe is love. There is only one true song, even though we may hear and sing it in different ways. There is a connection, a golden thread of love, between all lives seen or unseen. In reality, the threads of this symphony are the multifaceted life forms that are providing impulses to my words through the energy of light, truth and love.

The spiritual senses are activated through an established relationship with God and a passionate love for truth. Activation allows the mind to go beyond the veils of conditioned and corrupted thought patterns that have held humanity captive for so long. Regardless of one's belief system, "God is the Light of the heavens and of the earth." (the Qur'an, 24:35). The divine light is hidden within. Imagine the knowledge and joy that will surface when you bring forth the hidden and it blazes as a risen flame. The Beloved is never absent. It is with you whether your eyes are open or closed. Learn, accept and live who you are. Develop the courage to remember and kindle hope. A wider outlook will be the result. A wider outlook changes everything and nurtures it with Light. The Light of truth will illuminate your path towards wholeness and perfection. The journey is all about love.

Chapter Four
The Science of Light

To fully understand the invisible and visible, you will require both knowledge and experience with the Light of God. As the mind keeps moving towards a sublime opening of the soul, the unknown becomes the known. At times it may feel as if the road to wisdom and integration is unending. It is a personal challenge, which helps you embrace and penetrate who you really are. If you could see your real image, which came into being before you entered flesh, you would be willing to endure anything. True knowledge creates confidence. It is the awareness of Light that awakens the innate spiritual nature within you. Sometimes you must venture into areas that have been ignored and resisted. In doing so, you discover truth.

Life is lived as a science when you choose to master your thoughts, words and actions. To attain self-mastery, use the power of thought and the mystery will be understood. A truthful education regarding the unbroken Light, which comes down to the densest form of creation supporting even the lowest creatures, is required to be understood. The Supreme Light is connected within the highest regions of the heavens. This same radiant Light is also a part of your make-up.

God's covenant is with the highest divine messengers, the Brotherhood of Light. As your thinking consciousness becomes a part of the Light, greater knowledge is transmitted to you through God's messengers. Prepare your consciousness for the new program of Light and the Spirit of Truth will become an active influence in daily life. The program consists of mathematical light coding which is a celestial language manifesting in form. Trust and awaken to the truth, dear one, that you are a vessel of Light. Because you are made of pulsating light geometries within your consciousness, it indicates you are already an integral part of a divine circuit of information.

The teachings of the illumined ones cannot be fully understood until the mind and body is recharged by the Light emanations of the angelic hierarchies and the celestial masters. This is why every true teacher emphatically reminds us that we must seek enlightenment. Enlightenment is a map for physical, mental and spiritual evolution and the will of cosmic intelligence. Habits and attitudes must be purged that do not work towards soul evolution. Distortions, resistance and negative reactions are the blocks that generate falsity in life. As part of the science, it is wise to deliberately choose to remove yourself from anything or anyone who may hamper growth.

From the soul's viewpoint, when you are embroiled in a negative mindset, you stop spiritually evolving. When the mind refuses to study, understand and apply universal laws, the amount of life force available to the soul diminishes. If you persist in a negative pattern, the result is illness, suffering and loss. There is no sin in God. It is man who creates sin by clinging to a corrupted nature.

Once the personality is willing to change, the life force will return. Each traveler must eventually reach the clear understanding that there is an inherent order to the Universe and that high celestial beings maintain that order. Eventually, each soul will awaken to its own potential and power as a source of infinite love and wisdom. Spiritual growth is a matter of giving up resistance. Once the resistance is destroyed, life becomes a matter of celebration. The sublime satisfaction of striving to be a living Light is to have the power in giving to your higher Self and others wings to fly.

To understand life, evolution must be understood. Soul evolution is actually a spiritual science. It is the responsibility of the mind to nurture a relationship with the soul. The most common problem separating a soul from its Source is not being absolutely clear regarding the reason for physical life. To know that one knows nothing is the beginning of real wisdom. People are duped into believing that they already know who they are. The masses are falsely led until, after much suffering and confusion, a lucid point in understanding occurs where truth becomes a science applicable to all life. Once you witness and understand the Light, the illusion of separation is revealed and you begin to become a reflection of Light.

To understand the science of Light is to be aware of your own intricate design as Light, the blueprint behind the physical form. It is then that you receive knowledge concerning the Great Cosmic Plan. No longer will the personality cling to the familiar appearance of limitation. False identification keeps the soul at a standstill. There is a way out of the falsity through the attainment of self-mastery. Through self-mastery, you accelerate individual vibration, replacing impure particles of light with the more subtle and pure particles of the higher realms. The lighter and purer the element of your force fields, the more knowledgeable, harmonious and joyous life becomes. The river of darkness is crossed when the senses are controlled, a respect for all life forms is quickened and you work consciously with the Invisible Worlds.

You are already a creator whether this fact is understood or deliberately applied. Once the full meaning and purpose of spiritual Light is grasped, you will know the steps to take to regain a state of wholeness. Individual light energy varies according to spiritual maturity. You can only attain according to the level of your evolution. As you ascend higher in understanding, belief changes until you arrive at a final belief, which words cannot explain. You simply know and are an embodiment of true knowledge.

The past has created the present. The present is creating the future. You have the capability to increase and use the light that gives substance to your inherent makeup. The goal is to bond with God's primordial substance, which is known as Light. The Light is an energy that increases in power and possibilities as the soul integrates truth as a personal reality. A lasting benefit of an inner transformation is the ability to communicate with the Sublime.

For the higher celestial energy to exert itself in the duality of matter, you must increase personal subtle matter energy. Learn to work on matter in order to make it more and more subtle. Education regarding spiritual light is a required focus if you desire to spiritually progress. Physical light that normally emanates from the sun or the light we commonly call electricity is not the focus. Both are powerful and have their purpose. I am referring to the Limitless Light that was the first creation of God and cannot be described. It is the cause and origin of the universe. This essence or substance is present in all created things. It is very subtle and has many degrees of intensity. It can be seen with the "inside" eyes. The Light of God is reflected as intelligence, love, beauty, nobility and strength. It contains life and power. The intensity of Light differs according to the consciousness of the life form. The function of the heavenly Light must be freed from the cubic restriction of matter.

Divine Light can overcome conditioned limitation and override negative programming. If there are corrections and improvements that need to be established in consciousness, purify any negative energy that is attached to the memory and personality. The demons or negativity are frequently referred to as the shadow self. The soul is blocked from transmitting knowledge to the conscious thinking mind by the primate instincts. It is your choice whether you are the victim or victimizer in the negative areas of existence. It is all the same to the soul. There is a useful power in the shadow self because the pain it causes man actually serves to drive him back to a higher awareness of truth and the purpose of creation. These vibrations are in the energy of the aura. Transformation is the goal.

The divine plan is to transform and subdue the lower self, mind, emotions and body. Increasing the light intensity opens the gateway allowing the higher mind and its celestial influences to be in control. Light is the hidden gold. It is a symbol of God. When you are ready to be free and unlimited, you will have learned to love the Divine Light. A solid bond of love with Light creates spiritual wealth beyond imagination. The Elixir of Eternal Life provides nourishment and blesses all who recognize and embrace Its Presence.

When you are ready to witness Celestial Light through practicing spiritual exercises, It will reveal the reality of the subtle worlds of Spirit. At a specific point of readiness, Whole Light Beings may offer you instruction. Whole Light Beings are entities of Light that exist in pure bodies of energy and move in the midst of man under very special circumstances. A higher source of energy is now reaching our solar system, interpenetrating through arcs of Light. Invisible beings, active as love and wisdom, use the energy of heavenly Light to purify the elements of the Earth's atmosphere.

If you deny and do not pulsate love, how can you experience the redemptive light of the Greater Intelligence who is willing to help? Doubt and worry work against freedom. To be free, you must believe and have trust in that which you may not see or know. When a natural surrender occurs in consciousness, you experience a steady flow of beauty and love. The influx of spiritual energy provides the blessings of spiritual sight, hearing, feeling and comprehension, the gifts of Spirit. The Light of God becomes your truth. You become a windowpane, a transparency for beauty as you reach out to others.

There is an extraordinary power in spiritual light. The recorded truth that many individuals have a conscious experience with Its power and radiance indicates that the experience is available to anyone who has prepared and believes. It is not a rarity for a chosen few. Intimacy with God is for everyone. It is the substance of God, vibrating and bathing the entire universe. Light empowers you with an invincible certainty.

To create and nurture a relationship with the higher Self, choose to make changes that will lead to a spiritual goal. Daily meditation reveals a nonphysical reality of beauty and majesty. Witnessing Light provides a feeling of unity with God. When you have a momentary transcendent image where there is a shift beyond a conditioned dimension, you understand that both space and time do not exist. Firsthand experience is a true teacher. For example, you may experience a pulsating vision where the ever-expanding universe of Light surrounds you.

A vision intimately reveals the connectedness of creation and the unlimited possibilities of God's substance. Every heavenly body is vibrating light. Living streams of dazzling energy connect the heavenly bodies. The display appears as a giant network of living light, similar to a switchboard. The One God is not light. Our Creator projected Light and the universe manifested forth from the light. Light is the Absolute's first divine emanation and it contains all the qualities and virtues of God. You know God through Light. This Light appears within consciousness as pictographs, tracings, codes, geometries and spiraling radiations.

Your thoughts and emotions in the visible and invisible worlds create living forms that work for or against personal energy and purpose. Thoughts are actually living things, energies and entities. They are extremely influential as either a negative or positive force. Never underestimate them. Thought forms have no boundaries. They may attach to the physical body, a dream state, an out of body experience or physical death. Because you are the creator of your thoughts, they cling to you. Thoughts are the offspring of personal energy.

Thought forms created by other intelligences as well as thought forms from finer vibratory levels of the astral plane may also affect health, sanity, safety and your very existence. You can be protected from negative

BE: Embracing the Mystery

energy influences, whether they are visible or invisible, by taking command and purifying your own mind. It is up to you to release the mind from all vain endeavors. It is a healthy practice to ask whether a thought is truly an outside influence or your own. Influences exist everywhere.

The mind of a human is not complete. To be complete, you must take charge and liberate the higher Self. An ascending soul must rediscover the experience of being rather than doing. Eventually, you evolve into a larger and truly brilliant version of a human. You awaken luminous dimensions within. The finished product is a fully divine human. The path of freedom is for the courageous and the wise. The first and foremost assignment is to achieve control of the human personality and the normal activities of physical life. Many humans are experimenting and attempting to master more subtle planes of existence before they master themselves. They are inviting serious trouble. You cannot become fully enlightened if you neglect your own spiritual identity and growth.

When one is born with supernatural gifts, it is the result of having developed or received the gifts during a past achievement. It is also true that a student may develop a new talent through effort and training in his present embodiment. You must become educated regarding the complexities of life, both seen and unseen, if you are to grasp the full scope or higher meaning of life. It is your destiny to regain the lost coding which connects your consciousness to the original program of the One.

The purpose of physical embodiment is to be in the flesh what you are in the spirit. Self-mastery and visibly establishing heaven on earth is the assignment. The goal of the eternal Self is to experience perfection physically, emotionally and mentally while living in a dense world of thought. For many humans, the cupboard is bare. They have forgotten the high ideal and proven potentiality of the original design. True identity is a spiritual identity. The goal is completeness and perfection on all levels. Victory is achieved right here while in the flesh. You do not have to wait to be made perfect in a nebulous world.

There is nothing more loving or powerful than knowing the higher Self. There have been and are illumined beings who have conquered the lower animal nature. Through persistent striving and molding of character and appealing to invisible forces for help, they became victorious over matter. You, too, must make the effort to pass through the process of discovery, healing and victory. The levels of the complete self vibrate as consciousness, mind, emotions and body. Learn not to give in to the lower nature and drag the animal past along with you.

The important goal is to reach beyond the illusionary traps of both the unseen lower astral plane and the seen physical plane. The Spirit of Truth is the key to the hidden knowledge. Knowledge is revealed when intent is pure and you reach beyond the confines of the electromagnetic level. Your assignment in the flesh is to honor the Spirit first by increasing energy through purification, character development, training and living the Universal Law. For the moment, the best description of the Universal law is to quote Saint Ignatius of Antioch: "My law archives are simply the Christ." The name Christ is a title that represents a perfect state of consciousness, purity and oneness with the Absolute.

Victory is your responsibility. Once you seriously embark on the path of enlightenment, it becomes a natural blessing to access subtle realms of light and thought. You exist in the physical body because this is where mastery of dense matter and illusion is learned. If the sacred goal is not accomplished now, a return visit to Earth is required. Rebirth continues until the heart and mind is open to truth and something is done about it. Reincarnation offers the soul further opportunities to claim its true identity. Nothing is justified except by the diversity of an ongoing existence.

The light of consciousness goes wherever you are. Earth existence has seven divisions. The invisible astral plane, which is the most familiar region of invisible life nearest to physical life, also has seven divisions. Astral life is considered matter. It is less dense than Earth and the vibration lighter, but it is still vibrating matter. The seven divisions of the astral life differ in quality and vibration. The evolving soul is attracted to the level that is in harmony with personal spiritual evolution. The more you identify with the higher Self, the more assuredly you have access into loftier invisible dimensions of thought. The further away from heavy matter and the closer you are in consciousness with the Divine, the finer or lighter each dimensional level.

Generally speaking, family and friends who have discarded the physical body and have adjusted to their new environment eventually ascend to the higher realms and do not linger on the lower astral levels unless they have unfinished business. They may return to Earth's vibration if they feel a pull toward a loved one during a crisis. The length of time spent in the lower invisible worlds is determined by the age at physical death, the type of death experienced, the consciousness of the individual and the unfulfilled desires. The goal is always to evolve. Once the soul nature is healed, it is ready to ascend to greater heights.

No two situations are the same. If a recently departed soul appears soon after a physical death, he may be demonstrating that life continues and there is no need for grief. If there is confusion in the transitory state, an appearance may also occur. We never lose our loved ones. They are simply living in a different environment and will retain the personality, the familiar appearance and astral shell until they have reviewed, assimilated and healed the recent past life. The adjustment period has no set timetable. The length of stay in the Invisible realms is determined by spirit awareness and the needs of the soul. Our original spiritual home is loftier than the physical, etheric, astral and lower mental planes. We have our beginnings as individual sparks of light in the higher mental realms, referred to as the Heaven or Causal Worlds.

When your soul descends into matter, veils separate you from the higher serene worlds of light. For the souls who have been earnest students of truth in previous life experiences, the veil of separation does not hold the same influence and power. The higher mental planes are off limits to souls who are indifferent or resistant towards the Divine. Heaven to them is the astral level. The astral levels are similar to Earth and are referred to as the in-between incarnation worlds. Although there is definitely a greater freedom experienced in the astral dimension than existing here on Earth, the astral experience is only a step in the evolutionary process towards completion. When the soul is drawn closer to the Light, it will be led to grander vibratory realms, which offer infinite possibilities and the bliss of the Divine Fire.

Intuitive insights, flashes of genius and creative ideas are impulses emanating from the higher mental worlds of divine thought. The artist, the musician, the poet and inventor, the philosopher and the adventurer receive their impulses from the Higher Worlds, descending as drops of light into a receptive consciousness here below. The limitless ideas that are possible to the unhindered mind are planted as seeds into willing conscious minds as possibilities waiting to be born. The glorious lights and geometric forms that dazzle us in unexpected moments or deep meditations are the true angelic language, forever familiar to the heart and higher mind. Many souls experience moments of intense longing for a closeness that appears to elude them in the flesh. The feeling is an inner pull at the heart reminding us that there is something valuable missing in the chaotic world of appearances.

There are veils of forgetfulness in the lower invisible mental worlds as well as within the physical plane. They are created through self-imposed limitations and are similar, yet dissimilar, to the veils we experience as a spirit in physical form. The evolving soul gradually expands, awakens and purifies its energy. The awakening to the eternal Self usually occurs in degrees. It may feel like a very slow process to the earnest student. There are limitations that must be overcome in heavy matter. It is normal to feel frustrated as you strive to bring forth visibly and tangibly the power of divinity and the subduing of the weaknesses of the personality. Many are concerned about the brevity of life and that they will not have enough time to reach their goal. There is not enough time if this is the belief system of the mind.

The divine plan for you is to eventually merge with the good, the beautiful and the true. Through persevering and being vigilant, you are gradually readied for a greater receptivity and fulfillment of your divine Nature. As trust builds, divine wisdom will flow to you with clarity and power. The "mind stuff" of the universe will avail itself in accordance to your readiness and tenacity. If you are a laggard or doubter, it will not.

The higher life cannot be claimed if you have a personal philosophy that does not work. If you keep having serious problems and remain confused and saddened, your belief system is obviously not the right one for you. Many people do not value themselves or their abilities. Self-analysis and change are the required tools. The Divine will become evident once the mind becomes disciplined and you earnestly seek truth. A higher power will assist in uncovering the hidden treasure if consciousness is prepared. An expanded aura of light attracts our celestial friends like a magnet. Divine contact will help remove the shackles that hold you back from inner joy and peace.

It is through love that you convert the light force within into a living reality. The master plan will not become a reality if you waste life. Concentrate on the quality of life. Embrace wholeness. Support and inspire others with a willingness to transform. It is your belief and action that shape destiny. Deep satisfaction is one of the byproducts of soul awareness. In developing consciousness, you benefit and also produce something of value for others. Creativity is learning how to love self and all life. Your role is to be a conscious creator and convert the most painful experiences into wisdom. You experience good magic when your energy is fully alive. Prioritize your activities and do everything to protect, purify and respect life.

Ask All-Knowing Mind to help in exposing all hindrances of the lower animal nature that continue to block spiritual progress. With help, the veils and chains that separate the body, mind and soul from harmony and perfection will gradually weaken and finally disappear. The "whole" picture is not seen or understood from the human perspective. Train yourself to deliberately view life from the perspective of the soul. The soul creates patterns for life, but it doesn't control the outcome. Trust is a quality of the soul that will help unfold the inner potentiality quickly and efficiently. Part of the grand adventure is to experience trying situations where trust is developed. The more you trust, the more you are given. Some of the lessons may border on the bizarre; the result is what matters.

The science of self-actualization exposes the facade. Eventually, you realize that it is more important to have a strong spiritual foundation than to own an excess of material things or be in relationships that tear you apart. A choice is always given to impoverish or enrich self. True science is the science of Light, the science of how to live. An awakened life brings currents from the Invisible worlds, connecting and restoring you to a higher wavelength.

It is important to understand the difference between good and evil. Both have and will always exist on a planet ruled by duality. One view of evil is to look at it as the result of thoughts, feelings and actions that have violated the soul. What does it mean to violate the soul? The subject can be better understood by studying scripture. Paul in II Corinthians 4:4 states, "The god of this age has blinded the minds of unbelievers so that they cannot see the Light of the gospel of the glory of Christ, who is the image of God." Ephesians 6:12 states, "For our struggle is not against flesh and blood, but against the rulers, against the authorities, against the powers of this dark world and against the spirit forces of evil in the heavenly realms." Yes, the heavenly realms. Paul then goes on and tells seekers to stand firm and put on full armor. Who are these rulers in the invisible realms that are still influencing humanity?

False princes reign in the lower heaven worlds that exclude God from their programs. They are souls who disrespect ancient scientific scriptures of Light. They also contribute to neutralizing consciousness, causing a nullification of spiritual growth. There are false prophets and false covenants in both the seen and unseen worlds. There are negative brotherhoods under the control of angelic princes still operating in our universe. Fallen mind energies attempt to block the higher energy source, preventing seekers of truth from learning how to expand consciousness and attain higher bodies of Light. The lesser brotherhoods have interfered with Light reaching and educating the soul. Because of this ongoing interference, the higher teachings of Light have not been entirely given on the Earth plane.

The good news is that we are gradually moving into another cycle where more Light is coming to Earth. The heavenly light will expose evil and reveal truth. Spiritual education is what is needed, mastery not mystery. The return of a living Love will illumine darkness. We can be helped, reprogrammed to go into the image of the higher evolutions, if people are willing to be spiritually educated and not block wisdom. Individual action must be taken. The science is in our dedicating our energy to a higher form of creation. This does not mean we shun human responsibilities. It suggests we make time to think deeply and take steps to expand the heart and mind. To choose to be reeducated and unfold the spirit in flesh is to find the Self again in the pure ether of Light. It is a blessing that offers the possibility of understanding and participating fully in one's own divinity, one's inner gnosis.

The human body is a cosmic antenna capable of pulling energy from the surrounding universe. It is time souls be liberated from the restrictions of dualistic thought. Seek immersion in the Holy Light. It will enable you to come out of the lower worlds of darkness. Be consistent and balanced within your belief. True education, soul evolution, occurs when you choose to move your consciousness from being limited and earth-bound to living as unlimited love and heaven bound. This choice will move you from a biochemical slavery within a third dimensional consciousness to a higher life force and understanding where you feel and know as a firsthand experience that you are no longer disconnected from God.

Chapter Five
The Importance of Vibration

Many humans live unconsciously, without significant light or real love, polluting the atmosphere of Earth with unhealthy thoughts and feelings. What is sorely needed is a purification of the atmosphere, both individual and collective. There have been lone voices throughout recorded history that have cried out pleading that man shake himself free of the denial and stupor that holds him in bondage. The voices are generally ignored. It is time humanity recognizes a blinding identification problem.

The lost sense of true identification is not only causing damage to the soul of mankind but is creating overwhelming damage in the environment. If the masses do not awaken soon regarding the spirit within and the purpose of life, suffering will worsen and hope be dashed to the ground. Something has to be done now to stop the downward spiral into chaos and destruction. You can do your part by being responsible and paying attention to personal energy. When life is experienced as a dark pit, you must become your own candle. Be aware of the fact that you are a generator spewing out positive or negative vibratory forces through thoughts, feelings and actions. Ongoing unhappiness is the consequence of what your attitude and behavior send forth. True happiness and unconditioned peace emanate from the level of spirit.

Plato said: "To understand all is to forgive all." Understand the importance of vibration and how it affects every aspect of life both visibly and invisibly, and the knowledge will be beneficial. To have the capacity to learn, be eager and thirst and hunger after truth. It may be necessary for you to unlearn many things the world has taught you before wisdom can be claimed. Be an empty cup and the God-life will supply what is needed.

My intention is not to bog you down with intellectual details. It is far healthier and productive to feel my words, do research and then take positive action. What I share is my truth, but it also resonates with similar teachings of souls who have chosen a path that led to self-mastery. When it comes to the subject of survival, it is best not to place your entire faith in the intellect. The intellect does not increase spiritual vibration or make you wisdom filled. The soul and spirit, the two highest known subtle parts of us, are more advanced than the intellect in the realm of consciousness. The key is to learn to identify with what is holy.

What must become common knowledge is the great truth that when you vibrate in unison and harmony with your spiritual identity as well as with the forces of the universe, life becomes orderly. In contrast, by remaining controlled by the personality, various weaknesses and losses are created due to ignorance and unpaid debts. Eventually, causes and their effects must be faced. Life is sacred, a truth that has been cast aside. Contentment is never permanent when the focus is solely on matter. It is a law that you grow to resemble the focus. Increase a sense of the sacred and do something about controlling the personality. The goal is not to eliminate it, but rather allow the spirit of truth to take charge. By deliberately lifting your mind to an atmosphere of love and order, transformation begins within as well as in the environment. You become a power channel in helping others.

The physical body is a series of light waves. As consciousness is elevated, the light waves change in quality and vibration and you are a conductor of light. Discipline, effort, meditation, contemplation, prayer and changing of patterns will transform conditions. If your desire is sincere, you will begin to resemble the higher nature of the wise spirit within. Spirit is the source of all value and energy. Fusion occurs and a chemical union of true concepts and moral elements takes place. The result is an awakening intuitive mind. What is accomplished through effort is the removing of that which does not work and replacing it with something better.

A position of limitation is changed through inner knowledge. To receive inner knowledge, definite and scientific steps must be taken that will work towards becoming humanly what you are spiritually. It is possible to stop living in a way that is a direct contradiction to the order of Cosmic Intelligence. It is destiny to eventually be luminous, wise, pure and perfect. Why not become a rebel against weaknesses, mediocrity and laziness?

One of the roadblocks preventing peace and harmony is the tremendous influence of the subconscious memory. Humans live their lives for the most part reflecting the stored influences projecting forth from the subconscious. This has been ongoing since the beginning of the soul's journey. Progress is achieved when you no longer dwell in projections. When wisdom is regained, you will be able to look at someone or something with a nonjudgmental attitude. A pure and peaceful heart is one that is finally free of all negative projections.

You can see only that which you are like. One of the secrets of illumination and true joy is to harmonize everything within. By taking charge of destiny, equanimity will spill over into the outer life. This is easier said than done. The average person is ruled by fate and has minimal influence in the control of his life. Removing old established patterns that work against enlightenment and not repeating mistakes can change fate. What will effectively work is to engrave a high ideal into the new patterns. Freedom begins to be an integral part of personal reality when a willingness to be vigilant in thought, word and deed occupies the mind.

Destiny is in the stereotypes or patterns you create. To create balance and heal the body, emotions and mind, a strong desire to be free from suffering is necessary. This does not mean you neglect the material dimension. Instead, learn how to intertwine both materiality and spirituality and live outwardly the new understanding gained through right desire and sacrifice. Sacrifice in this context means to remove weaknesses and replace them with newfound strengths. No one can give you freedom. It is an inner experience that is born when you accept your eternal identity and no longer harbor fear.

Observe whether responses are working for or against you. The collective and individual negativity that is prevalent everywhere is a form of psychic poison. There are techniques that will help in combating psychic poison. Psychic poisoning can be a worse form of disease, decay and death than what is negatively occurring in our food and environment. Any area of life that is working against progression of the soul must be eliminated, although few people are aware or concerned about the psychic warfare going on all around them. Challenges are an opportunity for growth in consciousness as well as opening the heart to unconditional love. It is satisfying to make good use of what disturbs and use it as a transformation tool.

There are simple practices that will help you. When you bathe, envision White Light caressing the body, purifying every cell. Imagine the body as a sponge absorbing the healing energy. White light combines and unites the entire seven-color spectrum. Research the benefits of color and light therapy. It is also beneficial when color is lovingly projected on others who ask for help. Ancient cultures used color for healing treatments on various organs. The system has become popular again in recent years.

Think of yourself as a power plant. There are seven main power stations where energy is stored. The energy power stations are called "chakras." They are located in the next closest energy field, called the etheric. The vibrating stations are like interlocking wheels, which allow the energies to go up and down the subtle etheric body according to which special energy is needed. The wheels are located in the crown (pineal), brow (pituitary), throat (thyroid and parathyroid), heart (thymus), solar plexus (adrenals and pancreas), spleen (spleen) and root-sacrum (gonads and prostate). Each wheel has a color and a life assignment. The seven etheric charkas can be completely transformed into the Divine Image.

It is possible through an enlightened consciousness to evolve physical electrons to the next evolutionary step. Transformation of both consciousness and physicality is a gradual process. Eventually, through inner knowledge, growth and application, you will ascend to the radiations of a Master. If the plan is to be in step with a program where self-mastery and regeneration is achieved, the electromagnetic activity of your force fields will need to be adjusted.

By taking a few moments to mentally stop and visualize the body and its energy fields being embraced by healing rays, a cleansing and calming effect is created. Through daily reminders, you will either begin to create a new program in the subconscious or strengthen what already exists. It also is a convenient way to absorb the power of Light into your energy.

The first time that I was favored with a vision symbolizing the intricate pathways of the etheric health system, I was impressed by how complicated it is. The etheric field duplicates the interior of the physical body. It is similar to a maze of endless pathways of lines and curves. The energy patterns show weaknesses in health prior to the problem appearing in the physical body. It is this network of energy that must be corrected before a healing occurs in the dense form.

Have you ever given thought to the needs of the invisible part of your makeup? To nourish the subtle bodies, understand that these fields have always existed in varying degrees of power and influence. The physical-etheric body is built in the image of the emotional-astral body. The astral body is built in the image of the lower mental body. The lower mental body is built in the image of the higher Causal mind energy. God/Spirit dwells within you in the external world. The origin of individual spirit is in the invisible Causal Mental World. The imaging advances into the higher Celestial Realms. These "worlds" are states of consciousness. Appearances deceive. All parts of your makeup are within; they are not necessarily activated.

The physical body is a diminished version of the Celestial form. The physical body can, through a focused mind, attract the perfected non-polarized energy of the higher vibrations into the lesser through the science of mind and love.

Every moment you are creating consciously and unconsciously. Why not make a choice to deliberately create a new attitude and habits that work for truth and beauty? In other words, make new recordings and deliberately replace the old ones that have been buried in the memory archives, creating separation from wholeness and joy. Attention is required regarding old destructive patterns; they must be stopped and not allowed to surface, destroying any new efforts and purpose. Everything that has ever happened, both good and not good, is stored in the subconscious. The engravings constantly repeat themselves. To be free, deliberately change the engravings. When you change the engravings, vibrations improve. If you don't, misery and a sense of division will continue.

Dare to open your mind and heart. To be truly alive is to be filled with radiant Light. It is the soul's destiny to be whole, perfect and free. Spiritual growth is a process of purification. A truth seeker lifts the thinking mind to a higher level to discover the hidden essence. He directs his life to the sublime regions of the soul and spirit. To manifest reality, keep an image of perfection in both the mind and heart. You will need to cultivate a strong willingness to be unlimited. Most people act as if they have a death wish. They knowingly indulge in habits that are proven to destroy life.

Why not make a decision to change the direction of your life and make it more beautiful? Take charge. Transcend the worst enemy, the ego-personality, and spirit to soul evolution occurs. If a divided heart and mind lingers, duality remains a constant. When conflict lives in the mind and body, the soul cannot express and the immune system weakens. The devil is a symbol reminding us of the violation of Spirit that continues until this day. Negative intelligence and the lower vibrations, both visible and invisible, thrive on spiritual ignorance. Spiritual ignorance is the divider; it introduces confusion, fear and separation. Continuing to exist from the level of the primate lower self, spiritual evolution is delayed.

It is possible to achieve a balance between handling worldly obligations and pursuing contemplative needs. Look for the middle way and avoid extremes. Self-analysis and self-inspection accelerate healing, as does gratitude. Pay attention to what is felt within and quickly repair any mistakes. The sublime work is to transform the lower nature. Why wait? What a shame it would be not to take advantage of this life.

Destiny is to recapture and live the higher Nature. A student is required to embody teachings that work. To be successful, learn and understand the science of vibration. Vibration matches personal consciousness. Individual consciousness is the springboard to freedom. You will begin to look at yourself as an acrobat striving for balance. Skills will greatly improve through knowledge and the applying of them with enthusiasm, love and feeling. Higher knowledge increases vibrations and enables you to learn a new rhythm, a dance of life that is joyful and unencumbered.

Everything is constantly changing, including the physical body. What is frequently forgotten is the fact that all things live in rhythmical vibrations; all seek the harmonious and are repelled by dissonance. If intent is to live in harmony within and without, respect and be in charge of the physical, etheric, emotional, mental and spiritual environment. The physical body is actually two bodies, a dense body made up of solids, liquids and gases and an etheric body, which remains with it until physical death. Everything animate or inanimate has an etheric body. The etheric body interpenetrates the dense physical body and is composed of materials from the next four higher invisible levels of vibratory light.

The etheric body is also called the bioplasmic or vital body. The etheric acts as a medium through which the life-currents emanating from the Sun interact with the physical body. The etheric or vital aura is the matrix in which the body grows, just as the embryo does in the womb. It is filled with energy counterparts of every organ, cell, cell nucleolus, molecule, chemical atom and subdivision of atoms in a series of levels. If you could psychically see the etheric body, you would see that it consists of a structure of lines, force or energy patterns anchored to the physical matter of the tissues. The tissues exist because of the vital field constantly moving and shimmering. The etheric-vital body is the bridge between the objective physical world and the higher subtle bodies. No subjective or objective experience can reach the brain without it.

As mentioned before, the etheric body has moving whirlpools, vortices of energy, situated at specific points on the body, called chakras. These organs of the psychic aspect are part of every living creature. The etheric is intimately connected with the controlling mechanism of the dense body through the nervous system and the endocrine glands. A good fact to remember is how thought affects the etheric field. The etheric field maintains coherence and health as a result of your state of mind. Considering the enormous stress experienced in the world, meditation is one means of restoring order within where all positive change must first occur.

The energies taken in by all etheric forms are transmuted into the various life-energies needed to sustain order in the visible created form. Technically, we call the etheric body our health aura. The etheric is influenced both by physical conditions, nutrition and hygiene and the spiritual, psychological state of the individual. If neglect occurs, the currents' rhythmic flow is broken, irregular and can actually stagnate.

Pure thoughts, pure body and focusing on the Divine are the winning combination to propel you forward, leading to wholeness and freedom. Ask God what you can do to establish a higher consciousness on Earth. This prayer alone will transform your life. You will be doing not only yourself a favor, but benefiting the collectivity. A pure body and mind repels coarse particles because the particles vibrate at rates discordant with its own. A coarse body attracts them because their vibrations are in accord with its own. It is wisdom to accept the truth of how you attract or repel particles through what is placed in the mind and body. If serious about changing consciousness, consider improving the intensity of your vibration.

Increasing and purifying vibrations will build an armor of protection and strength. The negative easily bounces off the field and you are not usually beset with the ordinary problems that weaken humans. If a negative energy does approach, it is usually neutralized through a developed consciousness. There is a constant bombardment of collective and individual thought. This is why you may act, speak or think in a certain way

The Importance of Vibration

and not understand where that impulse came from. It is in your power through self-mastery to create protection and not be a target for damaging outside influences. Living the divine life has the power to lessen danger.

We are self-conscious beings evolving toward Christ and Cosmic Consciousness. It is our responsibility to be the ruler of our own kingdom, exercising order, sustaining peace, as well as developing and maintaining habits that work for and not against our ideal. The purity or impurity of conscious thoughts and actions will largely influence health, as well as the dream state.

To extract the true divine nature, be vigilant and guard not only the gate of the five senses, but do everything in your power to insure that products or psychic pollution do not corrupt personal vibrations. It is extremely important to be conscious of how to use energy. Without fully understanding the consequences, you influence and work with subtle matter every day. Whatever is said and done releases forces.

Build an oasis through study, contemplation, meditation, and a developed understanding. Love and accept who you are. When you do, life can literally be transformed. Why only be a recipient of secondhand knowledge? Everyone has the right and capability to achieve an intimate relationship with the Divine. Your assignment is to strive toward union. Begin now by choosing actions that create happiness and liberation. Genuine recognition of who you really are and a love for truth will bring forth a balanced life. A state of beauty and wholeness does not happen by itself. Embrace education and good changes that provide the ideal nourishment for a healthy body temple and an awakened mind.

To create rightly must be done through intense feeling, otherwise it is soulless. Harsh experiences can be eliminated if you choose to draw the hidden spirit into the conscious experience of daily life. No one else can do this for you. This is a moment-to-moment choice that is a certain path to liberation and joy. The shadows of the subconscious will continue to surface, but instead of drowning in them, the appearances will pass through you without pain. You will look at past mistakes as wrong choices and move forward in compassion towards your own journey into fullness.

Achieving the ultimate freedom, God Realization, removes the mind from confusion, suffering and the illusion. Enjoy being a conscious creator. The journey of integration and discovery is the greatest and most satisfying choice. With renewed and determined passion for wholeness, personal vibrations increase and wisdom may whisper into an attentive ear. Educate yourself and apply the universal principles. Knowledge is power. Right now in what is called space-time, you have the potential to become what you love and become what you know. Kabir, the great poet of India said, "Life is a field and you were born to cultivate it." It stands to reason, if you know how to cultivate and nurture it, you will reap the fruit.

Chapter Six
The Higher Self

Hope is renewed when we resonate with the eternal vibrations of the Spirit of Truth. The Spirit is divine love. It is a power and presence that infuses our energy as a crystalline structure and frees us from the vibration of old bondage that lurks within the subconscious. It is through the activity of the Holy Spirit that we consciously renew a conscious relationship with the higher Self. As God has spoken to others who are of pure mind and heart, God will speak to us through the Spirit of Truth and the vibrations of Light. When we choose love and wisdom, a stronger vibratory pathway will be activated and the Creative Spirit will make Her presence known.

Many seekers lose faith in religion because it rarely explains who we really are. Knowledge is power. To evolve you require a clear realization of the transformation process that must be undertaken. When you have knowledge of the fields that comprise identity you will no longer question the existence of God. The transcendent half of you, the higher Self, is an intricate part of your existence although it has been veiled for the most part. Because of forgetfulness and an erroneous sense of division, suffering and confusion exists. Once the complexity of what you are visibly and invisibly is clearly understood, it is impossible to deny the truth that God lives within you as the higher Self.

The ultimate goal is to rediscover the most sublime part of the Self. The sublime consists of three invisible layers of consciousness referred to as the Causal Mental Mind, the Soul and the Spirit. Since the energy of the higher Self cannot be intellectually described, I ask for your patience and understanding. It is remarkably indefinable. What I can share is your part in bringing forth the Indescribable. Only then will you fully grasp what I am talking about. Both the lesser energies of body, emotions and mind and the higher sublime subtle energies must be brought together and work as a cohesive whole. True mastery is when you have integrated

BE: Embracing the Mystery

all parts of your self into one vibrating intelligent unit of creative light. You are then capable of freely living as love in action because a sense of division is no longer a part of your consciousness.

Refusing to be only half alive will create a new race. By choosing inner growth, spiritual strength, calmness of mind and serenity of character, the flowering of the soul occurs. Misidentification and lack of acceptance acts as a restraint preventing you from being fully your true magnificent self. It is impossible to bring forth a complete transcendence over the lower nature if you have not accepted the higher Nature. What is real and lasting is the higher Nature. The human part of you is the vehicle used to return to the status of completeness and perfection.

A joyous aspect in becoming wisdom-filled is to achieve enough self-control to prevent future suffering. You will bury ignorance through knowledge, understanding and revelation. Once you fully grasp the totality of how the physical life depends on the subtle life, creation begins to make sense. The physical lower nature was gradually evolved over eons of time. This holds true for the higher Nature as well.

Understanding the infinite possibilities and potential for growth will give birth to enlightenment and eventually to a permanent conscious connection with the lofty worlds of Divine thought. This is the philosophy of sages and great masters. Union will free you from the base parts of the lower self. Union means to blend the thinking mind with the super conscious level of mind. Super consciousness is the active energy of the soul. Soul and spirit control the physical body although the subconscious and instinct is the primary influence on daily life. Consciousness is a common and neutral mirror for all forces. It is an inner screen where everything is projected on it.

Some people have the mistaken idea that they will automatically become similar to an angel when they leave the body. Others believe that resurrection occurs when they are physically dead. The resurrection is when consciousness returns to a state of oneness with God and has become as pure as the angels. For souls who are incarnating, transformation occurs on Earth. The universal assignment is to master the senses and matter. When the facts of reincarnation are clearly revealed, humankind will not be fooled by false teachings and the purpose of life will be finally understood.

The higher subtle vibrations are available to everyone according to the quality of thought, feeling and action. Within the highest realms, all is united. Within the lower invisible planes and the lower worlds of matter, separation and confusion is the norm. You have the power to bring your energy back to the fundamental Oneness. It is accomplished by placing the spiritual life in the center of your activity. Everything else will revolve around it.

In contrast, as long as you continue to live blindly and in denial of the existence of a non-material Limitless Light, personal spirit, universal laws and spiritual evolution, you will continue to stumble and be misled. To be permanently free of disorder and spiritual ignorance is to learn to control the human personality and identify with the higher Self.

Everything in the universe is part of a vast and expanding hierarchy of consciousness. Existence depends on the subtle world of intelligent and loving Light. If you have not made a permanent connection, how can you receive genuine knowledge and guidance? By training the mind to focus on the subtle, you eventually develop a realization as to how to grasp the Laws of the Universe and the absolute necessity of living them.

There is nothing that can compare to drinking the wine of God's love and wisdom. Be a thinker and insist on learning the science of spiritual evolution and how it impacts every level of creation. Life will change for the better because it has meaning and is nourished by the fire of discovery. Spiritual evolution is the path to joy and freedom. It is a science, a power and a living Presence. This Presence is Unnamable and unenlightened thought cannot comprehend it. It is who you really are.

When cooperating with the Science, you intuitively learn how to increase vibrations. Increasing vibration is a process that descends from the finer invisible Light Worlds filtering down to the planes of heavier matter. Keep the focus on the Godhead, realizing and encouraging the spiritual Light to become a stronger part of your physical, emotional and mental makeup. Protect, purify and illuminate your life, because, thanks to your efforts, you will obtain true knowledge, true clairvoyance, true riches and true powers.

The physical world is a condensation of primordial Light. Light is the substance, which emanated from God in the beginning. By means of Light, the invisible and visible worlds were created. The Light was drawn forth from within the unfathomable Supreme Creator.

The universe and all its creations are God's very own substance, the

One Power. In nature, examples are plentiful. Creation manifests when images are projected outward and are crystallized, becoming material form. Intelligent life are the seed children who can also choose to do the same creative work in varying degrees according to the level of individual consciousness. The next step is to lift consciousness higher than the intellect to the realm of Spirit.

The more conscious and intense personal light, the more easily you are able to reconnect with the Divine on a permanent level of activity. The stronger you become spiritually, the greater the ability to be a power for good. Intense vibrations animate the Divine World in contrast to the incalculably weak vibrations of matter. To consciously work with the divine levels of creation, you must be knowledgeable, disciplined, and maintain a selfless intent. In time, an increase in personal energy, both visible and invisible, is experienced and sustained. The purpose of intelligent creation is to increase our particles, filling them with purity, and become divine by being responsible and developing self-mastery.

It is through will and choice that you can actually neutralize and be free from the common negative vibrations of the collective human consciousness. Everything necessary has been given you to develop and become the image and likeness of God. The image is the invisible blueprint within that determines the direction of the inner forces. The likeness is the virtues and gifts. Plans for the evolution of intelligent life abide in the finer bodies that originated in the invisible worlds.

The higher Self is the Causal Mind, Soul and Spirit. From the viewpoint of the celestial hierarchies, it extends much further into realms that finite mind cannot comprehend. The first of the celestial energies is the Causal Mind. It is the gateway to the Divine. As higher Mind, it carries individuality from one life to the next. Eternal Self absorbs into itself only the experiences that can be reproduced in the vibration of its Causal Body. The vibrations are highly intellectual as well as lofty in moral character. Because of the make-up of the Causal Mind, it can only give to the lower human consciousness a vibration response if the individual has grown in moral and spiritual stature.

We cannot receive that which we have not prepared for, nor can we give that which we do not already have. The greater our inner wisdom awareness, the more likely the Eternal Self will use the Causal energy and contribute to each successive life. It is a receptacle and treasure house of

The Higher Self

all that has been assimilated from the past. The Causal Mind is the finer, highly developed Mind; it is a heavenly counterpart of the lower mind. It is an eternal substance. The two are linked together.

The next higher aspect of the Self is the soul. The soul is mystically looked upon as the feeling Feminine Principle. It receives, expands, and dilates and symbolically is water. It is our super conscious state of mind. Everything that comes from Above or below passes through the soul. The soul, in contrast to the physical body, never gets old or weak. It is still evolving. Human thought relates to images. We create a form to fit the various aspects of what we call our self.

The soul began as a seed, a germ of infinite possibilities, hidden in matter. It eventually changes into a full-blown masterpiece through the handiwork of patient effort in perfecting the lower nature through deliberate choices and scientific means. Bliss is experienced as pulsations of Light harmonically in rhythm with the universe. Visibly it can be witnessed as dancing light throughout the force fields. As I write these words, the Sublime is flooding my vision. Dazzling light is dancing over the page and expanding throughout the room. The feeling is one of intense gratitude and joy for something that cannot be described except to say that I feel overwhelmed by the Immensity of the blessing. Its Presence is a magnificence and beauty, a downpouring of unconditional love.

To be showered with God's Light is similar to watching an elegant display of fireworks. Instead of sitting on the ground looking skyward, you find yourself skyward in the midst of an ongoing explosion of light geometries. You are carried by the rhythm, knowing who you are, your relationship to the Whole and what God Is. The pulsating Light is intense. Pause in your reading and receive God's love, allowing it to caress and heal you. Allow your soul to expand and be touched. Being immersed in radiant celestial love while writing to you is no accident. The blessing is meant for you as well. God's love is available to all of us. Reach for It, embrace It and you will never be the same again.

Hopefully in this unexpected and special moment together, you also felt the overwhelming joy of oneness I fondly refer to as real magic. True magic is creative. It is a spiritual action that occurs at the right moment in the right setting. The effect is perfect accord. When in vision, you are at one with the essence of harmony, justice and beauty. When you receive the magic, no one or no thing can take it away from you. It is all that matters.

In my attempt to reveal a love of amazing magnitude and aliveness, a memory of another experience that was similar came to mind. I was in bed and fully awake. My soul felt a thrilling expansion, a harmonic movement. I suddenly found my consciousness free of the physical body in a way quite different from a typical out-of-body experience. I was lifted upward and immersed in a glorious realm of total joy and freedom. There were no restrictions, only the unlimited matrix of patterned heavenly Light. I found myself within a geometric flower petal design, which is referred to as a symbol for creation. The matrix is called the Flower of Life.

It is said that all knowledge is within the matrix. The exhilarating inner sensation was profound. I felt unbounded and joyous knowing within every cell of my being what true freedom meant. Separation did not exist, only union with God. The experience of being harmonically and mystically attuned without confinement has been a frequent visitor. It is a spontaneous and sublime oneness with all creation. Fusion, ecstasy, the mystical life is not comprehended through the intellect; it is a revelation directly from the higher Self. Fusion is ours for the asking.

Self Realization is the merging of the invisible vehicles with the visible. The form of light for the higher Self is developed through an expanding consciousness; it is a part of the eternal identity. When all of the seven spiritual energy centers are functioning in perfect harmony and aligned with divine Light, the eighth chakra, located above the crown of the head, becomes activated. It is at this point that you are consciously connected to the higher Self. The eighth chakra opens the gate to wisdom. Superior spiritual knowledge is received. The connection will be sporadic in the beginning of the regeneration program, but eventually it will be permanently established.

It is the higher Self who works with the Christ Energy. The plan is to evolve and connect to the Godhead and the many planes of Light. An evolving soul needs assistance. You are not alone. The celestial beings work with the higher Self and bring to your remembrance immortality, knowledge and unconditional love. They bathe you in beauty. Our brothers and sisters of Light assist in the reprogramming of the soul so it can reach a higher wavelength of Light. The result is a Light encoding that occurs between the physical body and the higher Self. The two become one active unit of consciousness.

The Higher Self

The higher Self includes the soul. It communicates through light geometries, which are symbols and pictographs, which link and fill the mind with spiritual information. The witnessing of the Language of Light and being able to consciously interpret it is a blessing that will support your journey to wholeness.

There is a radiation of Light called Merkabah, which allows the higher Self to connect with the physical body. It is a vehicle of communication and travel used by celestial beings to help seekers connect to the Divine. You also have your own Merkabah. When you seek and achieve higher knowledge, being creatively reunited consciously with the higher Self can override negative programming. It is the Christ Energy that assists in your attunement.

The unenlightened soul has much to overcome. Because of early influences by fallen masters misusing energy, many souls have been deterred from realizing their divine higher Self. A return to wholeness will happen through an intimacy with Light.

Very little is written regarding the higher Self and the forms that it may take or the worlds that it calls its own. For now what you can do is ask for guidance, love, healing power and intimacy. Higher knowledge becomes a living reality when you deliberately choose to evolve towards pure divinity. Once you begin to think, feel and act from the viewpoint of the higher Self, you are eligible to progress into the next level, the Christed Higher Self. Evolution continues.

When you are directly under the energy influence of your true identity, you are no longer kept in a lower world slavery consciousness. The goal is to cease being separated from the divine Limitless Light. Restoration occurs when the Christ Light penetrates both the physical body and its energy fields and the higher Self. This is perfectly stated in Isaiah 40:13. We reach a point of spiritual evolution where we are "Actively dwelling in a body of Light" within the body of flesh.

There is always more to understand and greater levels of growth. Awareness is a progressive realization of Omnipresence that brought forth creation both visible and invisible. The Soul and the Eternal Spirit are partners. They are the energy using the vehicle of the Causal Mind. Christ and Cosmic Consciousness are realized through the three higher invisible aspects of Self. The greater your understanding of what comprises spiritual identity, the greater the ability to experience the holy secrets of life. As the Soul is the super consciousness, the Spirit is the divine consciousness. The purpose of life is to become a whole light being and sustain a constant garment of Light.

The higher Self has its own form. The form is one of a series of invisible advanced vehicles of Light. To fully understand and demonstrate the higher Self and its vibrations and capabilities, the individual must be consciously connected to the higher Mind (causal), Soul (light-love) and Spirit (wisdom). The goal is to permanently activate the Power and Presence of the Christ Energy within your own consciousness. A Christ is an individual who is consciously intimate with all three aspects of the higher Self. He or she demonstrates the power of Christ in both a visible and invisible form. When an individual claims its highest identity, all the possible God aspects are at his disposal. A "sonship" is consciously established in the flesh.

Ask for the Christ Light to penetrate all your force fields. Focus higher. Being a Christ is the goal. It is the highest level of consciousness we can reach in form. When it manifests, it washes away the stains of the lower personality and all falsity. In the physical dimension, you are destined to know your true identity as a higher being, a Self of light, wisdom and love.

Chapter Seven
Cycles of Brightness

Man is ready for the mysteries to be revealed, and through an awakened mind, he will know the Divine. The answer to what God is becomes known in part as a result of a heightened consciousness. Our belief system determines reality. Divinity has a different form for each individual. Humanity hungers and thirsts for truth. For instance, the term "Son of God" according to Hindu, Egyptian and Greek initiates meant a consciousness identified with Divine truth and a will capable of manifesting it. The sons of God were messengers from the highest heavens. Jesus, an example of a Son of God, is also referred to as a Christ, meaning he demonstrated Christ and Cosmic Principles. He understood man as seeking after his greater Self. His role was to help man restore himself.

The higher purpose of physical life is spiritual evolution and the transformation of matter. Creation is destined to evolve. This means the solar system as well. Evolution is growth and development to the point of perfection. The new Lyman Spitzer Space Telescope can reveal what has been formerly hidden. In the past, telescopes looking at visible light found their view blocked by opaque walls of dust and cold gas. Under the new Spitzer telescope's gaze, those clouds all but disappear to reveal startling images of origins of planets, stars and galaxies that have been previously invisible. New faculties of intelligence are developing, making it possible for us to understand the hidden. Science is actually describing what an enlightened mind is capable of perceiving when the veils of ignorance are removed.

A re-education of the mind is necessary to progress. Each soul's responsibility is to personally unveil what is behind the opaque walls of ignorance through developed spiritual senses. To work on opaque, coarse, unrefined matter and transform it, we are required to call on hidden Intelligence. The new telescope has lifted a cosmic veil. It is also possible to remove the tangled mixture created by the senses with an awakened spiritual sight and mind. A grander cosmic view gifts us with the fullness of Light, a stability and peace.

The universe is made of Spirit and matter; it is a combined action. When Spirit Energy dominates matter, evolution of consciousness takes place. Train the mind and ask for Divine assistance. At some point of growth, it will be given. The world lacks serenity. When the motivation is an inner urge to return to unity consciousness, serenity and truth become visible and tangible elements.

If a new vibration from the outside physical world impacts the inner memory, the counterpart or finer vibratory power within becomes activated. A good example of this truth is in reading material. If you respond thinking that the words studied sound familiar, it is very likely that the inner vibratory power of the highest mental vehicle, the Causal Body, recognizes the material as familiar and true. If you are not ready to adjust conscious thinking and accept a new idea, the seed thought is stored for later germination. Nothing is lost. Stimulation is required to draw out what has been learned in past experiences. Look to teachings that work for the good of all. They will guide new thought. Call on a higher form of Intelligence within. Stimulation quickens the wisdom.

This is why it is very important to carefully choose associates, reading material, the messages listened to, and activities that may deplete energy rather than support it. The inner responds to the outer. There are limitless expressions of energy in space. The energy is as strong as the power that is given to it. Like attracts like. The energy looks through space for a place to attach itself, lasting as long as centuries. If any part of you is not guarded, wandering vagrant thought forms, which are a powerful form of energy, are bound to disturb any resemblance of order.

When the present form no longer exists as flesh, the growth achieved remains in the energy field of the Causal higher mental body. When a new human life is created after an assimilation and rest period in the vibratory in-between worlds of Spirit, the memory is handed down and will be awakened in a fresh mold and personality if and when needed. The higher Causal mind of the indwelling Spirit is the storehouse. It is very similar to a computer. Thoughts and feelings are powerful forces. A soul arrives on Earth with habits and thoughts that were formed in previous experiences.

Ancient thoughts and feelings may torment and are the consequences of past decisions and actions. It is important to free the lower nature of all false notions that linger. Growth is benefited when a good hard look is taken at what has been learned and inherited. Until new thoughts and habits are firmly installed, become an observer, which will place the thought process above the conditioning. Usually, conscious thoughts are from the past or looking into the future.

The goal is to attract more Light. Light is the symbol of the Present moment. The Present is outside of thought. It is in the reality of the Absolute. You know the Present as an innate experience, an intuitive thought, feeling or vision. Innate power will assist you in releasing certain forces and neutralize others by understanding that what was created that is working against spiritual growth can be changed. The physical experiment is a means to realize God in matter. The innate knowledge awakens through the senses. Spirit, which is an abstract, needs a concrete support in time and space of a form so it can be experienced.

A human-like intelligence has been found that lived 880,000 years prior to the written version of the Bible. The more that explorers and archaeologists unearth manmade evidence, the more it is realized that the human tree needs to be expanded. Enough solid evidence indicates Earth and its life intermittently go through cycles of light and darkness. In our present world cycle, the truth regarding the origin of life is still a mystery. Since we are slowly moving into a cycle where discovery of the past is being brought to our attention, hopefully more light will be shed on this subject.

If we choose to go further back in evolutionary history through private research, we discover written records that present another view of how a perfect Adamic race was intercepted and limited by fallen angels. Lesser brotherhoods have interfered with the evolution of man according to the Bible, The Book of Enoch, The Vedic Teachings and innumerable tablets and scrolls that are coming to our attention. It is still very obvious that whatever really happened, the human body is a marvelous creation designed by a Cosmic Intelligence beyond finite understanding.

There are also scriptural records of wars that have occurred in the invisible lower heaven worlds. The Bible mentions beings called the Nephilim who descended to Earth and mated with Earth females, creating offspring. The ancient writings claim that visitors made man in their image. The fallen Lords did not reflect the holiness of the One God. Was

Cosmic Law violated? If this turns out to be truth, then who created the intelligent beings who landed and manipulated the DNA of humans?

In contrast to the activity that happened long ago, the Infinite Living Light acts to restore Light to the lower worlds of duality and suffering. Out of love for the human race, the records mention that upgrades have been made in the force fields of man so he could have the ability to commune with otherworldly intelligence. Brothers of Light also incarnate in man to help in humanity's reprogramming, regeneration and eventual resurrection.

There are degrees of soul evolution, connecting the human species to a variety of possibilities. The more evidence scientists uncover, the greater our understanding and view of the whole spectrum of life. There are always philosophical and theological implications that arise with every new discovery. As additional information surfaces, we begin to comprehend the unity between science and religion, as well as receive answers that may leave us feeling uncomfortable or confused. Historical records are providing clues as to how the human race was originated. They are also indicating that there was more than one beginning.

The *Book of Enoch*, which was excluded in most versions of the Old Testament, was nevertheless part of ancient Hebrew scholarship and is included in the Ethiopian and Slavic versions of the Old Testament. The rebel group, the Nephilim, who I have already mentioned from Genesis, settled the Earth and interbred with the existing humans. Nephilim means 'those who came down' into the Persian Gulf area many thousands of years ago. Ancient peoples believed in gods of flesh and blood who had descended to Earth from the heavens and could, through advanced technology, soar heavenwards. The writings of the ancient Near East also clearly speak of a planet from which these gods had come.

There is growing scientific evidence from the Babylonian and Celtic cultures that primitive Earthman had physical evolutionary assistance. This new coupling mixed the DNA and created a race of intelligent beings much faster than if the Earth's evolutionary process was left untouched. According to recent discoveries, the alien intelligence was extremely high and had acquired a superior knowledge regarding genetic engineering of a species, as well as possessing physical life spans reaching well into the upper hundreds. Was there a special creation for selfish purposes or were the advanced beings solely instruments used to bring forth a higher life form on Earth? The beings colonized a civilization in Sumer, which flourished suddenly 6,000 years ago without a known precursor.

There already exist thousands of ancient Sumerian tablets that have been interpreted as literal descriptions of events as they occurred in one of the earlier advanced stages of development. The Sumerians had detailed knowledge of all the planets in the solar system, understood the precession of the equinoxes, and also had an understanding of complex medical procedures. The entwined serpent was used then as it is now as a sign of medicine. The entwined Serpent emulates the structure of the genetic code, the secret knowledge. Were the Sumerians the offspring of DNA manipulation?

The Puranas of ancient Vedic literature of India inform us that humans have existed for vast periods of cyclical time. Although there is fossil evidence that anatomically modern humans existed millions of years ago, living forms could not have been in existence if they were not governed by a vital force, which is the subtle invisible energy called Spirit. Creation is a concretization of cosmic energy entering into matter and eventually leaving it. We are all unique, creative expressions of a universal tune. Even our invisible blueprint is a symphony of expression that has been ignored. We are poetry, symmetry, harmonics and a song of life that humbles when understood.

Clues are also found in mythology regarding a race of giants/heroes who ruled over primitive humanity. The advanced beings were human in appearance and supposedly came from a far distant planet. As a result of the interaction between an advanced alien intelligence and the existing life forms on planet Earth, did physical and mental evolution progress more rapidly than it would have if Earth life evolved on its own?

The human bodies were not limited by instinct or lack of the potentialities of full reason. The new creation had the intelligence to evolve into enlightened beings. All space is ordered, whether the intelligent life form comes from another planet or our own. Order and balance are the law of the Cosmos. To fully express the divine potentiality within a physical form, a more advanced intelligence is required. One day the full truth regarding the origin of the human body will be known. Until then, all we can do is keep an open mind, realizing that anything is possible.

The human body is more than matter. Science is showing signs of agreement with the ancient wisdom science as a result of growing evidence that there is not only a body of matter but also a subtle mind element and energy, which never dies. Spirit is non-polarized energy. It is known through intuitive intelligence. Biological evolution, polarized energy, is not the whole answer, neither is extra-terrestrial mating with the fair daughters of Earth. Sanskrit histories as well as other ancient wisdom teachings speak of a third view where intelligent life descends from Spirit into matter.

A previous cycle called the Golden Age ended approximately 6000 BC. Seers in India, ancient China, the Old Kingdom in Egypt and the original Biblical Patriarchs knew the Science and Wisdom Teachings of Light. It was understood that there were multiple universes as well as multi-dimensional beings adapting to invisible and visible hierarchal creative planes of consciousness. Our human origins reach far beyond DNA, molecules and atoms.

The emergence of humanity has taken place in various Ages during the Earth's long history. Humans walked with dinosaurs and apes. In the past two centuries, archeologists have found human skeletons, footprints, and artifacts showing that people like ourselves existed during ancient cyclic periods. Each celestial cycle lasts 2,160 years. It appears as if man has made the climb from Stone Age to civilization more than once. Today, we are in the gap between the Dark Age of spiritual ignorance and moving towards an Age of Enlightenment.

As we awaken to a higher reality, new discoveries such as ancient texts will support inner knowledge. There is also growing support academically, scientifically and from scholarly known and accepted sources. Looking at the Hubble Space Telescope as an example, scientists believe that there are 400 billion galaxies and they are still growing. Finite mind cannot grasp that each galaxy usually has tens of billions of stars and many inhabited planets. We must be open to other viewpoints, realizing that we consciously know very little. Something remarkable occurs when we allow ourselves to connect pieces of information and "cross over" through time to the timeless vision of the cosmos.

When a constant connection is established with the higher Self, a profound Authority expresses through the thinking mind. Although we are temporarily in the flesh, we are destined to clothe ourselves with the perfect Authority whose seed exists within. We have direct access to the Divine through the spirit regardless of what plane we have adopted as our temporary environment. The complete spiritualization of matter is the ultimate goal here on Earth. Although humanity has a highly evolved physical body, we are obligated through our own effort to spiritualize the mind, emotions and the body. The goal is mastery over our own nature. Creation, whether an act of Divinity, DNA manipulation causing a genetic mutation or a natural process, is imbued with a life force, intelligence.

The life essence is within all form, whether it is mineral, vegetable, animal or man. All levels evolve according to desire and experience. Soul memory evolves as does matter. The cycle of the mineral world of form can be compared to the great unconscious. The beginnings of personality arise as does also the foreshadowing of sensation in the vegetable world, which is similar to the great subconscious.

The individual light, a conscious self, is placed in matter and experiences repetitive births allowing it to slowly evolve to a higher physical existence. When it advances to the animal kingdom, the animal will have developed both an etheric vital form and an emotional body. The cycle of the animal world is likened to consciousness. Subhuman life evolves through love. The more advanced the energy of the animal spirit, the less its collective group influence.

Looking at biological evolution possibilities, there is a specific point in natural evolution when the physical and emotional force fields are sufficiently evolved, opening the way for the descent of a higher energy from the invisible mental worlds. The soul/mind enters man. The process is supervised by the assistance of celestial helpers. Self-consciousness and the future potential ability to use intuitive thought and super consciousness are planted as a seed possibility.

To understand more than one possibility regarding evolution, a new cycle of brightness appears when a species is ready. It is time to acknowledge infinite possibilities and discover our role in the evolution of spirit through form. There are two general movements occurring on our planet. One is devolution and the other evolution.

The divine inner essence comes forth from the invisible subtle Light. Light is projected from the Supreme Spirit, the Great Cause behind all manifestation. Over millions of years, the seed possibilities for a higher consciousness and invisible life forms have been maturing, expanding in the same way that the physical body has evolved. Knowledge reveals that full spiritual impact and mental power does not take action until there is a suitable thinking mind, feeling nature and body to house it. The invisible energy fields are an impulse and an undefined energy field in the early stages of biological evolution.

Complication, multiplicity and estrangement occurs when any intelligences distance themselves from the Source. Desire is the architect that continues to live through the soul in matter. The changing soul is ruled by desire and nature, external events and interaction with others. What is gained in knowledge is stored for future use. Thought and energy is not organized during the early stages in the mental body. Reason is born when more than one mental image begins to appear. As desire experiences increase, the activity body is stimulated. The evolving creation learns about duality through experience, choices, desires, and in excesses of pain and joy. Duality is the teacher. Each new birth experience broadens understanding and the lessons are stored for future use. Form evolves whether seen or unseen.

The astral desire energy evolves slowly. It is the emotional feeling form. Eventually, the mental field is aroused. Through experience, the knowledge gained is stored in the Causal Mind, which is also expanding, and changing form. It is the highest mental causal energy that makes enlightenment possible. The physical, emotional, mental and moral experiences are stored in its treasure house. Continuity brings forth maturity. Although this brief overview is of a more complicated evolving life than most humans know, it will partially answer the differences that are evident in humanity. All areas of personal energy, as well as the exterior form, are refined when the lower nature cooperates with the Higher Nature.

Each soul-mind is given an opportunity to develop its latent inner power. A definite scientific order is involved which directs all the force fields. The joy of spiritual evolution is to be a channel for Divine Order. You become a transparency of Light when conscious effort seeks the high vibrations that bring forth wholeness. We differ as members of the human race because the particles of our individual physical, etheric, astral, mental and spiritual development are not the same. An individual is unique. This is one of many reasons why it is meaningless to judge another person.

As attunement is strengthened, the particles of light in the body purify. These particles at physical death will eventually return to the material of the invisible planes that they were originally drawn from before birth. What remains are the qualities recently gleamed from physical life. Everything is orderly in the higher worlds. It is a revelation to understand the ongoing struggle involving all life as it passes through the many stages of growth in order to develop a mind that is in resonance with the All-Knowing Mind. An intense desire to know truth is the required impulse. The soul requires knowledge, strength and a firm will power to not be enslaved to the five senses.

It is normal for an incarnating soul to experience loss of memory regarding previous Earth and heaven experiences. There are rare souls who do remember. To remember, spiritual maturity and readiness regarding the handling of information is a prerequisite. Eventually, the opaque veils drop and memories return in special moments, assisting the conscious awareness of the weary traveler. Before a new physical life begins, the mental seeds are vivified. The mental seeds are the powers that determine the newly created form. A different astral body is also created for the new incarnation. Memory is not totally lost; it remains in the higher causal body. Tapping into the treasure house within the causal body can access past life experiences.

The last cycle is a new physical body. When it is time to be reborn, the unit is influenced by the bonds of the past. The desire nature, relationships, developed mental-soul power, all affect physical heredity. The descending soul is assisted by highly evolved beings that guide the incarnation process. Environment and family are chosen as a result of the causes created in the past. A new subtle-etheric body, a copy of what the dense body will be, is built by helpful elementals under the direction of the Great Ones whose role is to govern the mental law of cause and effect. The new physical parent energy influences part of the building material forming the etheric and physical. The vital etheric body and the physical form match. One is visible and the other invisible.

Humanity has a choice to remain entrapped in a "jungle" consciousness, a "sheep" consciousness, or to be open to illumination and the secrets of life through direct experience with Light. Everything is ultimately Light. It is our reference point. Biological life evolves from a simple consciousness to self-consciousness and eventually to a Christ and Cosmic consciousness. An attunement to the Supreme Mind and Spirit as pure love is its highest manifestation. Intelligence on Earth, whether it originated as a descending or ascending movement, passes through a universal process leading to spiritual awakening, mastery of self and mastery of matter.

When the high road is chosen, the intuitive power of the right side of the brain is used. The wisdom gained will evolve outwards to the finer etheric, astral and mental energy fields. This is the return path of dignity to our original identity as a perfect spirit. Keep in mind that all the energy fields mentioned are aspects of our consciousness. Some are more developed and active than the others. Spiritual evolution is not escaping from Earth to remain in a heaven far away. It is doing your individual part in bringing heaven right here to Earth. A symbol for the bridge or interface between the earthly world and the inner world is the sacred geometrical shape called the Vesica Piscis as described by the first Gnostic Christians.

The symbol begins as a Circle representing God projecting into matter. Matter is the second circle. The center overlap between the two circles is the realm of balance, of Christ Consciousness. Every world civilization from Mesopotamia, Africa, Asia to India is aware of its cosmic significance. It is a vibrating, pyramidal, infinite structure that looks like an Arc and serves as a doorway to the celestial realms. The Arc is Living geometry assisting the receiver in remembering God's revelation. The symbolic Vesica Piscis is an intelligent and visible connection that I have experienced periodically all my life. When the sacred vision appears, it lasts approximately thirty minutes. As I watch the pulsations of living Light, the geometrical energy surrounds my force fields as well as moves through me. Spatial vision is incomprehensible. It transcends finite mind.

Lovers of truth are destined to recreate the lost paradise. With alignment of consciousness to the Infinite Indescribable, a vastness opens wide in the mind and heart revealing the secrets of creation. The opening breaks through the dualistic and oppositional experiences that mortals pass through. The result is to be consciously the full depth and breadth of life. Transformation occurs when the soul, mind and body is aligned with the pulse of Spirit. Metaphysical revelations intuitively make the unknown knowable. This is your capstone.

Chapter Eight
The Past Colors the Future

We live in an eternal evolving universe that is physical, mental and spiritual. Movement from one cycle to another occurs when collective consciousness, events or phenomena, is completed for that interval of space/time. Disorder in society is often the result of an expansion of consciousness. The current culture offers very little that is transcendent. A good aspect of disorder, division and lack is that it will bring forth questions and a search for a deeper meaning to life. When a passage from one zodiac sign into another occurs, a cosmic influence begins a new period. The soul of man is influenced by the influx of a different energy. The question of suffering surfaces and the desire for answers becomes dominant in the minds of thinkers.

Great teachers have all been great pupils. They have understood and learned well because they accepted and studied all people, situations and conditions. They learned from life what life and nature has to teach. The greatest teachers of humanity have matured through observation and personal experience. They are also part of a joyful family of souls who firsthand have the gifts and intimacy of the higher Self, the spirit of truth.

Think of yourself as Jacob climbing his famous Biblical ladder. Think of the ladder as a symbol for the many different levels of consciousness. This is why compassion is demanded of us. Regardless of our placement on the ladder of spiritual evolution, we have somewhere in time experienced the lower rungs. The cause of human suffering is partly caused by not having an ideal and living without active divine abilities. Unenlightened souls live without hope and usually do not receive guidance from a higher power. Power has many aspects. One of them is to understand who we are and why we are here. When truth and a higher knowledge are fixed in the mind, we fall in love with divinity.

Liberation depends on whether or not we agree to be influenced by negativity and false ideas. If the discernment level is weak, we may be swayed and dragged under by erroneous teachings and temptations. There is a prolific amount of parroting of wisdom. Because of this fact, many seekers have an unreal sense of enlightenment. It is an important tool to be able to unmask false wisdom. Misunderstood and false teachings are the fault of the spiritually weak, and those who have adopted an incomplete belief system are cut off from pure truth. The pure wisdom of Divine love is limitless and unconditioned. It is the level of consciousness that clearly interprets the sublime and sacred. Too many people function through the gross senses of perception and have no access to spirit. This is why they are never satisfied. As a result of a limited spiritual sensitivity, they are incapable of being open to unconditioned love or allowing forgiveness to manifest.

If moral character is not developed and we are unaware of Divine law, serious mistakes causing disorder and suffering will continue. Even the greatest and most exalted of truth seekers may experience moments of negative thoughts and feelings if the attention is allowed to scatter. Understanding the mental mantra "I Am that I Am" helps a personality remain centered. This statement is a Divine code of mutual polarization and communication. It actually is one of the highest statements a mortal can use in this world.

The patterns and conditions that oppose spiritual freedom have been lurking in the subconscious part of the mind for thousands of years. The struggle between the higher Nature and the human personality is an ongoing battle. As a direct result of past cyclic conditioning, both natures are part of the one Self but appear as divided due to ignorance and a human sense of separation. The feeling of separation is removed when the ego is surrendered.

Responses change dramatically with spiritual growth. An awakening soul learns to think before speaking or taking action. He scrutinizes and does not blindly accept what is seen or heard until it has been proven or intuitively recognized as feeling correct. It is easier to replace a weakness from the past with something new, nobler and more luminous when there is a willingness to change an attitude or habit.

Take charge and do your own spiritual work and suffering and confusion will be absent in your future. Take a big leap in faith by turning to a new and brighter direction. Effort is its own reward. Try not to worry about the results. Worry is a toxin to the system. It can poison and deplete energy. Do your very best at the moment and surrender the outcome, understanding that what is considered best may very likely change with time and maturity. Create and sustain harmony and the desired results will come when both you and the necessary conditions are ready to be healed and released.

If life is painful, it is to no avail to only wish for a shining future. Create the shining future by what is done today. The sublime teachings encourage us to work with the idea of transformation. What needs transformation is the personality. If laziness keeps you living in chaos, you will remain in the darkness of ignorance. Within is a pure power that will intelligently cooperate in fashioning the future. Instead of ignoring it, allow the power to take charge.

What is occurring in the inner and outer world is a manifestation from the past. When repetitive patterns are understood, taking new action will design a brighter future. The secret is to be mentally awake and pay attention and be the determiner. Stumbling blocks will be less likely to manifest ahead. Satisfaction is felt when you understand the influences of consciousness. The goal is self-mastery. You will become great by the greatness of your ideal. Achieving an ideal, you are no longer at the mercy of negative vibrations or intelligences.

What people generally do not realize is that there are lower invisible entities satisfying desires through weak humans. The entities are trapped in the physical/emotional vibrations of human life forms. The entities usually are invisible creatures or earthbound souls from the subtle lower emotional planes. Nuisance energies can also be negative thought forms bombarding the atmosphere. Through directed thought, you can build a strong aura that acts like a shield.

The shield is composed of particles of divine light. As an example, when you don't like a particular radio or television station, you search for something else. Practice the same action in your choices. Use the thinking mind and turn on a different switch and connect to a higher perspective and attitude that will activate the inner Light. Consciously trigger a positive channel and stop being a slave to a habit that does not serve your best interest.

The power of directed thought, character and preparation determine the authenticity of any communication. The true inner voice is the whisperings of God. To hear divine words, be alert and attentive. Messages

BE: Embracing the Mystery

may occur when you are relaxed or in a twilight state before sleep or just upon awakening. A single word or a simple sentence is my experience in hearing an audible celestial voice. To hear, you must listen. When you listen, you are given a deep unitive experience.

A good example was when I was still searching for an appropriate title for this book. I wasn't satisfied with any of the possibilities. One night after turning off the bedroom light and getting into bed, I heard an unseen presence clearly say the word, *BE*. As soon as I heard the word, I knew it was the perfect title. Being attentive to the inner Voice is a very stimulating and joyful activity. Instant remedies are one of the most loving parts of being consciously connected to the Greater Life. The Presence removes all the worries and anxieties and troubles and cares of the physical and mental plane.

It is your destiny to establish the light of wisdom as well as the power and presence of the sacred as a concrete reality. Expect good changes to happen and they will. Know that positive efforts will definitely manifest answers as well as goals at the right time and place. Remember, what is accomplished in Spirit Energy is beyond time and space. Your connection brings forth the ideal into matter. Maturity goes hand in hand with expanding Light. The stronger you are spiritually, the easier it becomes for the higher and the lower nature to work together as one masterful unit. Experience of the Divine is nondual and nonconceptual.

There is a definite pattern in divine communication, the direct experience of the mystical, whether a person is a public figure or living a life that appears quite ordinary. The validity of what is seen and experienced is a love exchange between Spirit and us. Many encounters occur unexpectedly. They also merge with our consciousness during meditation. It has been my experience when meditating to be suddenly transported into a realm that appears as a solid blue immensity of space. According to Vedic teachings, the blue "space" can mean the all-pervading Lord Vishnu, the Blue Being, the field of pure consciousness. It is the Ineffable Light of the Sephirah in the Kabbalah. When we are blessed with high experiences, it is our own divine Self in union with the Immensity! We are pure awareness.

Laugh, trust and do not judge. It is the greatest simplicity when we choose to observe without prejudice. Humans are relentless judges constantly placing conditions on everything. As a creator, keep in mind that you may use the wrong building blocks until you are ready to willingly surrender everything that is working against the masterpiece that is being created. The key to a strong construction is to allow the tools of inner wisdom to do the work correctly.

Everything required to access the Light is in the Causal Mind. It is the super conscious part of the mind and serves as a depository. Current human reactions stem primarily from present life conditionings and lingering subconscious engravings. Memories from this life are stored in the subconscious part of the mind. Many of us are able to consciously access data both within the subconscious and the superconscious parts of the mind. This power unveils what is helpful in understanding and releasing the patterns that have formed the ego personality. Conscious contact with hidden feelings assists in renewing a connection with the invisible Master Self.

Besides the five physical senses, there are five emotional-astral senses and five mental senses. The seed of full potentiality originally given to humankind at creation, when developed, gives us the ability to think, see, feel, listen, taste, act and travel to higher worlds of living Light. All of these possibilities are within the living cell originally implanted in our essence. When you choose to make Pure Consciousness first in your life, everlasting good will unfold. This means expanding the causal-mental field as a full blown illumined projection of God.

As an intelligent unit of Light, you have been slowly achieving this end for eons of time. Through developed faculties equilibrium is not lost. The talents and fruits of spiritual maturity become an integrated part of consciousness through personal effort. They manifest slowly and regularly with great patience, allowing the nervous system to become stronger. It is not necessary or wise for you to force powers and talents to materialize. Placing a love for truth and mastery of the personality as a priority, you naturally create heightened opportunities for growth, grace and the magical aspects of the divine. Growth is a heart experience, not an intellectual exercise. A healing attitude is to try every day to do your best and express more wisdom and love.

The readiness of collective consciousness, the timing of world events, karmic patterns and creation cycles play a part in what appears on the world scene. Creation cycles are rounds of planetary life. Mastery in human form is influenced to a great extent by the current Age or Cycle,

BE: Embracing the Mystery

whether it is one of darkness, light or the in-between gray vibratory influence. Because many humans are frequently disorderly and lack integrity and moral character, their behavior acts as a tumor inside nature as well as their own force fields. Both the individual soul and nature must fight for life. Nature records everything in a cosmic archive. Nothing is ever lost or erased. This is part of the science behind the past, coloring the future. To change ugliness into beauty, seek the middle road, the reality that is nondual, and discover divine spaciousness, joy and peace within. This is the original heritage of man's soul.

Science is based on divine justice. This is one of the reasons we are witnessing and experiencing chaos all over the world. The causes we create, whether they are good or bad, eventually bring forth effects. It is obvious that collective humanity is not in harmony with the forces of nature or with the inner essence. To be consciously aware is a full time assignment. Actions follow the soul throughout the cycles of the continuum. A soul cannot escape from the Law of Cause and Effect as long as it is unenlightened. This is also why life may appear meaningless when multiple embodiments are not understood.

Earth and her life are slowly moving as a collective consciousness toward a loftier vibratory manifestation. To make a positive difference, purification of the atmosphere must take place both inwardly and outwardly. The level of purity determines our vibration. Our vibration determines what occurs on this planet individually and collectively. Everything created is vibration, both visible and invisible. There are many degrees of vibratory influence within each creative sector. The next movement or collective world energy shift will not occur overnight, although it can be influenced due to individual and collective determination and dedication to the Divine. A physical form may experience difficulty adjusting to a higher change and more rapid vibration unless consciousness is prepared for the transformation. We cannot receive what we have not prepared for.

Each consciousness cycle has its group souls, a wave of humanity. We are still in the gap where darkness is running rampant and the Living Light of God is slowly revealing Its presence and power. The two exist simultaneously in duality. The hidden, whether it is of the darkness or of the Light, is manifesting in a very interesting pattern during the current cycle. The energy on Earth is struggling to transform itself, evolving into a lighter yet more rapid vibration. With each impulse of success, transformation happens on every level, both seen and unseen. Earth life at this time, being primarily selfish, feels like an abyss to many because it is by necessity a school of learning and indebtedness. The maturing process is similar to birth pains experienced in bringing forth a new life form. A new race will eventually emerge and usher in hope, inspiration and a greater ease for the soul-mind seeking a tangible divine life in matter. This is what it means to be born again. The soul is awakened after having come on Earth.

There will be a difference in the coming round in Earth's evolutionary history. Those who seek liberation will take responsibility for their own spiritual growth. All positive choices and actions will assist in bringing forth the eternal identity. In bringing forth divinity through the revelation of the hidden splendor, the beauty of Spirit will be projected in the personality and the physical form. The perfection that has been eternally sought will finally materialize as a reality. Humankind will be free to express as an awakened soul in physical form and no longer dishonor the inner by worshipping false gods or expecting someone else to save them. God will be felt and known as a visible force, a luminosity and intelligence freely expressing as unconditional love and not as separatism or a judge and jury.

Humanity can expect hope and a loving sense of community for the first time in a very long period of subjugation and denial. Presently, war exists on every level. When enough souls awaken from the illusion and darkness and choose to take collective action, the suffocating limitation will weaken and eventually cease. Humanity will be free at last to stand forth as people of the Light. This means that the kingdom we live in now turns into heaven as soon as the point of view has changed.

In the coming cycle, higher wisdom, kindness and love will be both an inward and outward force. More souls will be awakened. The inner light of aspiring individuals will have an accelerated vibratory rate. Intuition will be a common denominator blending human life into a fragrance of sweetness rather than selfishness and fear-filled energy. Trust, good change is coming. The physical world is meant to be the reflection of the higher worlds. A human being is designed for wholeness and joy.

Humanity appears lost because the darkness created by selfish and unenlightened men is in the process of being destroyed. The breaking

BE: Embracing the Mystery

up of the darkness-negativity always appears horrific due to the intense suffering and deprivation experienced both personally and collectively. What lies beyond the disconnected darkness is the Greater Light of Universal order, the sublime cleanser of that which is not real.

To view the whole pattern, both the heart and mind will look at the world scene from a higher perspective. To see clearly, the higher Nature is in charge. The best protection against evil is purity and the increase of inner light. Deliberately use light as a protection. Don't be at the mercy of every current. The universe allows evil to exist. What determines personal outcome is your reaction to it. Detach yourself from overly reacting to grief and the horror that spiritual ignorance manifests. Attachment to negative influences bankrupts consciousness by creating illness and suffering.

Detach in compassion and understanding and the inner life is liberated. Replace everything that does not vibrate as truth and receive the most sublime, subtle and divine realities of the universe. Celestial helpers will work with you to replace old worn out particles with new celestial particles made of Light. Lofty thoughts will find them. Reality, the sublime energy beyond time and space, will visit you. The luminous golden/white sparkles of the Celestial Presence may manifest as an exquisite delicacy and shower radiance and beatific powers upon your awakening consciousness. The gifts of the Spirit are stunning and frequent. The visitations are timeless, gentle, and extraordinary reminders that encourage, support and offer knowledge to souls who strive for the middle way of unconditional love.

When Buddha said, "Blessed are those who reach ecstasy through the knowledge of the deep and authentic truth concerning the world and our existence," he was speaking of the knowledge of the sacred interchange between men, all life and the unseen intelligence within the worlds of Light. Through the attainment of an inner peace, a door opens to ecstasy, restoring harmony within and without. To be peaceful, acknowledge and believe that there is a higher Love that will guide when in need. A simple example is what happened the other day. I was concerned about a loved one whose life read like the trials of the good man Job in the Bible. Sitting before the computer and concerned about my friend's troubled state of mind, three words suddenly appeared on the blank page. "I am Peace." My fingers had not touched the keyboard. Anything is possible. It is always a delight to marvel at the ingenuity of Spirit.

Mind has no limitations. The simple message of peace becomes our experience when we refuse to be swayed by appearances. Today is the past of a previous future. There are great advantages to change. Learn them by accepting the Light. Then you can live divinely. You will be lifted into a much higher and satisfying level of consciousness. It is then that the mystery is disclosed and understood. Embrace who you are and life becomes interesting. The right kind of help is provided, which is the real initiation. One day soon you will be empowered as the Divine Self.

Chapter Nine
Ancient Schools and Teachers

Today, the physical world appears to be polluted on many levels. The core of the problem is inside the mind and heart of man. The masses have become collectively vulnerable because the real identity is forgotten. A stagnant memory lapse manifests in the visible world. Toxins are the anger, hatred, sensuality, jealousy and greed that people haven't learned to master. The majority must pass through suffocating trials before they can come out into the open and breathe the Divine.

Man mistakenly keeps using the lower senses to seek what is lacking inwardly in the hope of finding what is sorely missing. Truth is difficult to perceive if the mind and heart are closed. Heaven forbids us to force the truth on others. When consciousness is open to the wisdom of the Living Light, a higher authority speaks and a soul listens. To develop compassion and love, follow a path that emphasizes introspection and transformation. When this path becomes your choice, divinity is regained in the senses.

There was a time in history when the few who yearned to achieve enlightenment were offered an option that is not common today. Although you may have heard of ancient mystery schools, I am bringing the past into the present to illustrate what was once provided for the few. The schools were an exclusive option. Sincere students entered the centers on a probationary level. Through trials and strict disciplines they learned that there is no truth without love and wisdom. They learned that the true life is in spiritual growth.

The great masters of the past had already evolved, attaining high plateaus of spiritual awareness. The teachers knew as their own singular intimacy, the presence of an Absolute Source. They understood that the world appears as a jungle and treats the unenlightened as an animal when mind is trapped in the regions of the lower nature. The way out was to lift the pupil's vision and understanding so he would see both sides of existence, the higher and the lower. Schools were opened to assist men and women who desired to be transformed, merging the divine nature with the human nature as a daily activity. Seekers willing to work hard for God Realization applied for initiation.

Religions teach man to offer himself to God in sacrifice. Sacrifice was understood as disciplining the lower nature and replacing it with pure light and good intent. The Mystery Schools were for the souls who had made a choice to be an emissary of a sublime Wisdom and Love. They understood that it normally took more than one lifetime to reach perfection. The intent was to accelerate soul growth through specific disciplines leading to the realization of spiritual identity. The master guides understood through experience that there was a celestial song within everyone although collective consciousness had stopped hearing it long ago.

The Divine teaching clearly emphasized control over the lower nature. In allowing the higher Self to be in charge, a pupil could live as a power generator of Light. The lower personality is transformed by giving conscious attention to the spiritual identity. The higher Self, when given the lead, has the power to make the selfishness and weaknesses of the lower animal nature disappear. The human personality changes according to shifts in consciousness. Through a cooperative effort, the lower nature evolves and is healed by allowing the hidden divine side to emerge.

The new students knew that physical existence had already become a prison for many. The proven method in removing one's self from limitation and division was through consecration, a means to open the door to enlightenment. It was a teaching of reintegration of the human being with the Source and Principle of Life. Students who applied no longer wished to be deprived of the activity of the Spirit; they desired to be free at last for having found the truth.

Spiritual energy begins in the cosmic realm descending into the mental, psychological and biological. It is a circular movement: an outbreathing and inbreathing. The soul ascends again as spirit awakening. God Realization is attained through a complete regeneration of the personality, mind and soul. As an evolving spark of light, souls journey through the veils of duality, which have been created through misplaced desire. Eventually, the soul seeks to liberate its self through conscious participation in the work of the Divine. To be accepted into a spiritual school was to be very fortunate.

The students learned that the emotional astral world was the center of the lesser force fields and not the spirit individuality. Negative suggestions, impurities and influences originate in the lower vibratory regions. If a student had not acquired discernment, misdirected energy, malpractice, usually was the end result. Pupils learned that the invisible lower mental plane could also gratify the personality's slightest wish. Desiring a return to perfection, they bypassed the lower worlds and reached upward to the higher vibratory planes.

Students understood that it was necessary to attune personal energy to the vibrations of real love, purity and selflessness. Apprentices were required to conform to the qualities and virtues of the energy of Divine Light if they desired the gifts to manifest here on Earth. Master teachers who lived what they taught, blessed them. These masters were mirrors reflecting the love, wisdom, will and power of a liberated soul.

To recognize a master teacher, discrimination, the faculties of the reasoning powers, and intuition must be awakened. If not developed, imposters may mislead. A true master is recognized by works, awakened divinity in the senses, creative imagination and a constant intimacy with God. Intuition, a heart experience, must resonate to the higher vibratory worlds of Light. It is in the heart that the Divine comes alive. The inner reality must be stimulated. It is that intangible essence within that awaits discovery.

What was once provided for the few as an exclusive option is now naturally available to all through every day choices. The individual higher Self will provide the experiences when the personality is ripe for truth. Activation of the higher level of the Mind is required to intuitively know and feel the truth. The same holds true as these words are read. Truth must be individually verified or one takes the chance of weakening the inner faculties. You are here in the flesh to strengthen inner faculties and senses and work for an exalted Ideal.

There is an old Greek fable that goes like this. "Even the wealthiest man must eat his own food. If he hires another to do his eating, the one he hires will gain the nourishment." For too long there has been a prostitution and commercialization of truth. Many unsuspecting souls are being misled and corruption of truth has been the result.

If discernment and discrimination are not acquired, at some point you will have to unlearn everything which was learned previously. There are false teachers who claim that there is no darkness. This teaching is a form of mesmerism leading students into believing that they do not need to protect their energy from the confused and collective vibrations that bombard life on a daily basis. Don't be fooled. Spiritual darkness is a manipulative energy. It has its own interest and pleasure in mind and not the soul's.

What is generally referred to as sin is the response of a corrupted nature. Learn to discern the true nature of any suggestion. Error thinking, evil, often appears as glamour. It entices, misleads and gives false promises. What must be clearly understood is that personal consciousness has created negative circumstances. Fear invites hostile forces. Pure thought and energy protects.

Imbalances can be caused by negative forces, which gained entry into the subconscious. Something thought, felt or acted upon opened the door to the enemy, the lower astral world creatures that can be malicious spirits. The lower astral entities are devoid of light and love. What they fear most is Light. God did not create negativity. Those with a diminished Light, the spiritually weak, are the creators. Spiritual ignorance and the belief in separation from the Source determine what is judged as good or evil. Purity is measured by the amount of light within a vibration. Earthbound entities, dark thought forms, are consciously separated from the Source, the Ceaseless Cause.

Removing negative obstructions or attachments was a practice taught in the old mystery school temples. There are many methods. One that I have used is through the power of laying on of hands. As an example, an acquaintance had a persistent pain in his hip. He asked for a healing treatment. As I slowly moved my hands towards the hip area an energy shift occurred. The troubled man began to speak in a rough and vicious way laughing at my intent to establish balance and healing in his body. It turned out that an invisible lower astral personality was comfortably attached to his hip. The negative entity was ready for a challenge and did not want to be removed from his comfortable home.

Other witnesses in the room could see the entity who voluntarily identified himself. The dark force spoke through the physical voice of our possessed friend. The technique that worked in this particular case was to bombard the intruder with the authority and power of the Spirit of Truth. The entity mentioned that he never knew anything except pain and felt quite at home attaching himself to a human body part. Pain, suffering and darkness are the absence of Light.

Attachment is a common occurrence. In questioning the entity, he said something very important that needs to be remembered. Whenever a human allows negativity or mind-altering products such as drugs and alcohol to take control of the personality and body, it is an open invitation to earthbound entities. This type of entity is comfortable with his existence. They look for an opportunity and human negativity provides an entryway. The small group radiated love and light to the entity. The angels were called and the entity willingly left.

There is a shadow side to creation and it cannot be ignored. God did not create it: misguided souls did. Our friend's hip pain immediately disappeared when the entity was removed. The entity's parting remark was that he would return to the man's hip if the patient again succumbed to depression and a negative attitude.

When temptation appears, it is not the tempter's fault. It is the fault of a weak human personality. Learn to say no. Think for yourself and decline any opportunity that harms life. Be stronger than the temptation. Temptations come from three levels: physical, emotional and mental. For these reasons, many sincere students sought Initiatic Schools. They chose not to run away from problems, but rather face and solve them. The seekers understood that evil and the forces of negative manipulation existed.

The dark forces will remain with humankind until the end of time. Duality exists in manifestation. Human inclinations create the negativity. Since intelligence has a family tie with the Creator, angels are also part of the extended family. Call on them for support in fending off dark energy. Archangel Michael is a perfect example of a defender against evil and injustice.

Ancient wisdom endures because it seeks to build character and set the soul free. Character purifies our energy fields. A true seeker wants nothing except wisdom, which is a form of love. The old wisdom schools demanded years of purification and preparation before the illumined instructors were willing to reveal the teachings of the Light. Teachers such as Pythagoras never instructed disciples in any of the philosophical concepts until after they had passed through a period of the strictest disciplines. The School of Pythagoras put students through horrific ordeals. Least expected by new students was the flood of scorn and unfair criticism to which they were subjected. This trial would last for long periods of time.

The students were given ordeals that would purify the heart and strengthen character. Anyone who applied to the schools was willing to be ground to powder and put through fire in order to be purified and become an exceptional being. They were treated with indifference and rebuked. The training was to root out all that was useless and bad for the student's balance and order. To be a student, one had to be daring, audacious. There also existed schools requiring twelve years of learning to control the emotions and another twelve years training the mind.

In the educational system, a student must attend a predetermined amount of years of public schooling. Although either unknown or ignored by seekers in our world today, a similar prerequisite is in force regarding private soul schooling. There are no shortcuts to wisdom. There are also returning souls who are spiritually evolved and have already completed a great share of their spiritual homework in past life experiences. Because they have a strong background of personal study, gifts and revelation as well as a high development of character, they vibrate in tune with the universe and all creatures making the disciplines of this lifetime less arduous.

Many of the trials and tribulations of life are sent by the invisible world with the purpose of teaching the personality to rely on an inner spiritual strength. The initiations that once took place in a temple are now given in everyday life, when least expected. This is another reason it serves to develop strength of character. Fortify will and align it with the Divine and it is easier to accept whatever vexations and humiliations may appear. Readiness can meet any force. Do not be in denial regarding negative intelligence.

As you spiritually evolve, the darkness is not completely removed although the influence is much less. A time may come when the darkness will deliberately put obstacles in the way and try to prevent soul advancement. All evolving souls are tested. The norm is to pass through initiations and eventually arrive at completeness through the choices made in daily life. Reactions are springboards in the quest for perfection. Regardless of the current level of awareness and receptivity, there are always greater heights to reach.

The more active the higher Self, the less you will actually discuss regarding the Absolute. This is one reason secrecy existed as students went through apprenticeship. Preparation is the most important part of being an initiate. If there is no work plan, the journey becomes a long hard struggle. The ancient schools provided the work plan. The intent behind the philosophy was to develop better humans who understood and accepted spiritual identity and were able to meet problems head on. Once identity was accepted and responses controlled, a higher level of knowledge was pursued. The awareness included transcended cosmic codes, phenomena and scientific technology. Eventually, the disciplines lead to the Profound. The mysteries were designed to bring a student to the place in consciousness where unconditional love rules and identity is claimed. This same intention holds true today.

A perfect example of the Profound is the response of Jesus while on the cross, "Father, forgive them. They know not what they do." The desired spiritual attainment is when we love the Creator, our own divinity and the divinity of others unconditionally. To be able to love with passion is to understand that harm is perpetuated by souls who are suffering from a spiritual memory loss. Their Light is diminished. They are wounded on many levels and are basically lost. They may appear outwardly as having the necessary material or physical wealth to live meaningful lives. The appearance is a façade.

There are sacred books, tablets and scrolls that have preserved the ancient wisdom teachings. They suggest we not stop seeking until truth is found. The ancient records provide a workable guideline clearly describing the evolution of the soul. When the known religions are carefully studied, it becomes obvious how the idea of God changes as the character, intelligence and soul of humanity progresses. In the very early periods of animal-man, humans were incapable of self-government. It was during that earlier evolutionary period, as well as much later, that beings from other systems came to Earth and taught humanity the ways of wisdom as well as advanced technology. Through exposure to a highly advanced intelligence, evolving man was given a sense of his birthright.

While advanced instructors were still laboring with the infant humanity of this planet, they chose from among the sons of men the wisest and the truest to lead. The chosen ones were prepared to carry on the work after the advanced intelligence had withdrawn. The keys of knowledge were left with the illumined sons who were looked upon as the ordained and appointed ones. Advanced beings have assisted evolution throughout the long history of humanity. The appointed ones founded what we know as the ancient schools.

Records have been found and are still being uncovered in the form of carvings, baked clay tablets, and papyrus rolls clearly describing the great temples, the priests and the chambers of initiation. The mystery schools disappeared when a weakening of consciousness occurred. As time passed, the teachers that followed were weakened and closed themselves off from the cosmic point of view and true universal brotherhood. A weak personal belief and lack of character does not attract lofty impulses from Creative Mind.

It has been said that wisdom lies not in seeing things, but in seeing through things. It belongs to the higher mind and the way we understand the principle of life. Myths and legends describe when advanced intelligence walked on Earth. Some of the advanced beings that chose to step into physical bodies gradually lost touch with the Sons of Light. Mythology is the authentic record of the periods of transition when the divine spark and the soul were slowly assuming the bodies of mortality. Divine assistance was given to humanity and is called a myth. Myths existed before religion.

The ancient schools demanded inflexible standards of consecration and virtue qualities almost absent in today's world of materiality and instant gratification. You can, through strong effort, build character, unfold spiritual powers and master the ego-personality without attending an organized school. Divine assistance is available when you are ready. Assistance from a superior source is not given to laggards. Take responsibility for your own spiritual evolution. Train the mind, be watchful and prepare for active participation in the Great Work. This is why you are in the flesh. It is possible to create a heavenly environment on Earth visibly and tangibly.

Wisdom is not a gift offered to selfish people. Wisdom gained is determined by how well spiritual studies are applied and how intuitive power is used. Power manifests naturally through spiritual awakening. It is not wise to force spiritual energy to rise within. You may harm your nervous system. Your force fields will naturally be bathed in spiritual Light when you are adequately prepared. Many seekers have made themselves seriously ill mentally and physically through personal attempts to break through the barriers of matter. The higher Self knows when you are ready. Readiness will gift you with the blessings of Light.

Choices exist regardless of the level attained. One path is to dedicate your efforts to humanitarian service. This does not imply the necessity for a grand public gesture. What has value is how life is lived day by day. There will be moments when there is no actual proof of the thing believed. When that happens, and it will, stop and reconnect to the still small Voice within and listen. This is your journey ... believing in an intangible Force that may or may not be seen or heard. The plan includes obeying a grander power than the personality, and molding energy into a fit vehicle for the Divine.

Every soul goes through a period of probation. It is during this period that mastery is gained over the little things, preparing us later for the bigger things. Mastery is a full time job that can be achieved in a material world living what is judged as a normal life. Conditioning from the past is the worst enemy. To receive greater knowledge, the soul passes through stages of spiritual ignorance and darkness, which may create more suffering. A cleansed soul is the final result. A great number of sufferings and trials in life are sent to seekers by the invisible world to force character development and reliance on Spirit. Suffering is also a means to remove a student from a wrongful path.

Question as to why an unpleasant event personally occurred and then learn from the experience, cutting short future suffering. Initiations are designed to teach man how to go within himself in order to find true love, strength, power and wisdom. None of the great teachers or masters of this world have escaped the sorrows and uncertainties of human experience. In the past, higher knowledge was given to the few. Today, with a greater influx of Celestial Light, truth is available to a prepared and pure hearted soul. Dare to be who you really are.

The true life lies in spiritual growth. The teachings of the great ones are meant for those who are willing to prepare. To find It, you must be It. When a transcendent level of energy is attained, you are finally free. Pure consciousness and matter merge as One Living Power.

Chapter Ten
A Developed Will

In the beginning of our journey eons ago, evolution was unconscious. Forms were more ethereal than physical. The deeper the descent into matter, the more refined the five senses became and less psychic the mind. Eventually, the brain and nervous system became more sensitive. During the later stages of mental evolution, the personality began to know itself as an instrument and physical body designed to express the higher Self. The physical body is a vehicle that carries us to our destination.

When man developed a will and chose freedom, more energy was required to become whole. To transform the restrictive life and evolve as intelligent Light requires proven disciplines. It is necessary to achieve a clear understanding of the physical body and accept that it is only one of countless vehicles that we have used to evolve. The ultimate goal is to purposefully return into our original design, which is perfection. When we look at any appearance, we see the outer form. We must examine both the inner and outer to know its content and value.

A student who applied for spiritual study in the past understood the rules and qualifications. He understood that he would need to pass through a probationary period before a Master Teacher would agree to accept him as a student. A major part of the probationary period prepared the student to step forward and learn how to deliberately change and develop a will that would direct him to his goal. What was true then is also true today. In order to observe the movement of our own mind and heart, of our whole being, we must have an unconditioned mind. It is similar to climbing a mountain. It is less of a burden to move upward if we discard all the things carried on the plain.

We climb to the summit through discipline and effort. Theoretical knowledge does not transform us. We destroy or build our world through our disposition. It is up to the individual to take responsibility for creative action. Will power needs to be developed and applied, otherwise the seeker will not follow through to his Ideal. A mental reframing must be used as a bridge to reach the state of being called God Realized. To achieve wholeness requires more than devotion. It is a deliberate science, a choice on the student's part to transcend the thinking surface mind and the feeling nature. Creation is thought taking form.

Through mastering and making the will work for our ideal, we are led to a point in mind where we can receive a higher understanding and apply it in daily life. As we expand thought, we discover that we go through an unfoldment, which creates a birth of ideas coming forth from a grander level of mind. Our thinking moves into an atmosphere of correct thought as we open to an evolving consciousness that functions as God's Will manifesting as our will. The two become one. Previously, they appeared as separate because the student did not understand or accept that the will of the higher Self is the same as the will of God. It is the same energy, but being used from a different perspective.

To master the lower world of matter, you must learn to think for yourself and hold a strong center in your life. It is the higher Self accomplishing what needs to be done. What are frequently thought of as miracles are in truth results stemming from a direct and scientific approach, which embraces both the heart and mind. Through the development of the mind and mastery over the personality, ability increases as to how to use the many tools available for spiritual growth. Directed will can be used as a creative power. Some of the tools are Self-Suggestion, Forethought and Character. By applying attention and interest, memory and concentration are increased. The magic key is the actual using of the will as a positive creative power.

Self-suggestion is an effective tool to use upon awakening and before retiring for the night. Repeat a statement of intent either out loud or mentally. This is called reframing or reprogramming the mind. The suggestion is offered to the One Creative Mind. Its role is to create the request and return it to you. Keep the goal alive and in front of your mind. If your thoughts and actions are the opposite of the affirmation, it will be either neutralized or negated.

If the soul comprehends the moral laws given to man through various spiritual leaders and ignores them, it will experience difficulty in working with any personal laws. A shift in consciousness must occur on every level of the mind to be successful. If models of divinity given are violated,

A Developed Will

how can the flame of your essence expand? Truth is an actuality when approached as an ideal with a spirit of scientific straightforwardness. Serious attention, an active observation, a real listening ability and a deep interest are means to developing and strengthening memory. Remain fixed on the subject of desire until it manifests. If you wholeheartedly believe that you can do something, it will be done. To be alive, happy and useful, discard the idea of limitation.

Repetition is the secret of success. Take a great interest in what you are creating. To keep attention fixed is to be clear regarding intent and desired goal. The daily practice of contemplation and meditation will assist in the application of mental choices. What works is to keep the attention fixed long enough for a new habit to manifest. It is similar to exercising and developing memory in weakened muscles. Self-suggestion is encouraged because it helps develop will power. When an image or idea is placed into the mind, give it a command to act in a specific way. It will impress the mind.

A vigorous imagination and strong faith complement an ideal. To achieve success with the science of learning to control the mind, these apply today as much as in the past. Stay with the course and use repetition until power is gained and results are achieved. A state of mind can reach such great heights that you can heal yourself. It has been proven over and over again that weaknesses and imbalances can be corrected by establishing a fixed state of mind that chooses to master the ego-personality and matter. Through the control of the human will, you tap into a strength that cooperates and eventually merges with the higher transcendental Will that is hidden within.

The higher part of Will is to be used as a marvelous power for creating spiritual states of mind and serving in ways that benefit life. It doesn't happen by wishful thinking. The end result is an ability to increase clarity of thinking, to act promptly when needed, and develop and draw out from the mystic depths of the mind a true and lasting talent. To ascend in consciousness requires serious resolve and steadfastness. When you consciously connect to the All-Wise Creative Mind, the possibilities of living an incredible life of harmony and beauty increase.

Pure Will is perfectly free. It is one with the Will of Divine Spirit. It is selfless, and to claim it as a constant companion, acquire wisdom and learn how to apply it. As free will is developed and guided by reflection and high moral character, the less influence from the personality is experienced. Mastery of self and bringing forth innate knowledge requires serious attention. Through the development of mental faculties, fresh experiences come your way. The future is made from the past. It is a magical art to recreate what is called the self. Disciplined conscious thought eventually leads to happiness and peace. There is no true liberation without love. It is through love that you reach beyond the lesser to achieve the greater. If a mediocre life is no longer desired, give the heart and will to that which is beautiful and truthful. Prove the inner power by personal experiment.

Thoughts must be your slaves. There is no greater example than the man or woman who conquers the human personality. Greatness follows when the will is lifted to loftier heights. Will in its perfection is genius. If you do not seek for what is hidden within, you stagnate and remain a lost and foolish shell of what could be. There is an unfathomable and spacious Nature, an infinite resource that can be tapped into by cultivating the Higher through the mastering of the lower. Self-command is in itself a very high mental pleasure. By training the mind, the ordinary will is transformed into a mystic will. No one gives to us but our selves and no one takes from us but ourselves.

To understand knowledge, a quiet mind is essential. When an alert and receptive state of mind is reached, a clear understanding is the result. In tranquility, truth is perceived. As long as the mind is in conflict, blaming others, resisting truth, avoiding change, denying reality, living from a conditioned consciousness or playing the role of victim, there can be little understanding or growth. The mind is thoughtful when it is truly interested. Regeneration is actually possible in present time when you are aware and apply this science. To be free of bondage is to investigate truth.

To expose how conditioning has affected your responses is the first step toward freedom. Look closely at daily activities. Are they the result of a conditioned mind? When the mind is attached to any particular conclusion, it is incapable of discovering something new. Previous knowledge and conclusions color any discovery. Humans respond to literally everything as a result of past conditioning. When a disturbance occurs, our responses demonstrate conditioning. This is particularly obvious when there is a struggle within the mind. It is also true that if we are comfort-

A Developed Will

able with our conditioning, we may become lazy and not put forth effort to further evolve. Closely watch the mind in action all the time.

A serious student analyzes all aspects of what is referred to as the self. The common human walks through life inattentively. A mind that is very clear loosens entanglements and attachments. Such a mind is a great Light. When deliberate steps are taken to end conflict, the mind naturally becomes quiet. It is then that the Sacred is heard. That which is holy occurs when there is no sense of time and limitation. There must be a cultivation of the totality of the mind.

It is through understanding the whole process of desire and conditioning that the mind can be free. When the mind is in a state of no condemnation, you can look at problems and mistakes and let the unnecessary go. The hidden mind, unconscious, is more potent than the superficial part of the mind. The conscious mind is occupied with the immediate, the limited. The unconscious part of the mind is ruled by past memory and deep time. Once there is a perception and understanding of the power of the hidden, the mind is free to respond as true intelligence.

As students seeking a conscious connection to God and wholeness, a good mind must be developed. Since conditioning increases with experience, try something new and lasting. All mental activity is a continuity of habit. The mind functions in the field of the known; the known are the habits. Why not look at things differently and step out of the known into the unknown? Break habits that work against soul progression and being truly alive. Habit is the continuation of action within the field of the known. You can know what you think, but not always why you think it. Watch carefully and everything will surface as understanding and growth.

Ideally, it is helpful to receive instruction from an enlightened teacher whether that teacher is in a physical body or a subtle invisible form. Spiritual assistance is eventually given to those who ask. When a student has prepared his consciousness and is ready to seriously take the necessary steps to be free from the hindrances and ignorance that he has allowed to ensnare him, the illumined ones notice. In rare cases, an invisible elder master teacher from one of the celestial dimensions of Light will appear and guide a dedicated student. The student does not choose the teacher; the teacher chooses the student. I am not referring to a teacher from the astral desire plane, but to the glorious possibility of a lofty illumined

BE: Embracing the Mystery

Master Teacher whose natural vibration is already established in higher vibratory dimensions.

A Master Being is wisdom filled, radiating divine light and love and may take on the role of guiding and protecting a soul who is ready for higher instruction. In rare cases, an illumined being will overshadow a truth-seeking student and be a living influence throughout the human's life rather than taking on a physical body of his/her own. There is a tremendous difference in the teacher and instruction emanating from a lower invisible plane in contrast to the sublime presence of a Master teacher from a lofty dimension.

When we listen to the song of life that is an inner melody, a Master teacher may visibly appear, looking like a familiar human, but the form is composed of brilliant diamond light. The experience is stunning. To catch a glimpse of a majestic presence emanating God's love thrills every particle of our being. The magnitude of bliss is overwhelming. There have been sublime moments when a Master Celestial Teacher appears as I call for truth. Responding in love, he creates vibrating letters of luminous Light spelling out a message of guidance. I can easily read the amazing words or symbols, which hover in the air. The celestial Teachers use the Language of Light, which is an instant communication within Infinite Mind. The communication allows a seeker to study the record of the mysteries. To know a master in this context is to be immersed in nonduality; it is indescribable. It is a pure heart experience beyond imagination or words. It is Divine Science in action as transcendent love.

Advanced beings know our intent and communicate with us through active intuitive faculties. There are also awakened students who do not spiritually see but intuitively sense the presence of a celestial being. When the sublime worlds of luminous Light are witnessed, we feel what it is to be in Paradise again. The inner eye sees both worlds simultaneously. It is a form of intuition that joyfully assists in perceiving truth within and without. In joy and gratitude, the sublime overshadows and the true meaning of love is magnified.

A genuine physical Master is also a being who has succeeded in controlling his thoughts, feelings and actions. Instead of the lesser human personality being in charge, life is directed by the spirit identity. A high Master may also have gained control of matter. A high energy rules rather than a personality. A realized being has control over his destiny, whether visible or invisible. Teachings offered are of the fellowship of Light. The work is accomplished as the direct result of unconditional love and infinite wisdom. Truth reigns.

When illumined beings live in physical bodies, they are the first to practice in their daily lives what they teach. Their actions are always consistent to the words they speak. They are living examples of a flowering spring. Light is central to the Master teaching for it is a perfect expression of divine reality. During the present world cycle, there have been few true guides. This is a result of man refusing to listen to the Illumined Ones. A Master teacher does not personally appear unless the student is actively doing his spiritual homework and has purified thought.

The ultimate achievement of a soul is to create and sustain a conscious connection with one's own Master Self, the indwelling Spirit. To achieve this connection creates aliveness. The ideal is to spiritually evolve not only for our own eventual liberation, but also for the benefit of all life. As our spiritual senses are quickened, we intuitively know and recognize energy fields through discrimination and the gifts or talents that are latent within. The energy, color, intensity, vibration and quality of what we experience is determined according to preparedness, willingness and a developed consciousness.

We are composed of varying energy fields. The etheric energy is not of the same quality and appearance as the astral energy. The astral-emotional energy differs in substance and appearance from the lower mental field. The mental realm and its vibrations differ in appearance and substance from the three higher celestial realms. The ascent continues; there is no end to evolution.

Occasionally, the invisible world leaves us without support, money or guidance so that we may discover how to find a dependable source in the center of our own being. We become wisdom-filled when we know which are the thoughts that save and which are the thoughts that ruin us. Through trial and error, you will learn what is the wise response that will help heal wounds, increase light and advance the soul. The more you correctly discern and are open to receive, the greater will be the influx of luminous and spiritual influences. The goal is to be a conductor for divinity. As habits and conditioning that work against the soul's illumination are removed, replace them with new thought patterns that bless rather than hinder.

BE: Embracing the Mystery

Understanding regarding the subject of spiritual evolution as well as the process of biological and psychological evolution will help open doors to the Infinite and the life we were designed to live. For instance, a major purification of the astral desire body is necessary for it to be vivified, protected, and erroneous impressions and stereotypes corrected. Being filled with passion and strong feelings can work for or against us. Guard passions and they won't plot against the plan of the soul. In the same vein, eliminate everything that dampens enthusiasm. All the vehicles that constitute a living package of intelligence must learn to work harmoniously together.

Although we are originally created with identical building material, soul patterns differ. What makes us different are choices, actions and reactions, and whether we live from the mind or from the heart. The mind seeks and looks for wisdom. The heart asks and is love. Both are required to be free. The will is used to create. Fuse them together and truth becomes our own. We create the causes and reap the effects. The four lower vehicles, physical, etheric, astral, and lower mental are all subject to evolution. We are not a finished product. As the latter two vehicles evolve, they go through the early primitive stage to a more advanced stage similar to the changes experienced in the evolution of physical form.

Everything created in form is subject to change. As we mature in our understanding of creation as well as our refinement of character, individual light increases and we reinvent ourselves into the beings that God intended us to be. The dedicated student is the alchemist who performs the transformation through an intense desire for beauty and truth. The secret of the true life is to seek nothing else but to be the higher Self, allowing it to rule the body, emotions and mind. When we are ready, spiritual beings present the right conditions and what is needed to continue spiritual growth.

A disciple is an individual who is focused on attaining his highest potential. He is one who is sincere, pure and passionate regarding the rediscovery of his own spiritual identity. A disciple is one who strives to create a world that reflects love, the great nutrient of life. A disciple strives to achieve an inner calm, which never fears. A disciple is one who respects and understands life and all creatures. A disciple feels and lives the oneness of all life. A disciple realizes that the union of peace and poise is power.

A Developed Will

Disciples may have supernatural powers. What is done with the divine powers depends on the world situation and what the needs are at the time. If losing a sense of self and identity is a concern as you advance in the Light, put fear aside. In consciously regaining spiritual power, the parts of the human personality that work against the Divine purpose and plan are gradually eliminated. What is lost is no longer needed; the hidden treasures are regained. Spiritual gifts are to be shared with discernment and love. We become humanly what we are spiritually, a grander version of who we thought we were. Discrimination and care is exercised regarding the use of a developed will because we now understand how the will determines destiny.

It is a recorded fact that the vibrations of the higher consciousness must have a balanced physical-emotional body to use as a conduit. Energy must be protected and not weakened as a result of disorder. Stress and strain can be harmful and cause an unpleasant nervous disturbance causing confusion or illness. It is very important to carefully watch that balance is maintained on every level so that energies will continue to flow evenly and beneficially.

Until the lower nature unites with the higher Nature, probation continues. Do everything in your power to purify the grosser matter through discipline and choices that favor balance. Develop equanimity and do not allow lack of control to thrust you into extreme behavior responses in daily life that jeopardize your spiritual Ideal. Quiet contemplation, meditation, fixity of mind and an authentic love for the Divine all work together for your lasting good and eventual wholeness. Learn to constantly be in charge of the body and control the thinking mind. Developing a higher state of mind will mold and expand lesser energy fields. Strengthen the will and control it at the same time. When an individual sinks into sorrow and sadness, he cuts himself off from the living chain. Negativity cuts the link.

The aura is a protective field. It is similar to an antenna and will receive heavenly vibrations if kept in good condition. Everyone has an aura-halo of light. The brilliancy and quality depends on the state of mind. A clairvoyant can see auras. For instance, one time when interviewing a young man, I was impressed by his outward appearance and flow of words. A closer intuitive look at his soul energy clearly revealed a character trait that represented deceitfulness. His aura was a sickly green color.

BE: Embracing the Mystery

I knew he did not speak truth. Being able to see someone's true character through the energy colors emitted is very helpful and will save time and possible future trouble. In the future, the gift of clairvoyance will be common.

Train the mind to be a servant of the higher Self. Discipline finally sets the soul free, enabling it to consciously express in finer vibratory planes as well as retaining memory of its learning experiences while yet in the physical body. The individual soul progresses through many worlds of thought, not only on this planet. Further evolution is experienced as you have mastered the little ego self in the present life. Everything is recorded. Nothing is forgotten.

You are an evolving, dignified and beautiful eternal being. As new choices are made, it may feel as if you are going through a long period of adjustment. The higher Self for the most part remains silent until you have achieved the right degree of readiness. This holds true for any advanced invisible assistance. I am not referring to angelic help during emergency situations. The angels are eager to help. I am in this reference stating that higher celestial assistance remains aloof in the area of wisdom teaching until the seeker's vibrations are quickened and receptive to finer particles of light.

The drawing power of thought works with universal law. Once you have exercised concerted effort and have reasonably cleansed the dark particles from the thinking mind, you will be ready for higher instruction and intimacy with the Divine. The war with yourself is won. The mind will no longer delude. Proof will be yours of a light driven, superluminal reality. Grace and a magical wonder enter your consciousness as you recognize the Garment of Light. A developed will that is aligned with Universal Law increases and blesses your being as joy and fulfillment. The Divine countenance is rediscovered.

Through a focused will, you have a remarkable power that intensifies all the good aspects of what you call yourself. It is understood that the physical body, etheric, emotional and mental fields are not separated from the higher mind, soul and spirit. The higher fields only appear to be distanced from you when understanding is absent and a directed will is not used to benefit life. You are a wonderful unit of intelligent activity rediscovering the totality of its Self. Developed will is used to reach the prize.

Chapter Eleven
The Prize

Divine Knowledge goes deeper than the rules of creating a new self. To be able to live rightly and improve consciousness, you need to be saved from the ignorance and forgetfulness regarding materiality, attachments and wrongful identifications. Everything born and created is interwoven and united with each other. All that is composed shall be decomposed. Matter is a temporary condition. If humankind continues to indulge in the idolatry of matter, wholeness and freedom will not occur. When enough of us take the time to hear truth and accept that matter is temporary and spirit is eternal, souls in greater numbers will detach from things and focus on what endures.

Words may sound inspiring, but what if you are living in ongoing pain either emotionally or physically or both? How can you escape the darkness that feels like breath deprivation? How can conditions be changed when you are choking in an environment of hate or disorder? One night, while feeling the pain of a loved one, I was shown a tunnel of darkness. At the end of the tunnel was the blazing Light of God. One does not need to have a near-death experience to experience the tunnel or the Light. This is the beauty and magic of being consciously aware of the Divine; hope is given. We can "see" with our own eyes another reality that is far grander than our temporary pain or situation. We rise above conditions because we know as truth our spiritual Source loves and cares for us. Yes, hope is ours as a result of a conscious connection to unconditional Love.

If disorder is your current situation, stand up to it with the power and light of your own inner energy. Be firm and reach higher for answers and relief. Relief may not materialize immediately in the objective world, but it will in the world of the soul. To transcend darkness, call on the Light and ask it to be a powerful force in your life. You have the right as an individual spirit to inherit wholeness and live in harmony and truth.

You have the option to rewrite your life experiences. Perhaps, you

BE: Embracing the Mystery

are the type who puts on a front and keeps pain hidden. Denial, secrecy, serves a social purpose, but it does not address ongoing suffering. Form is temporary and subject to change. The innate power within will help increase your Light, creating a new drama where you can regain dignity and integrity. Love yourself. Do everything possible to bring the truth of your spiritual identity out into the open. Everyone has the inner Light but most people ignore it and do nothing to develop it. This is what you can do to "save" yourself and recreate your life.

Call on your own higher Self to take control. Be insistent. Ask for guidance so you can expand knowledge and consciously express inner truth. In the darkest moments, mentally stop and call Divinity. Reach out. Repetition works. Do it and do it with passion. Keep asking that the higher Nature take control. It is then that the words shared will bring comfort and action. Write the script of your new story deliberately.

You are Spirit. Spirit is perfect, pure, a Knower. Its Ineffable Presence is indescribable and permanent. When Spirit descends into matter, it is not constant in its activities until the soul/mind has attained a consistent level of conscious awareness. Until the personality is ready to accept the truth of its eternal essence and allow it to influence consciousness, it functions from a lesser energy level and reality. You have the power through choice to awaken from the darkness and live what you truly are.

When you are finally disgusted with disorder and a false sense of separation, a form of surrender occurs naturally. The pattern of a soul's journey is to explore divinity and free self from the illusion. The mystery schools were given that name because higher truth is indeed a mystery to a soul that has not yet awakened to itself. The mystery can be penetrated, revealed and activated through desire. The teachings were guidelines to help the soul return to its Source. The evolving soul lacks knowledge, balance and healing if it resists the true identity as Spirit. As long as the human personality rules and is not interested in rediscovering Self, humans are basically the "walking dead." There is no real happiness when life is lived from a "less than" consciousness. Surrender places the focus on Spirit, allowing it to lead the way.

It is possible to deliberately change darkness into light in every area of life. Life force can be revealed. It is your responsibility to restore the link between condensed limited matter in the outward sphere with the higher sphere of limitless power. The higher sphere is like a Tree of Life.

The fruit will come forth when you allow the true nature to be its Self. The invisible sphere is Oneness, Light, wisdom, mercy, force, beauty, victory, glory, the foundation and a perfect man. The seed qualities already exist for a conscious God communication and connectedness.

Both the lesser and greater fields of subtle energy are patiently waiting. This is the mystery of the journey of the soul. No one is separated from spiritual qualities and energies, people only think they are. Erroneous thinking must be changed. You are a total package of magnificent possibilities waiting to be rediscovered, accepted and lived. In keeping this lofty truth of the higher nature in mind, self-analysis and understanding are proven tools to help manifest the divine in human form.

Reality is what is felt. It is the subjective world of emotions, feelings, and thoughts, and its roots are in the invisible. A higher world is your home. What is remembered here you knew there. Eventually, intense and prolonged feelings stir in the mind. The feeling world is located in the solar plexus, the astral region. The problem is the accumulated dust and fog that permeates the lower emotional and mental fields of our makeup. Negative memories of long ago still haunt, preventing a true sense of Self and freedom. Hardship is caused by internal conditions. No one can afford to wait for things to get better. Reach higher and do something about changing the patterns now. Every day, try and climb above the clouds. To do so, it is necessary to purify the mind and feeling nature. Deliberately work to keep them free of negativity. Effort will keep away any new invasion of inferior elements.

Typically, humans base their lives on the five senses, causing inner resources to run dry. When the focus is primarily on physical conditions, a soul can be literally crushed. Relief arrives by choosing true knowledge that teaches how to identify with the inner spirit and connect consciously with the finer dimensions of Light. Whether Earth is experienced as a heaven or a hell is the direct result of a belief system. The soul cannot reach the summit without purification in the various fields he calls himself.

As you master the balancing act between the visible and invisible, benefits are received. The goal is to understand the objective, concrete, material world and also the subtle invisible world. Understanding that they are not separated enables you to move forward. Passionate feelings will move you into a new direction where you are free to make a choice to activate the divine Source that is the true life and savior. Simply changing an attitude about a person, situation or environment will often work wonders. Make an effort to respond from a level of spiritual awareness. As perspective changes, good things occur. Learn to live by the laws inscribed within the soul.

There are many options available to help quicken a firsthand experience with a higher power. The secret lies in the knowledge that experience offers. A person is able to understand only when he solves the problem himself. If a seeker is oblivious to the spirit within and without, the inner source is inactive. Some people allow it to remain barren because they have felt betrayed. It is time to forget and forgive. Pollution comes from the inside. Desire must be strong and persistent to put facts and truths into practice. Eventually, the cleansing within will manifest in health and harmony without.

For eons of time, lovers of truth have been seeking power. It is not found outside of self; it is the seed of life within. If a seeker has not developed moral character, how can he gain understanding and ownership of what he seeks? He remains deluded. Study and apply Universal Law. Law in this sense means mind in action: it is an effect. Law is intelligence operating. Law is also Karma, a universal law of cause and effect, which provides us with opportunities of growth.

The higher part of the Mind must be recognized and understood for what it is. As a conscious designer of a greater life, you are capable of attracting Light, living in accordance with Universal Law and discovering how to transform yourself. Success depends on the quality of your love. Love unconditionally regardless of the circumstances.

Impurity destroys peace and is the greatest obstacle to a higher understanding. Contamination impacts consciousness through outside influences as well. An atmosphere of false thinking permeates everywhere. No one can afford to idly stand by and do nothing about it. Illness is usually a result of disorder and impurity in the body, mind or soul. Impurity includes self-judgment. One of the greatest favors you can give your self is to exercise will. Learn to work methodically and in harmony, trusting that effort will succeed in awakening the divine within and bring forth a better life. An alignment with your inner power increases by remaining focused.

Existence is guided and determined by the pictures created in the mind. Develop the habit of self-analysis. There is a higher plan. The plan is for all creation to evolve, attain spiritual understanding and be perfect. If purity and perfection are chosen as the foundation for life, all thoughts will gather around the central thought and actually obey it. The law of thought exists in every realm, seen or unseen. An excellent attitude is to strive and improve conditions wherever you are.

Typically, good or bad experiences depend on the nature of thought. Once having lost the true meaning of life, the soul vegetates. The spiritual vibrations will refuse to protect, guide, heal or inspire a soul that is disinterested. In contrast, the beauty of a definite soul plan is that you can deliberately change disorder and be healed, living a normal life that is actually filled with joy and meaning. Purity has to be cultivated inside. Learn to be selfless and undesirables will usually leave. We judge the world according to the way we see ourselves. The logical alternative is to wisely choose thoughts and monitor them moment-by-moment.

Physical matter is a condensation of Higher Thought. The life you are living is a materialization of your thoughts. If the idea of living as a crystallized fossil has lost its appeal, choose new thoughts, contemplate, pray and meditate with regularity. Develop a spirit of thankfulness and be kind and helpful to others. Abandoning weaknesses and making a disciplined effort to stop focusing on self centered thoughts and feelings will unplug the blockages. A workable plan is to throw off layer after layer of false human conditioning and ignorance. The more falsity is exposed, the more frequent the glimpses of an inner creative life.

To "let go" is to remove the traps, conditions and hindrances that bind the human personality to a falsely created belief system. Gossip, complaints, hate and negative behavior invalidate spiritual identity. Who is the master? Is it the inner Divine Spark or the personality who thrives on desires that harm and is riddled with fears seen and unseen? Why not control the temporary limited personality? It is your own fault when truth is known and nothing constructive is done about it. As spiritual energy increases, amazement will follow. People and things that would normally overwhelm will no longer have the same negative impact on the feeling nature and physical body.

Be bold and try. Many good people continually suffer because they frequently refuse to use discipline and change harmful choices. They deliberately choose pain rather than sticking with a spiritual ideal and striv-

BE: Embracing the Mystery

ing to control habits and thoughts that work against balance and peace. They continue to struggle with the same debilitating patterns. Usually this occurs when the individual has not grasped the great truth of his own spiritual identity and purpose. One must respect and love identity as divinity in form to make lasting changes. If identification is solely with the physical body, personality, and the appearance world, nothing is gained or endures that is worthwhile or beautiful.

Buddha stated that we must guard the gate to the five physical senses. The senses are real. They are the faculties through which we contact life in its expression. To guard them, we must learn to master weaknesses. Our five senses are like our children. Teach them to be obedient. If this is not done, nothing can be depended upon. Unenlightened behavior acts to bind the soul. It is a trap. Self-control is an acquired strength of character. It is one of the powers that will eventually set a seeker free from spiritual ignorance.

Self-mastery creates harmony. It is very easy to sound wise when everything and everybody is living up to expectations and fulfilling your desires. When the darkness of false thinking blocks the path and you cannot move forward, check your responses, because they determine effect. It may be that there is an energy within and without that is counter-productive and needs to be conquered. The challenge is, how do you react when the false and ugly appearance is staring you in the face?

Response determines the present and the future. Negativity multiplies when personal experiences appear bleak and hope disappears. A successful practice to help alter the energy is to learn to change the mind. This is a powerful practice that will assist in achieving self-mastery. A persistent problem is shortsightedness. In contrast, Spirit goes the whole distance. Give yourself the biggest favor by learning how to meet every challenge from a loftier perspective. Anyone who remains reluctant regarding the subject of transformation does not yet understand the purpose of existence. We dishonor our origin as pure consciousness when we rigidly remain less than we are.

To achieve the prize, do everything possible to create the best conditions for a spiritual life. Honor the higher Self. Communicate daily; ask for guidance and eventually a conscious connection is established. The soul journey and its blessings provide the light required to solve problems. It is up to the pupil to deliberately cultivate the relationship. Eventually, the soul will evolve as an incandescent form, a seed that will blossom into the incorruptible immortal body of light through self-mastery.

Self-mastery is the first prize. It requires a persistent love for truth and courage to live as a noble being. The souls who make this choice are different from the masses, but in this case, the difference is a blessing in disguise. The Holy Creative Spirit becomes an active partner. The presence within will emerge through fervent desire and persistence on your part. Create a spiritual ideal and be removed from the wheel of suffering. Constantly reach higher and in so doing the sacred fire is released and energizes you on every level.

It is the decision of the mind whether to unmask the light within or remain stumbling in the darkness. Once the choice for Light is made, adhere and fiercely protect the decision. No one is alone, although on occasion it may appear that way. Eventually, the "third eye," the eye of spirit, will permit a seeker to view things as they really are. Guidance is provided. True renunciation is living in harmony with the inner Self. It is a full time assignment and can be done in the flesh. Intelligence is fully equipped to reach a level of consciousness where spiritual harmony and wisdom is an Earth experience.

Change destiny through higher wisdom by learning to discern between productive and non-productive influences. No fairy godmother will do this for you. If you waver or become lax and lose sight of the goal, failure will occur and you will be required to repeat life in semi-darkness instead of living consciously in the Light. There are many seekers who have attained great book knowledge and have not lived it. They may lose their memory of the higher knowledge in a future experience if knowledge is not applied.

A force of will is required to control fluctuating moods. Strengthen and use the mind diligently and eagerly for a good purpose. A true healing instills order in the energy fields. When any one of these areas is in disorder, imbalances and mistakes are created. Meet each trial knowing that the Divine is everywhere. Fan the spark within and allow it to burn constantly. As the inner light expands, the power of the eternal Self begins to make itself known. Undo everything that has worked against freedom and transform consciousness. Keep silent regarding your progress. People who are less disciplined and are not seeking freedom may laugh and do their utmost to change the direction of your path.

BE: Embracing the Mystery

    Use common sense and realize that anything good and lasting is not built overnight. The dream of creating and establishing a masterful energy demands secrecy, patience, love, trust, vision and perseverance. Keep in mind the famous words of the great poet, Walt Whitman: "I celebrate myself." This is the confident attitude of true spirituality, realizing the presence of God.

    The irony of soul growth is that you may have already achieved a developed and noble character, experienced mystic visions, and be gifted with the ability to heal others, and still personally suffer. There may be some old negative karma lingering in the subconscious that the soul judges as unpaid debts. When this happens, accept the challenge understanding that the problem has presented itself because it is ready to be healed.

    What is gained in the Light must be lived. Self-mastery has many levels. Each grade lifts and expands the mind and soul to greater understanding and power. It is similar to attending a higher school of learning. Challenges occur because you live in a world where there is a collective false philosophy. Everyone is constantly being bombarded with negative energies from people, places and things. A conscious worker whose mind is focused on the Light has the right tools and knows how to neutralize, diminish and heal whatever appears. This is a solid reason to develop and maintain a healthy physical body and a balanced mind. Do everything in your power to make certain you are equal to any energy that appears as a challenge. Matter obeys the enlightened ones. A conscious and awakened soul only resonates with vibrations that match his own.

    Mastery enables you for the most part to rise above suffering and consciously live from a higher, Spirit-filled perspective. It is the winning perspective of the Divine, which clearly reveals the appearance world of man. Journaling is a tool that helps clarify consciousness. It can provide an excellent map, a good mystical philosophy where you can record a lifetime of inward experiences. Soul writing is not an intellectual exercise; it is a heart experience put into words. Never give up working towards an ideal. It is better to die in the line of duty and be faithful to the end than to live a polluted, unconscious, uncaring life that will only repeat itself next time around if it has not been transformed. Develop yourself correctly and you will become a living inspiration. Be the watcher as the new direction is firmly installed. As you awaken, Spirit becomes a great friend.

The darkness of fear and ignorance may attempt to make you falter. This is why it is vital that a strong foundation be constructed. Build the structure and its merits are yours forever. No fearful, angry person can create a chip in the foundation. If you are not strong in spiritual understanding and experience, the little ego will surface and perhaps create an explosive reaction. Secrecy, silence and a calm demeanor are the rule until a firm foundation based on action is acquired.

The more focused and comfortable you are with the truth of your own spiritual individuality, the easier it becomes to live a non-conditioned life. To live a life without labels, judgments or assumptions is ideal. Too many people cling to the past, reliving the suffering, abandonment and confusion of the fooled. Stop suffering by reaching higher to a perspective where you know that in God's eyes we are all equal. The equality is not as a human. The equality is the original divine seed within that is capable of expanding to a full-blown enlightened individual in the flesh. Human weakness occurs when we accept limitation.

To live in a state of conscious awareness, be attentive at all times, think deeply and remember to pay attention to details. This is a sound practice. It is your responsibility to consciously manifest a transformation in the atomic body, understanding and believing that authentic empowerment is yours already. The Beloved is already in your midst. Struggling with the acceptance of spiritual individuality is a crisis that may cause stagnation. Stagnation is a state of mind that will gradually cease as consciousness expands.

Meditation is emphasized because it provides an opportunity to experience the gift of completeness. If you do not meditate, the following is a simple suggestion. Choose a special place and time for daily meditation. It is not the length of time that is important, only the quality of mindfulness. Sit quietly alone, state intent and offer a prayer of love and gratitude. Divine assistance can also be requested. Imagine a golden ray pouring down through the top of the head. Work with the ray breathing slowly and diaphragmatically through your nostrils. An excellent beginning breath exercise is to inhale to a count of five, hold for five and exhale for five. Increase the number with practice. Visualize the body absorbing the transforming power of the golden ray as a sponge absorbs water. Imagine the cells being filled with light. Continue contemplating and meditating on the Golden Ray. If there is difficulty remaining focused,

BE: Embracing the Mystery

look at a candle flame or concentrate on the area between the eyebrows.

Meditation not only cleanses the disruptive subconscious memories, it can transform the physical/atomic body and sustain it in a permanent state of perfection through steady practice and attention. Poltinus said, "Let the body think of the spirit as streaming, pouring, rushing and shining into it from all sides."

A mental mantra, special combination of meaningful words, impresses the subconscious as well as the organs and cells of the body. Tools are to be used moderately; they will help you learn the steps to the dance of life. Through meditation you will learn to interact with Divine Mind. Real communion means to get in touch each day and hour with the living forces of nature, love and wisdom. Eventually, the ability to accomplish and experience higher frequency waves will manifest as a reality. These waves of frequency are spiritually heard by celestial beings that will be drawn to your personal light.

No one has to be a scholar to understand truth or increase individual light. What benefits a pupil most is to accept the immortal identity. This is the wisdom that knows how to listen to the gentle voice, which speaks within. The smothering darkness that can overwhelm a soul has visited my life. I have learned to transcend the abyss of corrupted thought and energy influences. Through personal effort, trust and love, energy evolves into a positive creative power. When we are willing, heaven and earth become one and the same. Hold fast to your ideal and persevere. Never waver. The efforts made remain beyond physical death. Once a spiritual journey is begun in earnest, you know what to work at and what to rely on.

In great joy and confidence, recognize your best friend as the Beloved within; the Beloved will help you recreate yourself. As you confidently move towards the waters of immortality, pain ceases and darkness dissipates. You will know truth and be the truth, and no one can rob you of your riches. You have chosen to come alive and change darkness into joy and experience fellowship with the Light.

Chapter Twelve
Seed Thoughts

If the spiritual hearing sense is not open, a pupil cannot hear wisdom. If the veil is not lifted on the spiritual vision, Light cannot be seen. If the Causal higher mind, the superconsciousness, is not contacted, pure truth eludes the thinking mind. No poet can give his true poem or artist his creation. Open your mind and heart and it becomes easier to grasp unconditional love and universal truth. Get past being a man or woman controlled by the senses. Learn to hush the human senses and yield to the highest within you. Choose a goal that will force the scales to fall from your thinking mind, thus achieving an unclouded consciousness of beauty and truth.

Sin is the great falsity connected with the outer self of the senses. It belongs to separateness and chaos. The spiritually ignorant, with their lack of understanding, make sin exist as a personal reality. When humankind responds from the habits of an unenlightened nature, life appears bleak and confusion and ignorance is rampant. Matter, the world, the physical body, are not sinful. It is humans who make bad use of the blessings of life. Nothing is bad in its pure form. When people do not know how to adjust or harmonize themselves with the higher Nature, disorder is created.

It is the perversion of reality that disrupts behavior, society and a natural order. It is an impoverishment that needs to be healed by those who created it. Many people automatically assume what they are thinking, speaking and demonstrating is absolute truth. How many verify information? Man assumes the unreal is real. It is a sickness, a betrayal of truth that fosters a false image of who we are.

When a great prophet, master teacher or Christ appears on the human scene, people are given an opportunity to follow a living example of an integrated consciousness. True teachings lead a soul beyond the falsehood of duality, emptying the soul, mind and body of all illusion.

Generally speaking, visible form is the feeblest and the most distant likeness of the real Self. The shadow world is an imitation of the celestial planes and your identity as spirit. Present conditions are an opportunity for spiritual advancement. To be victorious, grasp the idea that heaven is not a place, but a higher awareness of God, creation and the role we are to play here on Earth. The more knowledge awakened within, the more expansive the Divine. Faith in eternity and the All Knowing God is life and power. You always are and you always will be.

With a heavy heart, you may feel Earth is a place of unending sorrow. Knowledge is born of suffering. Suffering is often unnecessary and caused by opposing the will of Divine Order and denying spiritual identity. Eventually, you will look back at your struggle in gratitude. Until then, perhaps, you are hugging your chains. The worst barrier in the world is a sense of fear. Fear is the cloud that dims spiritual vision. Man, the highest known intelligence in physical form, believes in the appearance world more than he recognizes or believes in the Supreme Source behind creation. It is the destiny of humankind to yield to the highest within and experience freedom.

The weakest person has the whole universe to draw upon. To fulfill destiny, realize that you are entirely unlimited. Pierce through the walls of the human senses, yield to wisdom within and develop reverence for Earth and all life. Spirit is hidden in everything.

The current race consciousness is still in its infancy. A direct result of falsity has resulted in separateness worldwide, numbing the mind and soul. Individually, you can lift your consciousness and in so doing lift others. Learn to reshape every experience until it becomes transmuted. You have the power to bring those in need to a place of blessing. To do so, confront your own personality. It is the culprit standing in the way of freedom. You are on stage and the personality can easily be your worst enemy. Any point of view that works against harmony must be replaced.

Earthly existence is significant for one reason alone, a return to the Source. Realize what you are and why you are, your assignment in the flesh and the divine idea behind creation.

Unless spiritual laws and purpose are clearly understood, suffering will continue. Suffering will force humankind to take up the path of Love. Without understanding, the personality responds from the lower senses. It is mandatory that a seeker of truth ceases living in denial and in its stead allows the subtle, highest glory and wisdom to be revealed. It is time to let go of the fear associated with the unknown.

The soul is consciously alive to its true spiritual individuality by accepting it as Light eternal, with a purpose other than the mediocrity it has accepted. This is true empowerment. As Johann Goethe stated: "Boldness has genius, power and magic in it." The soul has a choice to step forward and be free or continue in a downward spiral that leads to misery.

To step forward and be free, accept that you are an indestructible spiritual being. Use the indwelling divine forces to spiritualize shadows and confusion. Love the Supreme Spirit who created individuality, love your true inner Self and move from a position of weakness to an enduring power. True spiritual love includes love of the light within and without. In our earlier moral and spiritual evolution, humanity worked with the law of an eye for an eye. Later, the law of love was given and the majority still rebelled.

Eventually, more individuals will stop resisting and demand to live as the brightness and not as the shadow. What is conscious thinking? From the point of Divine Wisdom, conscious thinking is only when you are aware that the spirit within is thinking as and through you. All other thinking is unconscious because it is not aware of a higher power. Most humans have been practicing error-thinking or minimized God-thinking. In other words, it is only the rare thinker who allows the spirit of truth to do the thinking through him. What you are consciously unaware of is difficult to maximize. As a result of being unconscious of the possibility of God thinking as you and keeping the power minimal, judging, thinking and believing from a separated personality view creates disorder instead of unity.

Through the power of thought, you have actively programmed every single person, thing and event into your life. Human beings for the most part are unconscious mortal creators. Since you already create both consciously and unconsciously, why not change a pattern that is not working? Instead, create consciously with a heightened understanding and deliberately maximize the already existing God power within and reconstruct the human experience. If this principle is understood and applied, you can change everything in life that displeases simply by changing your thinking.

The idea is in allowing the higher Self to be the Master and take charge. This will happen when there is a change in attitude and the reins are given over to Creative Mind. A seeker must allow the higher Self to correct and direct. When the change of power happens, transformation, joy and illumination is the result. The higher Self knows the entire tapestry of your existence. If you trust in the impressions Spirit gives and follow through, you will change into a limitless being.

Negatives destroy. They halt the flow of Divine energy. Stop taking sides with the whims of the temporary human personality. What you are likely playing around with is an excess of strong emotional energy that only pollutes your body, mind and soul, holding you back from the love, bliss and power that can be yours. It is up to you to rescue your higher Nature from the personality and negative energy that is collected from misdirected thinking and the dangerous energy of others. There are rules for creating an ideal mind and body, enabling the higher Self to function freely.

To change the downward spiral of the collective consciousness, allow timeless truth principles to come alive in your experience as practical methods that heal and create order. Stop separating the physical plane from the spiritual plane. There is a continuous progression that runs like a golden thread between all vibratory planes. To attain the higher knowledge, a pupil must have an open mind that is willing to accept that there is life vibrating simultaneously in varying degrees within all created realms of consciousness. We are multi-dimensional and co-exist with all levels of creation. Use your mind and ask questions. Accept the center of divine authority within.

From the viewpoint of wisdom knowledge, the masses are not projecting a divine image today. The true image is a sublime exchange of a relationship encompassing both masculine and feminine principles originally established within an individual entity. Humans mistakenly look for the other half of what they judge as self through intimate relationships and joining with the opposite sex. On a deep level, the seeker of union, or in this case a relationship or marriage, is looking for someone else to make him feel whole and complete. Unbeknownst to him, the other half he is seeking is an aspect that he needs to fully develop within himself. However pleasant, completeness is not normally achieved through merging with another human being. God is actually two principles, masculine and feminine, always together, yet hidden within our spirit. It is an erroneous belief that causes the principles to appear separated. Spiritual principle is not being fully demonstrated until both the masculine and feminine aspects are developed and balanced. Eventually, a union occurs manifesting God's Perfect Idea in form.

It is destiny to become a balanced human being and accomplish works of magic and wonder. Miracles are created naturally when you are of this understanding and energy. The goal is to have the two principles always actively present. Eventually, every man and woman must achieve unification. When you vibrate equally with the cosmic principles of both masculine and feminine, there is a choice available enabling you to switch from one polarity to another using a particular strength through your feeling responses.

"Know Thyself" is a well-known axiom. These two words were carved over the entrance to the Temple of Delphi. To understand one's Self is to make a conscious and permanent connection with your own immortal spirit beginning with the higher mental Causal Self. You do that through recognition, love and daring to visualize perfection. To thoroughly understand who you are also includes education regarding the physical, etheric, emotional and mental fields. Through the right mental and spiritual attitude, you will also receive glimpses, inspiration, and guidance and develop a strong connection with the three higher aspects of the Self. Real wisdom is to achieve a clear understanding of the entire energy package. Limitation will continue if you primarily identify with the physical body. It is spirit who is the rightful owner of your life.

Construct a true foundation cleared of false building material, erroneous thinking and wrong actions. As you progress, accept that the whole of good is yours. It is your right to release the wonder of the Great Mystery hidden within. It is through individual effort that you learn to live from the innermost Self. You are not alone. Eventually, a new race of beings will emerge and live from the heart center and not from greed. They will sweep away the debris of illusion.

Now is an opportunity to discover and be who you really are. You become God's masterpiece when the birthing of truth is allowed. God expresses through you when the channels are cleared. Be obedient to the dictates of your higher Self. Seek divine companionship. Unfulfilled and unsatisfied feelings will leave. Divine thought resolves all difficulties. It frees the soul from contradictions. The process is about learning to be unselfed. Use the present condition as an opportunity for spiritual advancement. Give love and give some part of each day to silent communion and growth.

To receive a pure message of guidance, lift the mind to a Greater Consciousness and not the obscure, manipulative hazy regions of the lower invisible planes. Erroneous advice can be given in the name of God. How will you know if the message is truth? Scrutinize what is being said and seek the same style, content and divine wisdom that support the proven teachings shared by God Realized Beings from all cultures and Earth cycles. Those who speak truth are of One Mind. There are many false prophets and claimants who are in actuality being influence by mischievous invisible entities that love to fool gullible humans. Or, it could be that the transmitter may be simply elaborating upon hidden desires.

Everything that comes to you on the path of life comes for a reason. You can deliberately step out of misery. It is not inevitable nor does confusion need to be the dominant note in your life. The false flame of egoism, possession and selfish desires can be snuffed out. When you succeed, escaping the whirlpool of fallacies, you escape unenlightenment.

The word fire also denotes the inner flame of the spirit. It is said in the Bible that God is a "Burning Fire." The Sacred Fire is the Fire of Love and burns within humans as well as impersonally as a symbol of the One Power, Presence and Wisdom. Life is actually the manifestation of the Sacred Fire. When the Sacred Fire is burning within, peace and harmony reign. Inner peace cannot be reached without the Sacred Fire. Higher Intelligence uses the fire as a powerful means to purify people and the planet Earth.

To see and feel the Sacred Fire is to be blessed. Sitting by an open fire serves as a purification for millions of people. As you ascend through spiritual initiations, different fire manifestations may appear in vision. In vision, I have seen three different forms of the Sacred Fire. The fire that specifically symbolizes the Absolute, the Supreme Spirit, is The White Fire. It is the ultimate symbol of purity, power, wisdom and love.

The White Fire is the Great Indescribable blessing us in moments of intimacy and bliss. This symbol has been described throughout the ages. As an example, White Fire is mentioned in reference to the Jerusalem Talmud. The Torah "was written with letters of black fire upon a background of white fire." According to Rabbi Isaac the Blind, father of

Kabbalah, there are two Torahs. The authentic one is the one written in White Fire and the oral Torah is the black fire. According to their teachings, when the Messiah comes, the message will be legible for all.

Be alert to the intuitive flashes offered in both times of need and rest. Long hours are not required to commune with God. Simply make quality time in your busy day to stop and acknowledge the Presence that is the substance of life. The more attention given to the immortality we have by Nature, the more divine light and sensitivity to the subtle worlds of thought are experienced. You will recognize the infinite power flowing through you. It provides deep knowledge. Pay close attention to the signs and symbols offered as guideposts along the path. The power and results of transformation is more than a mental event. It is experienced within all levels of your being.

A relationship with the subtle world is not always flawless. The rightness, the communion is definitely determined by the present state of mind. This holds true for any seeker who is connecting consciously with invisible energy. If the personality is doubtful, fearful or negative in any way, the communicative ability to be absolutely clear and pure will lessen considerably. To receive truth, develop and sustain a state of peace and receptivity. If you feel you are experiencing a direct contact with an energy that is beyond the known physical, discern its origin. Is it astral, mental or celestial? Is it limited, manipulative or false thinking? If discernment is not developed, many forms of mischief can manifest. Become knowledgeable in the ways of the lower astral realms.

Negative energies under the guise of love and concern for the unsuspecting and vulnerable human will mislead and cause eventual harm. A good example of unwanted excess noise in the mind or negative energy was the time I used a gift certificate for a massage. I had not met the woman therapist. It turned out she was a gentle person, but she lacked knowledge regarding the protection of her own energy or her clients' from the influence of possible dark forces. As soon as I stepped into her office, I felt heaviness and knew something was terribly wrong. Throughout the appointment, the feeling worsened.

My mother and a close friend had crossed over to the other side the previous week. Because I was tired and stressed from the two funerals, the negative energy in the massage office was felt more strongly than usual. I went home immediately after the massage and secluded myself in

BE: Embracing the Mystery

my bedroom. What I witnessed next would have frightened anyone who has not successfully participated in exorcism work. A large dark form as wide and deep as half of my bedroom appeared. The negativity existing in the massage office had followed me home. I immediately began to calmly and lovingly talk to it about the Light and God's love. My observation was that this conglomerate was indeed a collection of energies that had been left in the unsuspecting therapist's place of work. Attempting to see the good side of the intruding energy, I entertained the idea that perhaps this dark intelligence actually desired to be healed. I focused on the one Power and Presence and concluded with the Lord's Prayer.

The form was situated on the right side of my room. Immediately after saying the prayer, a lightning bolt in the shape of Archangel Michael's sword suddenly came swiftly from the left side of the room. The radiant blue-white celestial sword flashed past me aiming directly at the enormous dark form. In a short breath, the Celestial Light dissipated the darkness. Evidently, Archangel Michael felt that a stronger action was required than my loving approach. The heaviness left, my spirit rejoiced and harmony was restored.

The following are some of the proven suggestions offered in the area of protection when involved with energy work: Before clients arrive, offer a silent prayer. Ask for God's Light, protection and wisdom to guide the experience. Always ask for discernment. Because you are working in another person's energy field, pay close attention to thoughts that come to you. Are the thoughts your own or are they from an outside source? Are your thoughts from a spiritual perspective or from a lower animal/human nature?

It is very easy to absorb other influences. Anyone involved in energy or counseling work must strengthen his own aura. Build a personal light shield daily. This is not only a protection from outside negative influences; it will expand individual light so the angels or guides can work more effectively through you. Light a white candle. Dark entities avoid the light as a rule unless they, too, desire to be healed.

The therapist was allowing her clients to talk about problems during the massage. Insist on silence. Silence will benefit the client as well as assist the therapist in being a conduit for higher energies. If an intuitive message is received for a client, wait until the session is over before communicating. Whether you are a professional or are lovingly comforting a friend, it is a good practice to imagine a pillar of Light entering your head and moving throughout the body, extending through your hands to the client.

Call on the higher Self of the patient to help with the healing. Offer a silent prayer of gratitude when the session is completed. Make a habit of washing hands after working on a client. At the end of the day, burn incense such as sandalwood, which is helpful in clearing negative energies. If you have a water influence in your zodiacal chart, you may have a tendency to be emotional and easily absorb energies from outside influences. Be aware of this and take precautions. These simple practices work and are also necessary for any type of class or gathering where people are troubled and wounded.

There is an urgency being felt by sensitive humans, which is telling us change is on the way. What is needed right now is a new humanity, a brave and bold humanity who will choose to develop an inner thought power whereby we become conscious of our unity with life. Souls are being called who love and respect every living creature because they understand how all life is connected. The world needs individuals who seek self-mastery and infinite possibilities, beings who dare to reach out and take what is good for them. When this is actualized, we become one with a universal consciousness and draw upon a limitless fount of healing.

No one else can transform your consciousness. This assignment belongs to the soul who chooses to develop an intimacy with God. Suggestions, ideals, other beings both visible and invisible are waiting to assist when you are ready and willing to spiritually evolve. Do the "work" and take the necessary steps to free your self from false beliefs. What is required is a divine cleansing. During the cleansing process and reprogramming, you may occasionally fall flat on your face. When that happens, laugh and get up and try again. Learn through personal effort what is true and what is not. Experience is the perfect teacher.

Teachers of truth and scripture, books, lectures and life inspire in moments of aloneness and sorrow providing comfort and new insights. If you persevere and remain passionate regarding the inner quest, a time will arrive when the outward tools are not enough. The perfection in the spirit within is waiting patiently for you to remember and cooperate with it. Humanity has been struggling for eons of space/time with the opaque veils of spiritual ignorance that have clouded the truth of spiritual iden-

BE: Embracing the Mystery

tity. Separation and forgetfulness is not entirely personal. The key is to recognize this and consciously do something positive and lasting about it. A common obstacle is that many seekers are usually in a hurry and desire instant gratification.

The inward journey does not have to be harsh and laborious. Resistance, doubt, fears, a lack of confidence and a wavering mind will make the journey appear as an overwhelming task. In contrast, transformation can be a labor of love, a dance, if you completely trust and love Spirit. Guidance will come naturally and with ease. The future is determined by the choices made. It is attitude and what you consciously accept, trust and put into action that determines eventual freedom from suffering and removes a sense of separation from God. The more conscious you become as an ongoing individualized spirit, the easier the journey and greater the expanse and energy of your mind.

The Bhagavad-Gita states: "Only the man balanced in pain and pleasure is fitted for immortality." Although I am far from being an advocate of suffering, it does transform us. Many seasoned teachers think of suffering as a blessing. Eventually, when a student understands universal laws and lives them, suffering diminishes and in many cases ceases. The difficulties and subsequent trials liberate the powers of the soul and spirit and in time something magnificent occurs within. Old karma and conditions are healed and you become a compassionate being.

Accept and understand that balance in the mind and flesh is the goal. If a desire is a pure one, doors will open and the limited life will drop away through personal testing and verifying of what is true and what is not. You will know firsthand the hidden essence. Everyone is destined to live a divine life and live it in the visible world. Perfection is the end and not the means. Perfection will be yours visibly and tangibly through an enlightened and disciplined passionate effort. It requires perseverance and commitment.

Both the Eastern and Western wisdom teachings warn disciples that before they put their feet upon the path of wisdom, they must place their own life in a state of order. Don't worry about how long it will take to attain enlightenment and healing. A subtle reconstructing process will be taking place.

Absorb the philosophy of spirit, live with it and put it into practice day and night. Never make excuses; there are none. Waiting for the right conditions doesn't happen. Plunge forward trusting that the inner spiritual force is more powerful than any circumstances or relationship. This is part of the training.

When the mind and heart give priority to Spirit, the personality will rise above material conditions and what was judged as a bother in the past will actually improve or disappear entirely. To succeed, touch the center of your being for truly significant results. Eventually, you become a mystic. It is the mystic who is at rest. It is she or he who, in joy and certainty, experiences the Immensity. It is the mystic who knows the Self. The mystic understands that the higher wisdom is a science.

It is said that there are three steps to the ideal goal: right life, true life and truth. Learn to live a true life and you will know the truth. The principles of mysticism are a feeling experience. You already have an invincible Energy Body. Take good care of it. You have what it takes to draw out from the heart a lost inheritance and live your birthright.

Chapter Thirteen
Teaching Tools

God is uncreated consciousness. Uncreated consciousness is the substance of the universe. The substance is made of Spirit. Spirit is energy. It is within the smallest particles of our being. Spirit never changes; It is. Spirit is omnipotent, omniscient and omnipresent. When we purify ourselves, we create a filtering instrument for Spirit. Spirit descends and impregnates matter. We may not consciously know All Truth but Spirit within sees everything, knows everything and can do anything. Nothing ever goes unknown, all is known by the master Teacher within.

Everything is possible when Spirit is in control, and not the unstable personality and subconscious memory. If you do not consciously have a plan, create it. Design a plan that will encourage the manifestation of your higher Nature and it will expand the mirror of your consciousness. The voice of consciousness must be the heart center, the higher Self. The higher Self is supreme. It belongs to the lofty realm of Limitless Light. It only guides when you choose to climb the ladder of consciousness. When conscious thinking and feeling is united with Spirit, real life will begin. You will gravitate in one direction, towards God, the Uncreated Consciousness, That Which Is. Existence then becomes pure love; it is totally in love with itself.

It is up to you to become sensitive to the subtle energies. Spirit will grace you with clues that will assist in the joy of remembering. You will stop living within the narrow bondage of the flesh. Slip away from under the shadow of intellectual limitation and you will learn what it means to receive a grander vision of what life means. The right materials, people and events will suddenly appear to encourage and support your intent. Intuition may be stimulated as right brain activity. The higher Mind activity may manifest and teach through dreams, healing and dazzling visions of Light.

Dreams and visions are an integral part of consciousness. Pay attention to them; they frequently convey important messages. Recently, I had a dream where I viewed a woman walking down the street wearing a green cape and hood. She was looking downward. As I watched, I became aware of glorious music coming from her aura. I approached the woman and said, "You must come out and play. It is time for you to return to God." The message was for someone I had not yet met. A week later, a friend called and I shared the dream with her. She personally knew who was to receive the message. The woman in the dream lived in another state. We made contact. She agreed that the message was for her. She was depressed and uncertain as to what to do with her life. It was her custom to walk looking downward. She explained that the posture was due to her lack of self-esteem.

The woman is a pianist. The dream message was to encourage a human who was engulfed in personal anguish to literally step out of a deep depression and loss and give to others through her music. Sharing will also help the pianist reconnect to the divine within her. Each of us must fine-tune our own instrument, the body, mind and soul to be a receiver and giver of the Light. The inner music will transform the physical into the Holy and infuse the Holy into the mundane.

There is an ancient dialog that clearly illustrates the truth of spiritual identity. Although the source is unknown, the message is timeless. The story describes an old man who greets a stranger while walking down the street saying, "Good morning, master." Most of the people are either silent or think he must be an idiot. Every once in a while, somebody understands what he is implying and answers, "Yes, good morning, master." The old man asks, "Yes, good morning. I have a question for you master." The stranger replies, "What is that?" The old man states, "Do you remember?" The stranger replies, "Remember what, master?" The old man continues, "Do you remember that you have the power?" The stranger smiles and says, "Oh, now that you remind me, yes, I do remember." The old man concludes, "Good, I suggest you might use it. Good-bye."

To be master of the lower nature, use the available tools. When you remember and use the tools, conscious union with the beloved higher Self is your reward. Through connecting in consciousness, good can be accomplished. Reality differs according to consciousness. There are a myriad of discoveries waiting to be explored. When you successfully learn to meditate, you are tapping into ancient resources that help har-

BE: Embracing the Mystery

monically attune. Attunement will carry you into dimensions of matter and anti-matter.

The invisible worlds of the higher mind, soul and spirit are real as well as limitless. The energy is creative, beautiful and alive beyond ordinary imagination. The consciousness of the dreamer, the meditator, determines the integrity of the experience in the same way that consciousness creates cause and effect here in the physical world of separation and fear. Spirit is not limited. Open your mind and allow the higher consciousness to pour its majesty through you. When you cultivate mental peace and emotional poise, harmony as a spiritual state is the reward.

There are many practical steps that can be taken to increase the power of the conscious mind. As an example, the following two suggestions are workable regardless of physical age. It is well worth your while to organize mental powers. To increase the power of concentration, learn to train the mind. No one wishes to experience dementia. One cannot be vigilant nor have discernment to any high degree if the mind wanders or forgets. Five minutes in the morning is the best time of day for a concentration exercise because your body is more likely to be tension free after a good night's sleep. Close your eyes and focus on something beautiful or sacred. The training is more effective imagining a form such as a stream of water, a flower such as a rose, a butterfly or bird. Use an image that represents aliveness. A flame, or the calmness of the sea, billowing clouds, or a green meadow also provides the expansiveness and freedom that the inner self desires.

Use an image that is significant to you. Make it large and real. See it about two feet away from your body. Be gentle and use moderation. Evaluate the image. I recommend you use the same image every day until it becomes real and lasting. It will take repeated attempts and regularity to establish a rhythm. When I first began my mind training, I would stare at a blank wall. Universal symbols of Light Energy would appear providing a tool for knowledge and investigation. To keep the mind focused requires discipline and is an ancient practice exercised in cultures on the far side of the world. The Greeks also developed mind exercises for improvement purposes and memory perfection. Pythagoras taught perfection through release of all the potential powers of the Self.

At bedtime, exercise retrospection. If your lifestyle does not provide for a mental exercise when you retire, honor your own choices by keeping the time under ten minutes. Seek privacy just before you go to bed and try the following practice. Use the discipline of order and repetition to review your day. This practice has been proven to strengthen the thinking mind. Start with the last thing you did before sitting down for the exercise. Think backward over the entire day from the end to the beginning. This practice will sharpen the mind and increase an ability to remember, focus and to meditate in a more meaningful way. If the mind wanders, bring it back to the last remembered action.

Mentally live over the day and contemplate what you could have done differently and visualize it changed. As a side benefit, this exercise is a helpful tool for people with insomnia. If you fall asleep, the process will naturally continue subconsciously. The ability to do this will increase and memory will eventually be strengthened. Practice on a regular basis. The idea is to take charge of life. Blessings come when you do your own thinking and take deliberate steps to create self-mastery. As you plant new seed thoughts into Mind, you will reap great rewards and push past old self-imposed limits. Concentration and retrospection practiced daily lead you to the path of power. Both are prerequisites of a spiritualized state. Paracelsus said: "The beginning of wisdom is the beginning of supernatural power."

The gifts of the language of God are variations of Light, symbols, numbers, vivid geometric energy forms and intelligent, loving and majestic beings, all of which help a serious student come alive to an enduring and powerful reality. Although there is only One Mind Thinking, it appears to humans that there are at least two minds when we are in a physical body. The one part of the Mind is busy with simple living and survival, and the activated higher part of the Mind has a direct contact with higher dimensions, creativity, beauty and truth. It is through the activated power of the higher Mind, the mind of the Spirit, that you receive the gifts of God and communicate with beings from finer dimensions.

A vision experience is the direct result of the higher Mind communicating. It has nothing to do with the human brain or planetary thinking process. Recently my dad's spirit appeared to me with an important message. Near the close of our conversation, he changed his known appearance and displayed one of his higher vehicles of Light. His familiar form changed into a being of radiant golden Light. His energy was beyond definition. When we make contact with perfection it is because we know,

BE: Embracing the Mystery

see and identify in consciousness. We momentarily escape from limitation.

Remembering and learning is also quickened through visual enhancements. There are thousands of symbols that help clarify the language of Light. Pay close attention to any symbols that come into your life. They are a gift from your inner Teacher.

Guidance may come as an animal totem, a means of receiving important messages from the higher Self. The animal world is a great teacher. There is a mystical side to animals. They offer assistance and support if you are open to it. When you know what to look for, use them for the development of character, true prophecy and higher perception. Every aspect of nature is woven into your life. In allowing this truth as a teaching tool, you receive guidance and support when needed. The prophets studied symbols, dreams and visions.

Lucid dreams are also an indicator that the superconscious is active and a higher intelligence is attempting to contact and guide the personality. Lucid dreams are experiences created through the interaction of the unconscious and conscious part of the mind. In dreams, a storehouse of unconscious knowledge is available to our conscious experience. For more than a thousand years, Tibetan Buddhists have induced a lucid dream state where the mind is fully awake when the body is sleeping, maintaining an unbroken continuity in consciousness. This is the focus of one who meditates.

Mind forces, thought, soul attainment and spiritual strength are made of different speeds of Light. The key to all life and the universe lies in harmonic interaction of Light, which is mind and heart. The art of unconditional love is the companion tool that enriches the mind and soul and not only the body. Love is the very breath and essence of life. Be gentle and patient as you attempt to remember and consciously be the divine. Begin in earnest, be realistic and accept the truth that there may be obstacles and inner resistance at times that will hinder your focus. This is normal.

Eventually, energy will shift and living a life of genuine thanksgiving and Light will come effortlessly. There is a proven pattern. Spirit disseminates its energy and matter collects and unifies and rises to meet it. True spirituality consists in never losing sight of spiritual identity and the Cause behind it. Its rightful place is at the center of the mind and heart.

Teaching Tools

You are to discover in matter, which is condensed Spirit, how to try and test greater things in the material world.

Another tool is to gain knowledge of the Science of Astrology. It might help clarify any karmic negativity that appears in the human personality. I say might because many astrologers today do not take into consideration the continuation of the soul and its level of evolvement. In ancient times, the astrologers had a greater understanding of the process of soul progression. Searching for a thorough and good philosophical astrologer, who is seriously on the path towards enlightenment as well as knowledgeable regarding the subject matter, can assist in pointing out past and present influences in your life through the power of the stars. Since both invisible and visible creation is connected, reality includes the stars and planets as well.

In our current cycle, astrology more commonly applies to the human personality and not to the soul or spirit. The aspects at the time of birth indicate the available growth potential. Humans will only escape from a planetary prison by transcending weakness and the astrological chart will clarify both the strengths available for use and the weaknesses that need to be conquered. The goal is to come into harmony with the highest qualities of planetary energy. It is possible through right knowledge and effort to neutralize or transmute character traits.

Ancient astrology conformed to the foundations of wisdom teachings in the minds of the first astrologer priests and philosophers. The ancients understood the philosophical aspect of astrology. They considered the mysteries of the heavens as a revelation of divine principle and divine will. Astrology and religion developed side by side. In known history, the Hermetic Egyptian philosophers, Greek philosophers, Druid priests, Hindus and Lamas of Tibet understood the Law of Cause and Effect. They understood karma as the result of previous thought and action.

For thousands of years, the Asiatic astrologers helped people understand problems in the current life by looking at the past. They also understood that conditions vary according to the various levels or degrees of spiritual development in the individual. Since the universe and man is vibration, we are born with planets that are consistent with our own karmic vibration. What we have earned comes from the stars, administering cosmic justice.

Be cautious and do not go to extremes in your transformation process because that will only cause problems. Walk the middle road by not becoming overly materialistic or overly spiritual. Balance is the goal as well as concentrating on harmony in both the material and spiritual world. Many people are buried in matter and haven't a clue as to how to make themselves free and weightless, full of light and joy. Remain flexible and adaptable and eventually you become enlivened with the wisdom of Spirit.

A periodic reminder check as to the truth of your spiritual identity will help sustain a focus. There exist elements that are beneficial to soul progression in every one of your energy fields from the lowest to the highest vibration. The tools are available; start using them. Remove the restraints of matter and doubt from the thinking mind and watch with astonishment a remarkable metamorphosis come upon you.

Progress occurs when you are conscious of the inner master Teacher. Through the growth process, problems may continue to surface due to an environment of disorder. Train yourself to look at disorder from a new and heightened perspective. Accept challenges and realize that they surface to force the personality to face a false sense of life that has only duped and entrapped. If you are serious about spiritual growth, difficulties will even make you more determined to succeed. The pleasure begins when you stop being robotic and positive intuition develops. At some point in your journey, you willingly sacrifice the weaknesses of the human personality.

Spirit is subtle and elusive and needs to grab on to something material in order for it to be concrete and visible. The physical, emotional and mental part of what you are is the medium through which the invisible subtle energy expresses on Earth. Accept and work consciously with the cosmic energies and suddenly you will achieve the union, the divine completeness you have been seeking. Respect and guard personal energy so that you do not become discouraged, depressed or sad, all of which separate the mind and emotions from the soul and spirit. Your higher Self is not off somewhere remote and untouchable; it is near and waiting to be recognized and loved. It is not a location; it is a state of being.

A stubborn denial of truth and lazy habits holds one back from engaging in the activity which is truly worthwhile. Recognize that you are destined to participate in the work of God. Go beyond the physical body, negative emotions and intellect and penetrate the totality of the quintessence of life. Know the truth of who you are. The truth is a synthesis, which can be known only by the spirit.

Prepare for the supreme moment when you recognize your identity as kinship with the Ever Present Greatness behind natural manifestation. When you become aware, the spiritual identity is determined by what you are in mind and heart. Place your own being in a state of order. The moment of truth is when your true Self comes into being a Tree of Knowledge. The inner transformation occurs with acceptance and choosing to live the reason for your experience in the flesh. This is the second prize.

Mind is the tool to begin with. The state of the mind determines everything that happens to you. The power of thought, speech and action determines success or failure. Learn to make the thinking mind an obedient instrument. Deep thinking is required to see whether the use of mind is right or wrong. Train the mind. If conditions are hard, it is usually due to the fact that you are not in harmony with the conditions. Always analyze thoughts, words and actions. Do they reflect your inner Self? Be a vigilant trainer. When non-productive thoughts appear, change the energy by mentally stating a personal mantra of power or simply reverse them.

The true origin of life is Spirit, not physical. Internal comprehension is discovered in meditation. Some people feel connection and exaltation when the emotional nature is stimulated with music, pictures, perfumes, colors and light. Another prefers absolute stillness. It is all a matter of temperament. If you are sincere and have a strong feeling to rediscover and develop an intimate relationship with the divine, that is all that is required.

A true meditation is experienced when you have prepared for divinity. Some of the many benefits are these: A new courage and higher purpose is developed. A greater vision and broader view naturally occurs. A peace that has eluded embraces you. A temporary release from falsity and disorder provides greater strength and determination. Doubts dissipate and contradictions are cleared away.

A meditator can escape from limitation. A positive intuition develops. A natural unfoldment of super physical faculties eventually manifests. A realization that you are part of a greater Plan makes sense to you. Consciously, you are brought into the presence of the Divine, a contact with perfection. The truth that God is a non-sectarian Deity becomes

BE: Embracing the Mystery

evident. You joyfully discover and recognize that the indescribable relationship between the individual Self and the Universal Self is a living truth. The Light of God is received as a personal experience. A choice to use inner power for Good fills your being. The final achievement is the realization that you are part of the Whole. The ability to know and to see with love, discernment and understanding rules the mind, rededicating the soul to the enlightenment of humankind.

Use inner power to pierce the illusion and become consciously aware of a more sublime reality. Learn to communicate and work intelligently and scientifically with your own consciousness. At first, the connection may be sporadic. Light and awareness increases through acceptance and living truth knowingly and with love. Longing and an awakening love will return you visibly and tangibly to the Divine. The journey is not meant to be a hardship; it is a love affair between God and creation. The greater your understanding of the implications of spirit identity, the easier it will be to accept your original beauty and perfection. When the truth is finally accepted, Love reigns supreme as the underlying expression of the Living Light. The true meaning of love is understood.

The journey of the soul is long. It is your choice as to how you are going to live each new opportunity. As you seek a conscious presence of God, peace is the reward. A spiritual state results from the development of peace. A grander support is experienced. In joy and gratitude, you have found your identity once again. Regardless of what happens in life, the support and peace remain undisturbed. The rhythm, which is in the depth of your being, moves you beyond images, theologies and cosmologies into an open-ended universe. True religion is unfolding the heart, mind and hand that will gradually grow into divine realization. It is natural to love for the sake of Love, serve for the sake of service and live to uplift life. Are you ready? If so, you will bless life and help others live as one compassionate people.

Chapter Fourteen
The Actor

Do you ever stop and imagine what it would be like to be someone else? What if suddenly you could change gender, birth sign, family and friends, occupation or geographical location and be a different person, one who is living the kind of life that you secretly yearn for? For those of us who have been actors in the theater, it is understood we must completely drop personal identity and assume the identity of the character we are to play. This is what has happened to humanity unconsciously. With each new embodiment, a different character is played. In the process, the true identity as an evolving soul sustained by spirit is forgotten.

Most people see through a glass darkly. It requires an awakened spirituality to grasp the truth that behind the role of every individual is a divine spark. A corrupted personality masks the dormant life essence. The whole truth is beyond present comprehension if you yourself are not attuned to a higher perspective. Regardless of appearance or personality, what you see in a mirror or in another is divinity playing a role.

When we understand the possibilities of our own life, it may feel overwhelming. The physical plane is the shadow of the brightness. You may long for harmony, but the world cannot give peace; it only pacifies. True harmony is a process of becoming. In the process of awakening to your light, you grow wings. Strive to be in harmony with whomever and wherever you find yourself. A helpful choice is to study the life of a master teacher such as Jesus and the veil will be removed more and more. What you read is not about falsity, but the truth of being. When you take inspiration from a Master, you have an example of true health and balance. A God-realized man or woman is completely human and fully divine. You, too, can be a blessing to others by reflecting the blessings of your own growth. You can be just as much of God as you are prepared to manifest. In other words, you can be as large or as small as you think yourself.

When it is finally realized that you are looking in all the wrong places for your own divinity, you learn to extract purity from physical matter and creation. Do not always believe in what you see, look behind the appearance for the real truth. Find your luminous Self. From a spiritual perspective, you are already one with all creation. You have flesh so you can manifest God. Reach out for that which is behind the visible. You are a spiritual being here on Earth to do God's work and will. Begin to seek out a quality that gives meaning to life.

People, who have not yet discovered the Supreme Light, live an existence that is more quantity than quality. What is lacking in their lives is the pure, intangible, imponderable something that gives meaning to life. Quality comes through a direct contact with a higher Intelligence and the mental ability to control thought. The common man normally functions within the outer surface of reality, the dream world.

Many current science fiction stories depict humanity as ruled by machines. Machines are matter and, when analyzed, we realize that collective humanity is dully submersed in the lowest existence. Value is placed on material things. You have the most sublime power hidden and waiting within. Stop allowing desires for materiality to be sovereign. Accumulating things and manipulating others never bring lasting happiness. It only perpetuates the delusion and fills the mind with non-essential thoughts and buries the soul with additional burdens. Ironically, everyone must leave behind material things at physical death. If they are controlled through the medium of matter and have not evolved spiritually, they arrive in the invisible worlds empty-handed.

Spirit is authentic power. All states of existence are determined by the inner life and its expression. Why not give Spirit a chance to make the crooked places straight in life and develop mastery instead of being governed by lesser desires and energies? Stop pretending you are someone you are not. Why not drop the false self-consciousness and claim the godlike essence that you already are? Think deeply about this truth. As we enter a new evolutionary cycle, renunciation of false conditioning is demanded of us. Instead of a belief in two powers, which delude, souls must wake up from the spiritual ignorance and take positive action to discover the One Power behind life, thought and form.

Matter is the primary focus of the average mind. Lower energy coupled with the astral desire energy will draw a soul into darkness rather than the illuminating light of Spirit. A misplaced focus will trigger experiences that can be extremely painful with the purpose of shaking the unenlightened out of a stupor of forgetfulness. The thoughts, feelings, sensations, failures and suffering that are part of individual experience will actually extract the lessons a soul has chosen for further education and eventual enlightenment.

Pure spirit is the only available means to bring direction and harmony visibly and tangibly into our lives. It is too easy to relinquish an ideal and choose a path that will lead to disorder. Disorder leads to false thinking. Too many people are already experiencing the reality of hell.

The majority of humans who live a pleasant existence without soul challenges normally do not seek truth as passionately as souls who are faced with trials. For instance, if an individual were blessed with perfect health, beauty, a loving family, a comfortable home, sufficient money in the bank, what would the reaction be if suddenly he lost his blessings? Reversals occur and what was once considered normal no longer exists. These are the moments that reveal true character. If true identity is understood and lived, you remain positive and reach for the superconscious state of mind. A magical connection with the Divine strengthens and supports regardless of the severity of the challenge.

There are many people living in a situation that makes them feel that life is a hopeless round of joyless events. It is difficult for them to believe that there is light at the end of the tunnel. At some point in the awakening process, the higher Self may reveal a sudden vision. The vision will vividly illustrate the Light that illuminates the darkness. It requires a great determination to gather courage and trust to be who we really are. God never leaves us; man leaves God.

The Divine is present, although thinking mind and body feels chained in a prison without a door. There is a way out. It is during the horrendous periods of life when everything is seemingly lost that you are closest to victory. Support will come in unexpected ways if you trust and believe in the boundless Light and the power of the supremacy of Spirit. The mind is the seat of pain. Conquer your mind here in the body of flesh. This is where you learn. Understand that trials are molding tools for the mind and soul. Eventually, you experience as reality the tangible greatness of the Spirit.

Do not forget your body while you are training the mind. Once both the body and mind are in harmony, it becomes easier to focus on who you really are. It is the actor, the inner force, who has the real power. The mind and body have the choice to express it. The spirit is imprisoned when the mind is weak. When the body is neglected, bondage also occurs. The higher Nature must act through the lower nature. It plays its part when the mind is open and the body strong. When there is imbalance, the actor cannot experience the vibrations of true harmony, joy and love.

Liberation as expressed in the Upanishads is understood as the conquest of immortality. The supreme ideal is freedom, perfect health and immortality. All can be gained in this life. The physical body is important. If we neglect it, how can we attain the true and powerful knowledge? We must learn how to care for the body and realize that it is actually a temple of God itself. The body may appear as a form with flaws and defects. Once you spiritually see the ultimate reality existing within the body, the mindset changes. You realize that you can transmute the physical into the divine body. To accomplish your goal, use the disciplines and develop the will to master and perfect it.

Disciplining the mind and strengthening the body is also enhanced through correct breathing exercises. Deliberately using the vital energy will actually increase the span of life in proportion to the role breathing is used. Controlling the breath is particularly good if you have trouble sustaining a mind that is focused. During training, the universal and divine vital energy is first exhaled, slowly inhaled, retained in the heart and then slowly exhaled. Breath control is one of the many intimate aids for controlling the mind and body and diving inwards.

Learning to be outwardly what you are inwardly is choosing to live a healing and mystical life in the everyday world. Never give up. Believe in yourself, in your existence. Find out the Source from which you came.

Although you are multifaceted like a diamond, you remain one package of evolving intelligence. To function in matter, each field of energy sustains the other. At any given time you have the option to maximize in any area of your being. What if you choose to maximize and focus on the limitless Spirit, the eternal part of what is the true Self? Instead of isolating your connection primarily with the body, emotions and mind, why not include the Causal higher mind? What would happen if you did this? The opaque veils will fall away. A different reality that is limitless and eternal, healthy and ageless, wise and loving and totally free from the mesmerism of matter and its many forms of bondage gifts you with its presence. Instead of matter being in charge of life, the higher Self would be master.

As you gradually become a soul without boundaries, you become more human as well as divine. You are capable of experiencing the highest freedom and love in the present moment. Subconscious influences cease to hinder. Consciously be alert and change your attitude every time you begin to identify with limitation and unworthiness. Say with conviction, "I am the eternal Self in form," and falsity will drop away. Use discipline, feel passion for what you are striving for and focus on the goal. The higher Self will help you materialize intent.

There is a power that creates from within Itself. It acts through desire. Live and work with truth daily and God-power will externalize at the level of your thought. Decide to be permeated with Light and creativity. Focus on a virtue that is lacking until it becomes a natural part of your behavior. Call on the Angel of Fire to purify the head and its outlets, the Angel of Air to balance the throat and lungs, the Angel of Water to cleanse the solar plexus, stomach and sex organs and the Angel of Earth to remove hindrances and blockages in all the force fields. Imagine limitless Light flowing unimpeded until that glorious moment when your soul is filled with awe and bliss.

Real effort is the effort of the mind. Disciplined behavior and new thought patterns will trigger forces of a higher order and establish contact with regions of power and purity where help and support is available. The decisions made moment by moment create the future. Something shifts within and a decision is made to change now, not wait. What prompts change is usually an issue of great importance. When you fully understand spiritual origin, returning to the ideal becomes a valid reason to live in balance.

By choosing truth, you are no longer normal in the typical sense. Good results are experienced in many areas of life because new spiritual elements are drawn to your energy. The new spiritual elements may also manifest as friendships with higher beings of light as well as attracting like-minded people into your circle of life. You live outwardly a normal life, but also attract blessings from the higher realms of Light.

People usually can tolerate pain and unhappiness for just so long and then something happens inside and they have had enough. At that point, a decision is often made that will dramatically move life in a healing direction. This was my personal experience. The story emphasizes a few dramatic decisions that changed the mold of the ego personality and physical body and brought forth visibly and tangibly the higher Self. The higher Self waits patiently for our attention and love. Sadly enough, many do not fully turn to the Divine until a dire need arises. Establish a direct connection and solid foundation with God before everything falls apart.

I have tested for myself everything that is shared throughout these pages. I pray that the sacredness of real life experiences will be the medium through which your soul will respond and perceive a higher meaning to existence. The unimaginable and seemingly impossible will manifest in your life in stunning ways just as it has in mine.

Divine intervention is a bridge between the absurdity of matter and the grace of the human condition. We are a bridge when we allow ourselves to be fully human and fully divine. Reality is the son of man who is also the emanation of God. Humanity is the bridge between animal and angels and plants and archangels. Grace will guide and comfort when we have opened our hearts to infinite possibilities and recognize that we are already living in a spiritual world. The world of matter is an ongoing drama within it.

My life dramatically changed after a post-surgery emergency situation. A decision was quickly made which changed everything. I gave birth to a healthy boy. We were a family of six souls. While still in the hospital, I chose to have additional elective surgery on my lower abdomen. After being home a few days, it became painfully evident that the stitches on the lower abdomen were not healing properly. Being extremely busy, the signs of a serious infection were ignored. The pain became uncomfortable. The area around the two-inch long incision was swollen and red streaks appeared showing how rapidly the infection had spread. A fever developed and the pain had to be dealt with.

What was happening in the body was serious. I did not have a background of prayer although our family favored a universal belief and love for the Supreme Spirit, accepting all religions as varying expressions of the One God. At the time I did not fully understand the wisdom teachings or accept my own divine nature. Intellectually, I understood that there was a spiritual force within who was the real me, but I had not understood its power and presence nor did I use it properly. I was a human who had not deeply explored Spirit and Its riches.

A very serious decision was made and a totally new action was chosen. It was unusual because it was a spiritual idea, a new way of reacting as a human personality. I chose not to call an ambulance. Please do not assume anyone can do the same. It was early morning and all the family members had left for the day. Our baby had finished his ten o'clock feeding. I decided to go back to bed and handle the developing emergency situation through prayer. During that time period, alternative healing or prayer was not a part of my life.

Lying in bed, I placed my hands on the painful and infected area. A soul decision was made. The decision was not to seek human help or tell anyone about the urgency of the infection. Instead, I chose to not struggle and instead surrender the worsening situation to a higher Power. Somewhere out of the depths of my being a faith and trust surfaced in the activity of the Holy Spirit. I did know at that time the Holy Spirit was considered to be a perfect Power who could change things man judged unchangeable. Making the choice to give an emergency to an Unseen Power was highly unusual for my personality.

After making the decision to be healed, I fell asleep. This was abnormal in itself. Awakening one hour later, my hands were still lying on the infected area but there was something very unusual about the feel of the skin. A sticky substance had spread all over the area. To my joy and utter amazement, the infection had drained through two small holes divinely created on each end of the two-inch long incision. The Holy Spirit had accomplished Its glorious work.

I was intuitively instructed to wipe the area with rubbing alcohol. The swelling, pain, red streaks and fever vanished. God healed the life-threatening infection during the one hour of unconsciousness. Two small indentations remain as a reminder of my first physical-spiritual healing. A decision was obviously made on a very deep soul level to be healed by a power beyond my conscious understanding. That one decision changed life in surprising ways. In the following days, months and years, the gift of healing became an integral and intelligent force of love that could be used to help not only our family, but also others. Prior to the healing, I believed in a Higher Power although I had no in-depth knowledge regarding the subject. A change in consciousness as well as a physical healing dramatically became mine as a result of belief and surrender.

There are people who have tried to control matter and achieve healing without success. Why did it work for me? I truly believe readiness affects timing. The inner fire must be lit so that the celestial Presence can find you. God works through high beings. They are celestial helpers. I believe the Holy Spirit worked through the invisible beings of Light because I was ready for the intimacy and power of the Divine. This question hopefully will be answered to your satisfaction as you study the variety of personal examples offered throughout these pages. Firsthand experiences are sacred and consciousness-elevating.

The greater our understanding that it is done unto all, as they believe, the more likely we experience what is referred to as miracles. It is important to clearly understand how thought shapes our lives. Hopefully, personal favorite dramas will ignite new possibilities within your mind and heart and plant seeds of inspiration and hope. Everything that is sublimely good is more real and natural than the physical world we take for granted.

We learn what love truly is when we align ourselves with holiness. When we reach out to the Divine Fire, it does not burn ... it transforms. The Holy Spirit is the sacred fire. When we recognize It, It recognizes us. The experience is like being struck by a Divine thunderbolt. Nothing of a material nature can be compared to this Perfect Power nor is there anything more precious, rare or wonderful. Divine light impregnates every fiber of our being when we are receptive. True happiness is to cooperate with divinity.

When you make a decision to heal, there can be no doubt, no fear, no guilt or conditions. Make the decision and immediately release it knowing deep inside that a strong trust and conviction will produce positive results. Accept that in God's world anything is possible and anything can happen. However, God's timing is not always the same as our desire.

Every day we are manifesting new ideas and forms. Why not deliberately use Creative Mind for good? There can be no wavering or questions regarding the outcome. Be definite and trusting and know with a certainty that the outcome will be good. To experience a miracle, which is in truth only a natural occurrence resulting from belief, consciousness must be prepared to receive. Believe that you deserve to be touched by holiness.

Matter is condensed Spirit. Spirit is the essence or substance in all that is seen or unseen. Stop standing in the way of truth being fully actualized. It is a challenge to accept proven truth as a reality and live it not only in moments of need or drama, but also in everyday life. Practice faith when everything is fine in life. When something unpleasant comes along, you are prepared. It is your destiny to live your own divine Nature. The plan is to cooperate with God. Don't put off the inevitable, embrace it! Take off your mask and be bold. Allow the real Self to be on stage. It is then that you will demonstrate that there is absolutely nothing outside of God.

Part II

A Message

Look deep within and see the Self
What is seen is a Christ unadorned, simple and pure
You have been confused and lost the way
It is time to return to the glory exalting God.

Now is the time of remembrance
Now is the time to gather the many and commune
Now is the time of demonstration and rejoicing
The past is over; freedom is now.

No longer look back; step forward in the moment
Realization is to live as a Christ in form
Find peace in understanding and totally trust
Spirit is God's perfection living as you.

In accepting true identity as holy
The body as the Word made flesh
The mind as All-Knowing
The Father and son are one.

S.

Chapter Fifteen
Special Moments

Symbols, numbers, visions, dreams, divine thoughts and healings are keys leading to truths temporarily forgotten. The material manifestations are extensions of a great law and truth. When you begin to develop the spiritual senses, you are able to penetrate beyond the veil. Materiality is but an unconscious form of manifested consciousness. It is the development of consciousness, which allows the spiritual eye to see color and light revealing the keys to the Kingdom. Perfection is the goal of the soul. Do not be satisfied with anything short of it.

When touched by grace, it is important to understand and use the gift regardless of the form it takes. The gifts help you remember. Humanity has been so attached to the bankrupt material worldview, resulting in a mind that has not been open to the possibilities of a universe(s) of awesome diversity. Civilization as a whole needs a very serious redefinition of life as it is presently lived. Because humanity has lost its connection with holiness, assistance is coming closer. The mysterious supernatural Source sends archetypal symbols and emissaries from the Creative Principle. The Creator has a variety of messengers calling us to continue soul evolution. We are at the beginning of a spiritual renaissance where everyone can be touched by special moments through the power and beauty of the pure energy of our Source.

Reconnection with God is life's purpose. To relieve the anguish of the soul's separation from the Source, more and more people are being given glimpses of a finer reality. Once an individual chooses unity over duality, transcendence begins to instill its magic. What appears as supernatural is a refresher course in experiencing the natural, or wholeness, in an unfathomable way. We begin an amazing adventure, an awakening program that gently helps us remember. What if unexpectedly a series of unknown letters, symbols, geometric figures or numbers appeared on the screen of your mind? What significance does this hold for you?

BE: Embracing the Mystery

Nothing happens by chance. It is to your benefit to research what you are shown. For instance, if Hebrew letters appear suddenly, you will learn through research that the Hebrew alphabet is considered a language of Light, an angelic language. The ancient Hebrews also had an important and strong connection with the Land of the Nile. Once you respond through research, you may be given a vision of words of power used in Ancient Egypt. One clue leads to another. Your soul may be urging you to research hieroglyphics and Hermetic literature. Look at spontaneous insights as a clue leading to your spiritual identity. Eagerly approach what has been brought to your attention and think of it as your own personal archeological dig.

Our culture has shut down and lost touch. To ease humanity up the ladder of Light, dramatic shifts happen. The following example shatters barriers that have been erected between matter and spirit. It definitely is one of joyful playfulness and freedom. I was a member of an astronomy club that met once a month on a Sunday afternoon. This particular Sunday the weather was hot and muggy. Class was ending and everyone was concerned with the sudden downpour of rain and crashing thunder. As a group, we walked to the front door and waited under the portico. The rain looked like white sheets making it impossible for people to go to their cars. The drama and power of the elements were in full force.

Although I was minus an umbrella or raincoat and clothed in a lightweight summer dress, a spontaneous decision was made. Removing my shoes, a goodbye was said to everyone. Without looking back, I deliberately ran into the downpour without protection, creating a leap beyond time and space. The car was locked and located a distance from the portico. In delight, I ran through the downpour like a child. The grandeur of the experience was not fully grasped until I unlocked the car door and sat behind the wheel. In amazement, I discovered that I was completely dry although I had no outer protection. Even my shoeless feet were dry. Later, a friend telephoned who had watched me run the distance to the car. This is what she said, "When you ran to your car, you looked like a butterfly. Your feet seemed to be fluttering above the ground!" She wasn't surprised at all that I had not been soaked to the skin because she, too, believed in the great truth that anything is possible. At that moment, action transcended limitation.

What happened? Evidently, somewhere within hidden memory, the playfulness of my own soul took action. When I deliberately ran into the rain, it was in freedom and joy. The experience was an ecstatic union with the elements. The four elements, earth, water, air and fire are part of our make-up as nature in expression. These same four elements exist, but as finer vibrations on the physical, astral, mental and spiritual planes. In this adventure, I was in a state of harmony with God communing with nature. Befriend nature and learn about the inner quintessence.

The next story has to do with time travel, a subject that is indeed fascinating. Scientists have been intrigued with the idea of manipulating time, moving it backward and forward with ease and control. The idea of dematerializing and materializing people and objects has also attracted the attention of students who accept that anything is possible, and is verified in many of the sacred teachings of mystics. I had recently purchased a new car from a dealership approximately an hour's drive from home. The car was being rust-proofed and an alarm system installed. The salesman had loaned me another car for three days while the work was being completed.

On the day that I was returning the loaner, a sleet storm arose about halfway to the destination. The four-lane traffic was moving at a fast speed. To my dismay, the windshield wiper was not working. A very serious problem developed. The sleet was gathering on the window and freezing rapidly. Cars were speeding although the weather conditions warranted caution. Automobiles in front and back and the right side blocked the car from changing position. I was fast approaching the right side exit needed to reach the main street leading to the dealership. Not being able to see because of a broken windshield wiper and the sleet, the car remained in the fast lane, surrounded by moving cars. Very concerned about missing the exit, I called for celestial help. With limited visibility, I was at a loss as to where I actually was and how to exit off the highway.

In a blink of an eye, I experienced what it would be like to be in a scene from a futuristic science story. I instantly found myself at the top of an exit ramp, which led from a right lane. The car was in the correct position to make a left-hand turn on the road that led directly to the dealership. What an astounding display of power! Can you imagine the shock in finding the car transported from the fourth outer left lane of a highway to the top of a right-hand exit where I was safe in less time than it takes to inhale a breath? Humanly, I did nothing. No steering or maneuvering of the moving car. I couldn't have done anything even if I had tried, because the windshield was iced over. The car was locked into an unchangeable position. Everything was methodically attended to by a higher Intelligence. An invisible Power dematerialized the car and immediately rematerialized us at the top of the correct exit ramp. The movement happened so quickly that if there had been a driver on the ramp, he probably would have been oblivious to the change.

Jesus stated, "My Father doeth the Work." The Work is bringing Creative Mind into action through desire and directed thought. We think and Spirit produces the activity. When we align our will with God's Will and are immersed in an Infinite Creative medium, it is literally done unto us, as we believe. Without belief, the opposite may occur. The Invisible world is far more alive and powerful than anybody or anything we commonly see or experience in the visible world. With focused thought and right choices, life becomes an ongoing miraculous tapestry that is woven with all the pleasures we need. It is a partnership whereby our life is in God's keeping.

There are some things and situations that human thinking cannot fix. When such occasions arise, call on a High Power to do its marvelous work. You may question as I did, who dematerialized the car and then again materialized it? Was it an angel or a celestial guide? Or could it be an encounter with an 'otherness" who lovingly came to the rescue? When ready to embrace the cosmos, we are required to accept infinite possibilities. Humanity has been repeatedly shown that when consciousness is prepared, a higher Intelligence will step in when needed. The luminous energy that handled the rescue is available to any soul who has developed a relationship with the Supreme Source.

There is a pure force that works with matter and transforms it. This Force impregnates everything around us with the higher Light. It sees only Itself and Its infinite ability to create. Divine Energy delights in offering assistance. This means that we enjoy a higher consciousness, a partnership that is amazing as well as loving. We become a free universal soul acknowledging and vibrating harmoniously with life. It is an outreaching, an identification with an All-Pervading Spirit. As acceptance expands, we learn how to trigger constructive forces. We also learn to be vigilant and able to recognize what is stirring both within and without. It is in the subjective world that God has hidden every potential. We become a genuine creator through the power of thought because creation takes place through the higher Causal mind, the place between the senses and spirit.

Man is robbed of soul-power when matter is his only focus. Grace becomes an activity of mind when acknowledged and respected. Anyone may receive guidance, inspiration, protection, assistance, healing and God's truth as a living reality. Dramas such as the ones mentioned beautifully demonstrate a sampling of the diversity of a higher Love. Miracles are a result of the Law of Correspondence. Thoughts and feelings attract similar energy from the Invisible world.

When you pray and reach higher to the Divine, use passionate words capable of moving angels and archangels. You can also reach out to Saints, Patriarchs, apostles and prophets, Initiates and Masters who have lived on Earth. Expand your mind and accept the truth that there are embodiments other than our human form and that we are all an integral part of the creative life. Reach out to the spirits and even the elements. Departed loved ones may desire to be of assistance. Speak out loud and bring the energy down here to the physical dimension. Words are an energy that creates movement.

Learn to believe in the Invisible worlds; it will expand and harmonize the visible world. It is a wonderful science of reality manifesting. As you give love and attention to the eternal Presence, love and attention is returned in manifold ways. Once the meaning of life is discovered, a quality of confidence and joy will always be yours. Comfort and a strong sense of being loved is your experience. There is a peace within that no one or anything can diminish. Extraordinary beauty and harmony is your truth. It is a reward that results as inner as well as outer transformation.

The key to releasement is within. Joyfully transmute the darkness of ignorance into the Light of understanding. When you yearn with fullness of heart to be your real identity, a connection with the Divine is established. Pay close attention to what appears unexpectedly in the mind and experience. One evening, I watched in awe as a sudden manifestation of a large luminous diamond-shaped energy form gently floated across the room. Many possibilities came to mind as a result of the diamond vision. One of them was to investigate The Diamond Sutra of the Buddha.

The symbol of the diamond is purity, perfection, beauty, and hardness, the balance of masculine and feminine principles or heaven and

BE: Embracing the Mystery

earth melding together. The secret is to look beyond the obvious. Buddha was teaching the Diamond Sutra in a community of 1,250 fully ordained monks. The theme of the Sutra discussed what a seeker should do to master his own thinking, become more generous, how not to become ensnared in rules and regulations and how to put the teachings into practice. There is a hidden message in every symbol of Spirit. Look for it. Subtle phenomena, moments of grace, are natural happenings. They encourage us to think. Hold on to them in joy and thanksgiving as a permanent state of consciousness.

Keep the moments of wonder alive by reviewing them periodically. They have been earned. Truth is allowed in increments so it can be received and digested properly. Eventually, the supernatural becomes a natural daily experience. When the focus is on God-Realization, the Light will shift the energy of darkness. It is like having a spiritual bank account that you can draw upon. Through struggle, you actually learn to not accept limitation in any area. The true science of the Spirit manifests when you give it greater freedom to express and act. To walk forth is a command to action. It is your responsibility to discover the experience of being whole and enjoy true freedom. The result is a joyful soul participating in the activity of the Cosmos.

I urge you to find your own inner strength and then use it. Real love for the eternal Self is dropping all conditions. To be negative on any level is malpractice. Keep trying and a dazzling and intelligent world of light and love embraces you. Visions arrive unexpectedly. A glorious example was the occasion when I was with a few other people participating in a yoga routine. A feeling of ecstasy came over me and it was necessary to leave the room and go elsewhere for privacy. As soon as I secluded myself, a Divine Merkabah, a golden vehicle, which moved like a chariot glided through the outside wall into the living room. Three luminous beings stood within the vehicle. The vision was an ineffable moment of total merging, an ecstatic spiritual epiphany.

The message is simple. We are multi-dimensional, not alone, and have a far grander identity and purpose than most minds can imagine. Higher beings are very interested in our progress. They give us symbols and visions to help us move forward. To see with spiritual vision is to temporarily use your own higher consciousness. It is not the personality who learns truth; it is the soul who remembers. It is time to regain the dignity of the Spirit.

Research states that all souls who have established a firm foundation with the Living Light speak familiar words and have similar experiences. All the truths that have been offered to humankind since the beginning are practical, healing, transformative, intellectually satisfying, emotionally stabilizing and inspiring. They offer a connective hope because we came from the same Source whatever our form or history. There is nothing new. Discoveries that appear new actualize when you move past the influence of our Sun and space/time. There are no limitations. An emancipating journey occurs when you allow the mind to expand outward into a limitless Creation that is full of love-powered emanations.

All aspects of wisdom are integral parts of the One Wisdom and One Love manifesting through diversified channels and multiple planes. Life on all planes, visible and invisible, is a continual revelation. Loving and intelligent beings share the energy they have achieved. When you are given a key, gratefully use it. Destiny is the final blending with Light. Nothing happens by chance. Pay attention, dear one. The future is not fixed or stable. Consciousness determines it. You may feel bound in the body, but by the power of the spirit within, you are free. There is no secret initiation, no mystery in God. You need the heart of a child to be unlimited, understand and grow. Exalt in your true Nature, it is the real you.

Chapter Sixteen
The Cause Behind Effect

Why do some people suffer and others move through life with ease? Why are supernatural experiences normal for many people and others are denied access to the invisible worlds of light? Why are deformities, lack, misery and abuse part of the human experience? There are fortunate souls who have answers to these important questions because they have an inner realization of what Mind is and think deeply about it. They have answers because they are educated regarding Universal Law, the Law of Correspondence, Divine Rule and Justice and the methods required to govern life by inner realization. They also know enough about the Law of Cause and Effect that they can begin to draw true happiness into their lives.

Karma, simply said, means the conscience is working and restitution is in process. The spirit part of us prevails over the personality. Although most people associate karma with negative effects, this is not altogether true. The higher Self is wise. It desires that consciousness evolve. The Self desires certain experiences. It desires us to understand pain. Suffering eliminates faults. Pain comes to us through our faults. If this process was understood, we can confront pain-karma with a totally different perspective.

Ideas and concepts are dependent on karma. To fully understand the completeness of who you are, going beyond the physical plane is required. Some of what you discover may be uncomfortable to hear. But these are the things you need to know that will lead you to self-knowledge. Negative karma can result from guilt stored in the soul or it can be created by the inner Self to awaken the personality to its faults. The personality would avoid a path of pain.

Throughout the ages, scriptural records have been either ignored, removed, mistranslated or been hidden and as a result, millions of good men and women continue to suffer and remain in spiritual ignorance.

Lack of pure universal knowledge promotes ongoing disorder as well as distortion of original truth teachings. How can anyone have a genuine happiness or peace of mind if truth is not understood? Spiritual ignorance occurs when people do not comprehend the power of the mind and how that power creates experiences.

The mind must learn to be managed. Man's word becomes the law of his life. Any extreme, whether joyful or sorrowful, positive or negative, can create defilements. Defilements are feelings, people, objects, as well as anything that we are attached to at that moment that work against order and evolution of the soul. The personality may not know how to stop the defilements because it is in a state of denial or bondage. It is at this juncture that the inner Self may choose a road of pain and suffering.

When thoughts and emotions arise within that are out of balance, they must be controlled. Higher spiritual education teaches us to look and react in a neutral manner. To be able to achieve detachment, learn to stretch thought to the level of the Causal Mind, which is luminous and neutral. Causal Mind is the part of you that is God's Mind. Expand and use more of It. Mind in its self-knowing state is spirit. The first step is to grasp what this means. The Mind of God functions in you according to your understanding. The second step is to learn to control the thinking mind by lifting thought beyond the appearance world.

The One Mind is the indwelling spirit. It is the truth and substance of your being. When you are in alignment and believe, conform and obey the truth of your being, only good comes through your mind. It is necessary to control all thought that denies the Divine Presence within. You are an incarnation of God. There is a divine plan for you. It is through your mind in harmony with Spirit and Law, that you become aware of it.

When you are clear as to how your mind is part of the One Mind, you can increase your mental equivalent and vision transforming your life. It then becomes possible to remove yourself out of conditions that are nonproductive. The idea is to not have obstructions in your consciousness. All manifestations are effect and subject to Cause. In other words, cause and effect are spiritual. When you recognize and accept that your mind is one with God's Mind, you are able to create as well as receive unlimited good. Although the universe is mechanical, you are not. God's Nature is part of your own nature.

You attract what you comprehend and believe in. This in itself is good enough reason to enlarge consciousness and receive. Start believing in the power of God as your mind and spirit. Be willing and allow the power to help. When you understand, mistakes will lessen. Law responds to thought. Removal from bondage happens with enlightenment. Train your thinking and learn exactly how it can reflect the inner Self and happiness will be your experience. There is no medium between you and God except your own thought.

The Indescribable One is the Cause behind Limitless Light, invisible worlds, visible creation, as well as the neutral substance that exists everywhere. Although finite mind cannot comprehend the Infinite, it is in your best interest that a serious study takes place regarding the cause behind physical, emotional and mental experiences. Become aware of the impact and resulting creation that has been brought forth through corrupted thought, feeling, word and action. Corrupted thought is the garment covering your light. It is darkness, cravings, ignorance, jealousy, false wisdom and attachment to matter.

The negative vibrations accumulated in the past influence and manifest as your experience today. This is the interplay between the invisible and visible. Past causes determine everything in life including the present physical body, how the brain is constructed. Associations, length of physical life and the creative powers of Spirit at your disposal are all a result of former choices. If that wasn't enough, you are obliged to other souls and social conditions. When harmful thought and behavior continues, future falsity and pain is created. Mind as law must be directed or it will do nothing of permanent worth for you.

Soul, the subjective part of the mind is law. The Spirit must put the soul nature under its rule. The subjective soul accepts every thought, feeling and experience you have as its truth. Since the soul executes law, guilt may be the result. The lingering guilt that you feel creates negative karma. As spiritual evolution moves forward, past actions and thought will re-emerge. Study and learn this mental law of justice. It is a law supported by the soul. It is wisdom on your part to accept and work with conditions and do your best to neutralize or improve the already established patterns. Simply stating a quick "I am sorry" will not erase the damage. Universal Law expects you to expand and use the part of the wise Self within. If resistance continues, challenges will continue.

The Cause Behind Effect

From a spiritual perspective, there is no fate. It is your belief in fate that makes life situations seem as though predestination has stepped in. An unpleasant event is usually caused by ignorance of Divine law. The individual has forgotten that there is One Perfect Power and has immersed himself in duality. The trials of life stimulate spiritual growth. Instead of complaining, accept the challenge. Somewhere in the past, a universal law has been broken. It could also be the result of groping in the dark and not giving thought to results. In other words, mindless behavior creates suffering. Whatever the weakness, the universal law of balance at some point will bring the past into the current experience to be corrected and healed.

Many people blame God for their circumstances. The Source behind creation neither punishes nor rewards. You are the determiner to bring forth restitution and balance. Chaos or order manifests according to thought, feelings and action. Out of any chaos, harmony can be produced. When you are a serious student of the Greater Consciousness, the dark world of confusion and separation is left behind and the energy of Light and understanding is entered. How to see clearly is realized.

It is vital that the soul be strongly impressed as to how thought, whether positive or negative, will eventually solidify into action in visible form. Everyone reacts unconsciously or consciously to vibrations. All creation is made of the One Substance. The vibration determines the difference in the form. When an opportunity presents itself as a result of repetitive thought or action, it is possible to actually transform any future negative manifestation by reversing your own thoughts. In other words, change the mind. Because of a deep-rooted guilt, this practice may not occur.

You have the power to change the mind and bring forth good. It is possible through a higher knowledge to deliberately command yourself to drop all the conditions that are working against freedom. New thoughts create new conditions. Learn to think from the God part of your mind. The path toward Self-knowledge is a pilgrimage. The movement is towards becoming a good person.

Limitation is the result of ignorance of how to use the law. The belief that you are separated from God must be destroyed. It is the higher Self who is guiding the personality to strengthen the weakened threads of the design. Correct thinking transforms consciousness. Decide what you wish to have happen. The idea is not to limit self in any area. The problem lies in not recognizing that you have become a prisoner of your own making through repetitive and negative behavior that does not serve a good purpose. Ignorance joins with fate. Fate does not want to stunt spiritual growth. Its role is to awaken and increase the influence of the hidden spirit. When thought is controlled, you have the ability to undo what has been mistakenly created. Desire only good, it is like opening the gates to Heaven.

In Western culture, people are not as knowledgeable regarding the subject of cause and effect. They are less likely to be understanding of their role in creating suffering. The tendency is to blame God or an outside force for everything negative that happens. This is foolishness. An individual is responsible for his or her use of creative power, whether it is expressed consciously or unconsciously. Reluctance to achieve something in a spiritual way creates stagnation. It behooves us to understand human karma, which involves both inner and outer suffering. Suffering may not be experienced if the individual is already mature and practicing universal law.

Subjective Law is sensitive and creative. It indifferently receives all images you impose on it. Mental suggestion operates through the subjective part of the mind. It is receptive without caring what it receives and creative without caring what it creates. It is your responsibility as to what is allowed inwardly because it will definitely manifest outwardly. This law works both for good and that which is not good.

It is prudent to pay close attention to all personal negative patterns and intense feelings that appear to control your life. Also, look at connections and communications with others in the light of karma. Acknowledge the harmful habits and situations and learn from them. Disorder contains truths that will uncover and rectify. Divine justice cannot be escaped because the laws of the universe rule created existence. The mind is the cause and justice is the effect. Creations belong to the individual who created them. Pain may transform shortcomings into positive abilities.

Karmic effects may be removed through conscious sacrifice, love, and changes in mind. Noble acts of character, genuine forgiveness, humility and making different choices accelerate maturity. Remember, the mental, emotional and physical fields that comprise what is called the lower nature constantly change. By changing a belief system, thought, action and fate can be altered. Change can work in a positive way. Don't fear change; accept and work with it. If your personality understands the Law of Cause and Effect, it will be less likely to cause harm to self and others. Lift the focus and you can finally free yourself from future pain.

An unenlightened being simply does not understand how spiritual law goes into action. In contrast, the effects are more devastating if the mind is fully aware of the laws of action and reaction and continues to create harm. The laws are absolute and powerful. Understanding and applying them will eventually liberate the soul. It is then that it is possible to state with confidence and knowing, I am that I Am. The mind is free. The goal is to be able to grab the reins and take control of destiny. This is a quality of mind that has attained a very high degree of sacred realization and is ready and willing to be free from the nonsense of self-imposed entrapment.

The effects of negative causes created are dramatically weakened when character is developed and love is the focus. The idea is to understand which thoughts, feelings and acts will continue to empower and make it a positive. Dark and negative actions continue to create grievous effects because civilized people generally have a conscience, which places guilt in the soul. Guilt and the belief in fate can be healed. By switching on the inner light, you can take refuge in it, remove fear and free the mind to be itself.

You know as much about your higher Self by what you have learned through experience. As you learn to understand the law and apply methods that will help in reaching a higher state of mind, obstructions will be removed. The key is to activate inquiry and learn spiritual science. Learn to be a watcher who recognizes what fear creates. An attitude of objectivity will assist in seeing clearly all life patterns for what they are. The conscious mind observing, rather than the emotions uncontrollably reacting, will free you from restrictions and bondage. The God part of your mind is the realm of cause. It is the spirit who guides. In contrast, the subjective soul as law is neutral and creates whatever is given it. Expect the best and the best will become a part of your experience.

Look closely at the process by which you become wise. Imagine, seek and make the eternal identity alive and real. Even though virtues and setting noble goals are a subject basically ignored in today's world, it is vital they be cultivated. If not, you will have to wait for another opportunity.

Service to others develops an enduring strength. Besides benefiting everyone, the soul of the giver spiritually evolves. You always project what is within the soul. Remember, it uses thought and manifests what is truth to you. It is the creative medium of Spirit and is changeable. You retain the lessons learned from error as strengths for a future time.

There is a Great Work, a Plan of God. An Ideal is part of that plan. God's ideal is for creative intelligence to achieve a true bond between all peoples and nature as well as bring forth perfection in form. Ignorance will follow until enlightenment occurs. Whatever is discordant does not belong to the Spirit of Truth. To enlarge personal consciousness, drop all contradictory thought. Choosing to be an active participant in God's Plan will nourish the greatest soul growth as well as offer an opportunity to help others. Truth must be lived. Arrange your life and relationships so they reflect a healing consciousness. Peace and happiness will remain and not dissipate.

Misuse of the mind in the past has created conditions today. People are now asking for help and are ready to face and accept past obligations. To be successful, correct thinking must be practiced daily. The soul must be purged of darkness and become pure in mind and heart. Impulses must be of the Divine and not built from carnal or material considerations. Generally speaking, many people feel dissatisfied and imprisoned. They do not understand why. A crime against the spirit has been committed. Crime is an appropriate word for behavior that impedes the soul and prevents its perfection and freedom.

Cause and effect is a profound subject experienced in both the subjective part of our being as well as the objective. A special woman in my life was healed after forty-five years of daily physical suffering. A healing situation was provided because All-Knowing Mind gifted me with a vision of what caused my friend's crippling spinal pain. Although she was not consciously aware of a past life wrongful action, she had outgrown the hidden guilt through self-inflicted suffering and was ready to be healed. Dramas are created for eventual maturity.

I suggested that she go to the bedroom and forgive herself for any past actions of cruelty. By genuinely forgiving herself and removing the guilt, she could be completely healed of the daily back pain. She accepted what was revealed, forgave herself and was instantly and completely healed. The transformation from severe daily pain to comfort and healing occurred over thirty-six years ago. She is at this writing an alert and healthy 102 years young. It is the hidden memory within the subconscious part of the mind that clings to pain and punishment. By forgiving and healing unsettled energy now, the past is corrected and a debt-free tomorrow is created. Forgiveness is a power tool.

It is wisdom to understand that failures can be our greatest victories. They become a victory when allowed to influence and develop character in a positive way. We can evolve by making an effort in spite of negative conditions. Pain can transform shortcomings into positive abilities. When it is correctly understood, we realize that the subjective side of life is the universal part of us and is one with the objective state. When we think from a loftier perspective, cause and effect are in harmony. Damnation only occurs within thought. Punishment is inflicted through ignorance of Divine Law. To the degree we become conscious of our true identity will the darkness disappear.

If a goal of God Realization is not reached, realize that sincere effort is never lost. Effort carries over as newly acquired qualities of character in future life experiences. Instant healing happens when an individual has exhausted negative karma regarding an old condition and the time is ripe for its release. The body is usually not transformed unless a healing first takes place inside the mind and feeling nature. God did not create guilt, negative behavior and suffering. Weakness is the culprit.

The ancient teachings of the Initiate caused the veils of Isis, nature, to fall away one by one. The initiates understood that removing the veils of delusion and ignorance was an individual responsibility in order to achieve perfection, the goal of the spirit. The wisdom, seekers and teachers never dreamt of wallowing in pleasure or self-pity. They prepared themselves for spiritual ecstasies through effort, disciplines and a trust in teachings that were tested and proven over time.

There are seven veils. The veils are the physical, etheric, astral, mental, causal, soul and spirit energies. Veils are the exterior appearance. In trying to see others as well as our own self from a higher point of view where the spirit dwells, is to see behind the veil. This is how you know your true self as well as the inner light of another. Contemplate divinity and do not be content to only function as the surface personality. The greatest privilege is to become a suitable instrument of God. When this truth is known, the true purpose of life is realized.

BE: Embracing the Mystery

God has condensed the entire universe in man and woman. We harbor thousands of memories, which are neatly stored in Mind. Everyone has an intricate tapestry, a history, and a story to tell. Perhaps, you have felt a surprising familiarity when visiting a new city or meeting a stranger and instantly liking or disliking what you see. Something is triggered in the hidden memory bank. Meditation and contemplation will help access the past. Although glimpses of the past may help in understanding yourself, it is far more important to consciously live to the best of your ability God's perfect ideal right now in this embodiment.

There are many things you can do to help create a future without negative conditions. Spiritual integrity is being able to look into the future and see the consequences of your choices. It is possible to determine what future effects will surely manifest by sending a true force of love back to previous causes and neutralizing them, burning karma through knowledge. This can be done even though you do not have a conscious recall of the past. The secret is to change attitude and feelings about people and situations. Reactions today reflect emotions lingering from the past. Personally, neutralize every force of hatred and resentment, fear and greed within. When Gandhi, the Indian holy man, was assassinated, he bowed to his killer standing before him and blessed him. Gandhi understood effects. His act of forgiveness discharged any future karma with his assassin.

Each life is molded by the lives that precede it. Life is not unjust as it appears. Everything and everyone is connected. Imagine strings of Light as the connection between all creation and you grasp the idea of Oneness, a Universal family, and our responsibility to respect and love one another. Justice arrives at the doorstep as a result of the causes we originated. We are not robots; we are will creatures who design life through choices.

Transformation begins in the mind. Become a conscious shape-shifter. Anyone who exercises discipline and has a plan for growth can, with practice, consciously control and reshape life according to imagination, will and belief system. It is in the learning to be the true Self that future effects are controlled. Different teachers will come to you until a point has been reached in consciousness where an intimate communion with the wise inner teacher is experienced. God's law works according to belief. Train the thought, have faith that the law works for you. Satisfy the Divine Urge. There is nothing too great to undertake. You are in the midst of an eternal opportunity.

Chapter Seventeen
Steps

Scripture states that it is God's good pleasure to give to us. To fully receive, we must understand who we are and why we are. We desire happiness and in clear moments we desire to be perfect. The Apostle Paul in his statement "Christ lives in me" was referring to the perfect Christ Mind. To receive, stop being a crippled version of your true Self. Bondage is not God-ordained. Spiritual ignorance causes suffering. The way you believe sets the limit to your demonstrations of a Christ Mind.

Totally believe in the Power and use it. Begin by changing your objective self and conditions. When you accept that your mind is a point in God Consciousness, God's good pleasure becomes your reality. Allow God awareness to flow through and bless you. Think of it. Believe and trust in it. Allow the power to expand as your mind through mental awareness.

Consciously tap the subjective part of mind, soul, through specific thought using focused power. Impress your ideals into the subjective part of the mind and it will obey the orders given. Create a mental picture of what you desire and through belief, persistence and acceptance it happens. Periodically during the day, draw the power of spirit through the channels of the mind and you will make the great discovery of your inner Self.

The closer you are in reaching Christ consciousness, the more intensely you live in an ongoing state of harmony both within and without. True Knowledge is received through direct connection with the higher vibratory realms of thought. If a conviction is absent, it means knowledge is incomplete. Be filled with courage and live your knowledge, taste it and practice it until it becomes an integral part of your consciousness.

Remove conditioned beliefs that limit. It is for your benefit to refuse to believe in the image of limitation. The personality must expand and also invite the highest part of the mind to take charge. The challenge and

BE: Embracing the Mystery

ultimate goal is to bring the two aspects of your nature together and consciously live as one cohesive unit of intelligent energy. The only way this will happen is for the lower nature to be controlled by the higher part of the mind. Learn how to think deeply and the creative force can be consciously directed and definitely used. Because the Source is all pervading, the higher part of you is never absent. Draw the Infinite Mind into your thoughts and meditations and the inner nature is understandable.

There are many steps leading to infinite possibilities. It is easier to move forward when you understand exactly what the Mind is. Because God cannot be described, we fumble around using descriptions that confuse more than help. A good explanation is the one given through the brilliant mind of Ernest Holmes, the founder of Religious Science: "God is the First Cause, the Great I Am, the Absolute, the One and Only. God is Spirit, the creative energy, which is the cause of all creation." He goes on to say that the Formless is God as Spirit. Spirit knows itself. It is active. It is our Parent, life, God in man.

Soul is the Creative Medium of Spirit, the mirror or subjective side of life. It acts on the thoughts of conscious mind. Soul contains within it the formless, the Light. It is part of the One Mind. You glimpse both the soul and the spirit through mental and intuitive awareness. Thoughts are movement of consciousness. They take form on the subjective invisible side of life and manifest in the objective visible side. Consciousness is both objective and subjective.

Think of God, Universal Consciousness, consciousness, Mind and Spirit as one and the same thing. Spirit is within as the Divine or Christ Mind. None are separate from us, but you and I are separate entities in it. The Whole is experienced when we dig deeper into the multiplicity, which comes from Unity.

Commitment is a major step in consciously achieving a Christ Mind. Commitment is a state of being that is both emotional and intellectual. Permanent harmony will not be experienced until the false becomes unacceptable. Work on spiritual things first in the mind. If the mind is not trained, you remain a slave to falsity. Learn to still the mind and direct it towards whatever point desired. The mind sees perfection. Use the mind to fulfill the purpose of your creation. This is a scientific means of building a new matrix and demonstrating truth.

Making a sincere commitment and stepping bravely away from the

Steps

vicious circle of suffering will help shape a new mindset. As you build and work on the invisible spiritual, mental and emotional vibrations, acquired merits will spill over into physical life. Patience, a necessary virtue, is required to bring forth spiritual identity. Diligently cooperate with scientific proven universal laws and apply them through intelligent action.

Humanity has been struggling with an ancient slave consciousness. It is time we move into a higher consciousness. When you design a new pattern of thought through desire, an image begins to form. Thought creates a mold in the subjective where the idea is accepted, poured and eventually manifests in matter. What you are doing deliberately is working with causation, understanding that form can be changed. The pattern must be habitual. When commitment is given to a spiritual ideal, a new course of action begins to manifest.

Decide what you desire and make a heartfelt pledge of honor to fulfill it. The inner Flame has been watching and waiting patiently for you to take the first conscious step. It is relatively easy to take vows and sign contracts in physical marriages. A wise soul will reach higher and gladly commit to a grander eternal vow, a spiritual realization that lasts forever. Commitment opens the heart and mind to the merging of matter and spirit as one, a true marriage. Why fear that which is real and choose to remain hidden in the illusion? When fear rules, it prevents the soul from evolving. It is time to honor the higher Self, a being with a thousand forms. It is also respectful to honor all the teachers and experiences from the past that have led to this decisive moment in the present. Mind remains limited and spirit is silent when the truth of being is neglected.

In the physical world, wealth and power are admired. This is not true on the spiritual level. What is significant in the higher realms of thought is whether an individual acquires virtues, has pure and noble thoughts, right actions and has learned how to use the principles of creative thinking. If true freedom is desired, prepare for the sacred. As long as the mind is limited, it shall never be blessed with any form of lasting creativity. Out of necessity, truth is learned the hard way. At some point in the return journey, the soul will finally grow weary of the illusion and seek help. Commitment begins the alchemical change and is required in controlling and transforming life experiences.

Surrender is another step in understanding commitment. Humans fear surrender because they do not understand it. Fear does not see clearly. Surrender in the area of spiritual growth indicates a willingness to let go of everything and everyone that is working against an ideal. Results are produced according to belief. Cherish life and do everything in your power to regain a permanent and dependable relationship with the Ultimate Reality. This is the "strength of all strengths" Hermes Trismegistus wrote about. Remove all thoughts and feelings not in harmony with cosmic forces. Replace what is not beneficial with something that creates, not destroys. Totally believe in the One Power and use it. Know that faith within will neutralize all lingering doubts. Surrender does not imply giving up the good life. In truth, it is the beginning of a truly remarkable life.

Be aware of choices and understand that surrender of harmful habits, thoughts and actions is a proven method that will open and energize personal spiritual centers and expose them to cosmic influences. This is an active form of surrender, a beginning leading to purification. Since the majority of humans are oblivious to the cause behind suffering, they do not comprehend that purity leads to understanding, gives strength, creates good health and opens all doors to spiritual gifts and divine exchanges. Suffering is categorized as a raging fire. It burns away the lesser so the greater can manifest. It is possible to substitute the devastating fire that burns and destroys and replace it by cooperating with the inner celestial fire of the spirit.

Be faithful in your efforts to recreate yourself. Lip service is not enough. Sacrifice is rarely understood. It is through willing sacrifice that wholeness is reached. Typically, sacrifice is judged as a painful experience. Mistaken thinking does not understand that real sacrifice is a voluntary act. If a personality has been blessed with a glimpse of Reality when experiencing the light of Self, there is less fear and pain. Disorder arises when the ego personality abandons the Ideal. A true seeker, one who is fixed on the Divine, works toward an Ideal and will gladly turn away from everything and everyone who stands in the way of spiritual evolution. At the same time, he realizes he has practical, intellectual and spiritual needs.

Flesh limits. Limitations are removed one by one through commitment, surrender and a willingness to sacrifice, that which works against the soul's purpose. Physical science states that everything can be scientifically reduced to one ultimate essence. This essence is God substance and is everywhere. The Limitless Light, essence, is behind all creation; it projects parts of its Indescribable Activity into matter through outward emanations. The Absolute One sacrificed a part of the original Sublime Energy to create the invisible and visible worlds. The projection is a glorious example of Creative Mind thinking and loving. Befriend the Light and be a conscious projectionist for the Divine and it will work through and for you.

Souls are given an opportunity to know themselves as superconscious beings. Limitation occurs until the soul evolves and is free from restraint. Limitation ceases when awakening to the truth that you have a God-given right to desire and create good. This understanding is a valuable truth to know and use. God wants the spirit part in you to manifest health and peace. It is necessary to direct will correctly to fully experience the life within. Totally believe in God's plan for you and use it. Concrete evidence is the result of using intelligence and directed energy. Creation first happens in the invisible world. Form requires Spirit to give it life. Now, it is your turn to sacrifice that which is not of the Light and mold a better world.

It is beneficial knowledge to understand that there is a vast hierarchy that descends willingly to Earth. There is also a hierarchy in human consciousness polluting the flow of life as a result of uncontrolled thought. Life is colored, polluted or purified according to what it encounters in the region it flows through. As the river of divine life flows down into the depths of the Earth, it is our choice whether we work with it or against it. Choosing to accept, believe and desire a world of harmony, we automatically lift other souls to greater heights of understanding and happiness.

The greatest joy is in the releasing of the Divine force within through the act of selfless giving. As a higher physical creation, you have received the gift of life. The collective consciousness of humankind needs to be exposed to the true purpose of creation and take action through the returning of the gift to the Great Giver. Sacrifice is not resignation to a higher Will. Believing this way is a false notion. The Will of God is the will for perfection and full expression of the part of God within you. Sacrifice is removing everything that hinders the inner divine will to freely express. It is a blending in purpose. In truth, it is the only sane action to take if the desire is to be the extraordinary being you really are.

Generally speaking, evolving beings began as a spark in the mineral kingdom. On every level of evolution, one form has been sacrificed for a higher form. Struggle has always existed in nature because form is transitory. A dramatic energy change occurred when the spark of light, the higher Self, received a more finely developed intelligent human form. Man was able to choose. He was not left to his own devices. Master teachers and celestial beings have always been ready to train the awakening intelligence of man. Eons of time and experience have gradually led the evolving child-souls to the heights where more and more invisible helpers are voluntarily offering loving assistance.

The visible universe is the body of God. We are units, cells, in the body of God. Life has varying degrees of intensity and vibration as it flows downward through Nature. All of Nature supports us. In Nature, evil does not exist. We are obliged to Nature and must not rape or abandon her. We must work with Nature by giving to Her. If we love, She will speak to us from within for we are a part of Her. The divine joy of giving and returning the obligation to Nature is a great truth that must be grasped and lived by all humans or there is no release from the wheel of rebirth and suffering. We cannot only take from life.

Nature is also evolving. She evolves as consciousness. Man is similar. He does not reap great rewards without ever having planted a seed. He must do the groundwork if he wants to receive what he asks for. The more the thinking mind expands, the easier it will be to grasp the true significance of sacrifice as viewed from a loftier perspective. Understanding offers a willing relinquishment of attachments to form in exchange for immortal riches.

At a special point in spiritual evolution, an inner Voice whispers, "Honor thy Self." Very few humans understand this profound suggestion. How can you honor the inner God if personal energy is scattered in every direction? Is it productive to be so busily occupied that you no longer have moments for deep introspection and communion with the Divine? To honor the true life is not a solitary selfish act; it is a joining of a soul to the universal community of souls who choose to remember and honor the eternal spiritual identity. This day will not come again. Begin and cherish who you are.

A very real and powerful spiritual community exists. It is both visible and invisible. It is a brotherhood of the Spirit and not the flesh. Helpful kindness towards another is an integral part of the brotherhood and sisterhood of life. Giving includes extending our hearts and minds to our own sublime God spark as well. Self-mastery is mandatory; it is the means to live the real life and create a permanent connection with the Divine. Passion must be felt to make adjustments in the daily routine. To discover the sacred, listen to the call of the heart. Changes are necessary. Sacrifices are required. There is one Universal Mind and individual mind is a part of it. Inner joy is when you learn to expand and experience your portion.

It is normal for seekers to have guides and angels who are ready and willing to help in times of inquiry and need. In gratitude, allow the Spirit of Truth to guide. A Master Teacher from the celestial regions may appear. To view a Luminous Being from one of the Higher Worlds of Perfection is an experience never to be forgotten. Pure Presence is beyond words. Sublime radiance is beyond definition. The all-embracing completeness communicates through a transcendent power that is felt in every cell of the soul, mind and body. When you feel deep love for God, love reflects back in amazing ways. True love rejuvenates, strengthens and empowers.

Hermes Trismegistus said, "You must separate the subtle from the gross with great diligence." Love for God teaches us how to do this. It is a great treasure to learn to extract the wisdom latent within. When desire is only for the Divine, wisdom smiles, new doors open and life becomes magically directed. God whispering encourages us forward. There is no greater joy than being a conduit of the Divine. When you voluntarily choose the road to happiness, sacrifice is empowerment. Fear is a stranger.

Sacrifice does not mean to neglect daily duties. Always be responsible. Eventually, a level of understanding is attained that is beyond human nature. Do what must be done. Accept that all creation is indeed One Life moving in rhythm to a greater harmony. Know without a doubt that you are prepared and available to live as a channel for the highest purpose, a carrier of Light. The secret is to anchor the personality to the living Light within, stabilizing intention. Never expect other people to provide your happiness and do your spiritual work. Give authority to the inner Identity.

The physical body is influenced by all our force fields from the greatest to the least. If the goal is visible, tangible completeness, establish harmony in every aspect of your being. An invisible world of beauty already exists. Find it. When harmony manifests, everything becomes clear. Misery occurs when disruptive activity mars inner balance. Shun disharmony as the worst enemy. Do not allow anything to sabotage the hidden desire.

BE: Embracing the Mystery

What greater joy is there than to be able to assist in helping the evolution of life? Honor the Sacred. What is within begins to be visible without. In the meantime, perspective changes dramatically. Pleasure is in simple activities, understanding that divinity is everywhere. A developed awareness of the Light of God is acknowledged in everything and everybody. Attachment to materiality and temporary things no longer imprisons. Learn to extract the most precious elements and stabilize them as part of your own makeup.

The Divine is practical. It provides a life of personal grace although suffering may surround us. It is a loving and natural behavior to be an example and serve souls who are not ready to make a higher choice. It is never comfortable watching the pain of others. Every thought, feeling, word and action will be an offering to the Divinity within. You will understand joy as well as sorrow and even accept past causes not yet exhausted. The desire for completeness will act out as part of the great mystery and majesty in allowing an expanding creative power to rule.

To be free at last, make an offering of your life as a gift to Nature, to God in exchange for the life that you were given. Voluntarily take the steps necessary to be liberated. Liberation is true power. You are then free to serve. What have been removed are the chains that bind in the lower nature. Consciousness will rule and bring you closer to the sublime goal of self-mastery. Be attentive to the inner promptings establishing a heightened relationship with the Divine. Concerted effort will open the way to a grander life of order and fulfillment.

Destiny is what you are making. Freedom manifests through the intelligent use of Nature's forces and law. The slave mentality is dissolved. A developed and perfect belief will materialize the purpose of creation. Pure thoughts, efforts and an unspeakable love are preparation for Christ energy as an extraordinary poetry waiting to be written.

Chapter Eighteen
The Eye of God

It is helpful to our spiritual growth to be knowledgeable regarding the hidden language of symbols. We are all on stage before God. The "Eye" is a perfect example of a universal symbol. The gaze of God looks upon the soul and not the outward appearance. Whether we feel comfortable about this truth or not does not change the fact that the "Eye of God" looks deep into the depths of a soul exposing every thought, word and action. There is no place to hide because nothing is hidden from God. The Eye emphasizes the role of the perceiver in all creation, the One Absolute God. We cannot hide from God's view; it is only our attempt to hide from the Whole of our self.

A human may react strongly to an eye staring at him. Perhaps, it is a race memory going back to an ancient time when created objects depicting an Eye of a Goddess or God were open and looking at the beholder in judgment. In Mesopotamia, archaeologists have found many objects they call "eye idols." Ancient texts refer to devices used by extraterrestrials that were used to scan the Earth from end to end. The millennia-old depictions of Earth scanning satellites are very similar to our satellites of today. Since the beginning of creation, we have been observed, whether the watcher is from nature, the higher Self, the invisible, unknown worlds or the Supreme Being. We are never alone. The universal symbol of the Eye is a reminder.

Myths are disguised truths. With the help of science now supporting what is received in meditation, visions, intuitive insights and sound research, we are being inundated with corroborative evidence regarding our physical origins. Humankind cannot fully comprehend identity unless both the physical and spiritual origin is understood. As of now, the collectivity has only a general idea of the history of Homo sapiens and less understanding of what Spirit is. The more clearly the facts are comprehended regarding both the inner and outer reality of what we call our self, the greater freedom is available to live as magnificent beings of love and wisdom.

Small tablets made out of clay were used from 5500 BC and later from 4th millennium BC onwards as a writing medium in Sumerian, other Mesopotamian, Hittite, and Minoan/Mycenaean civilizations. Other tablets have been found that may be older. The tablets were used as archives. Since the discovery of over 500,000 clay tablets, long forgotten answers are rapidly becoming available. Documented and detailed historic evidence is serving to liberate a thinking mind. The latest translation and revelations reveal humanity as having a long and painful past. Whether life began as a mineral and eventually evolved into a primitive man and was made more intelligent by others technologically advanced is not an unthinkable possibility when you compare the procedure with science today and what is being done in laboratories. Regardless of our physical origin, a human being is not the appearance form alone. In order for the form to live, it must be imbued with a spirit.

Symbols carved in the past on clay tablets had many different uses. As a religious symbol, an engraving of the "Eye" symbol suggested the idea of a Supreme Source behind creation. It has been recognized since antiquity as the One Divine Presence, Power and Wisdom by the physical gods of ancient days who ruled over primitive man as well as the evolved man of today. This vast and mystifying subject is offered only as a brief overview in this writing. It is included because many of us have had Divine visions of the Eye occur during special moments.

There is a prolific history and writings regarding the Eye of God. References are found in world religions, the Old Testament and the Gospels, in Mysticism, in Nature and in symbolism. A triangle with an Eye or Sun in its center, radiating rays in all directions, is called a glory; and symbolizes the Yod, or first power of God extending through the primal air, water, and fire. This symbol is much used in Kabbalistic, alchemical, and Masonic work and is found on the Great Seal of the United States. It is the Eternal Light of Wisdom, which surrounds the Supreme Architect as a sea of Light or glory, and from this common center lights the world. In ancient days, the circle or pupil of the All-Seeing Eye was interpreted as the Eye of the goddess, the original Mother of Truth.

Carvings, paintings, poetry, as well as the language of symbolism such as the Eye of Light, the Eye of Shiva, and Eye of Zeus in mythology provide evidence of the importance of this ancient symbol. Boatmen around the shores of the Mediterranean still believe that eyes painted on their boats protect their journey. Egyptian mythology associates the Eye symbol with the All-Seeing Eye of Maat, of Horus, of Thoth, and of Ra. In ancient days, the advanced ones understood that a biological restructuring could occur through the region of the eighth chakra, invisible energy center above the head, and used as a model for new creations through the "Eye of Horus."

Eye amulets were very popular among the Egyptians and are not to be confused with the human "third eye." The Eye of Horus was used as a model for the super-human who has acquired higher consciousness. It was considered by the Egyptians as a device used by advanced beings on other planes to view events on Earth. In other words, it was the "Eye of the Lord." Some sources considered Horus as an extraterrestrial supranatural figure.

Many ancient peoples would use invocations/mantras calling upon the All-seeing Eye for protection, strength and vigor. Chanting the Eye of Horus mantra could be utilized as a personal protection against psychic attack of any kind. The goal was to become a perfected one, similar to the gods who descended to the Earth early in human history. The Greeks later took over the symbol; it was considered magical. The Druids believed to "lift the veil" covering the Eye would reveal the secrets of God. The Eye is one of the most powerful mystical teaching symbols given to humanity. Any basic world symbol can represent many different things in various times and places according to the beliefs of people who have interpreted it.

In nature, the Sun is known as the Great Circle, the presence of God. Modern eclipse observers metaphorically call a total solar eclipse the "Eye of God." The Eye is also part of an Aztec symbol. The "God Eye" is found in American Indian weaving. Carvings of the Eye are engraved on walls in churches throughout the world. There are also references to two eyes in ancient scriptures.

The wide-open eye commonly symbolizes God who sees all and knows all. It is comforting to know that the All Seeing Eye watches over us. Sacred symbolism is considered a lost language. It is a blessing to receive spiritual sight and understand how powerfully intimate the Eye of God is as a symbolic experience. Conscious awareness of God Intelligence

BE: Embracing the Mystery

as part of your inner nature, may gift you with an Eye vision.

Periodically throughout life, I have had visions of a vividly alive Eye of God. It looks identical to a human eye except it is very large and the energy of it is radiant white diamond Light. The Eye actually moves, blinks, looks right at the beholder and gives a strong impression of feeling and knowing exactly what is going on. The Power behind the Eye determines its appearance. When looking at the center of the Eye, I am frequently psychically pulled in and through the Eye and thrust outward into the infinity of space amidst the stars. From my understanding, the symbol is a reminder that there is a Mighty Presence and Power who does care about individual existence.

A totally different form of a vision occurred recently. In wonder, I watched the movement and expression of the breathtaking Eye of God and suddenly a teardrop formed within the Eye. I had never seen negative phenomena with the Eye visions. We have heard of tears forming on statues of the Mother Mary and her feelings regarding the suffering of humanity. To watch a tear form in an Eye of God vision was disquieting. The implication is serious. We are endowed with personal will and what have we done with it? Understanding the soul's connection to the Divine and how collective consciousness has turned away from its own divinity, it was difficult and sad to witness a negative symbol. Symbolism is the language of the angels and is the most poignant means of communicating with humans.

As a result of awakening to a conscious connection with God, we realize that suffering, fear, and division can be softened and eventually eliminated if misdirected souls would only choose to be "saved." The majority does not fully understand what being saved means, nor realize they are living a self-created illusion by not accepting the inner eternal and true identity. This is one of the reasons I am impelled at this time to share spiritual experiences. Perhaps, more people will do likewise. The intent behind sharing is to give hope. Hope is a foretaste of perfection. Under no circumstances abandon hope, because lack of it will halt spiritual evolution. Many live, but few think. Deep thinkers know that they have the ability to resurrect their lives.

There is only God thinking, but the majority is in a confused state of consciousness, which is referred to as misthinking. From a spiritual view, to consciously think is to think from the perspective of the higher

Self, the God portion within. This is a lost talent that is waiting to be rediscovered.

We have access to the wisdom of God and can help remove the tear by choosing to think higher and achieve a universal understanding. It is our destiny to be one with divinity and actually live in a state of grace. New ideas and methods must be something that can be applied in everyday life. Consciousness sleeps in the mineral life, dreams in the plant life, awakens in animal life and becomes self-conscious in man. Cosmic Intelligence gave humanity the power to think and reason.

Although we have both an animal lower nature and a higher spiritual nature, we are capable of reaching higher to the Christ and Universal level of consciousness. We must know the truth of our physical origin as well as spiritual origin to fully evolve. Acceptance of the spiritual identity and purpose opens the gates to the waves and currents emanating from the higher regions of Light. When the intellect understands and cooperates with the soul and spirit, life becomes good.

The higher Self is luminous and omniscient and part of the One God. It is God Mind and can of its own volition create a form. The real Self exists forever. The human personality is deluded because it accepts the mind illusion that it is separate from God. This is a false belief. The majority of people identify too closely with the personality. The personality can be the worst enemy as far as understanding and demonstrating truth. It is attachment to the physical and material limits on every level, cutting ties with the Invisible worlds of Light.

This is one possible reason for the tear in the Eye of God vision. Ignorant clinging to the false belief that we are only a physical form creates a high state of agitation. When Reality is seen from a clear perspective, life can be spiritually directed. Nothing can hinder the movement toward enlightenment except the individual. Egoism does not project Light. Light is a manifestation of the Spirit. When we allow our mind to expand, it is possible to become god-like. The shining, translucent, transparent, intangible essence comes forth. We begin to resemble our Creator.

Humanity is gradually moving into a new era, a cycle of re-education where we attain knowledge of our complete identity through scientific and scholastic discoveries and spiritual insights. Everyone has an opportunity to reconstruct him or herself. Thinking correctly with belief, understanding and expansiveness, we can eventually, through a focused mind, match the physical template geometry of genetics with the invisible and perfect body of original Spirit.

A trained mind is God thinking. It is possible to become whole in the physical form. The souls who make the right choice become alive to the invisible Reality. They are the ones who benefit from the heaven-sent blessings as well as comfortably tolerating the stronger vibratory influences. To be a conduit for Celestial Energy, which is an aspect of the One Mind, learn to rely on a Supreme Power if you wish to be liberated from the falsity. It is a cooperative effort.

Once real progress is attained, do not take divinity for granted. Always analyze and seek meaning for what is being presented to you. Curiosity coupled with wrongful desire can also plunge a soul into mediocrity. It reminds me of the popular story of several celestial beings observing the life of animals. The one invisible being decided he wanted to experience life as a pig. He descended into the pig's body and immediately forgot his spiritual identity as he stuffed himself with food and wallowed in the mud. He soon connected with a female pig and they had a family. Being totally immersed in matter, he lost contact with Spirit. His celestial friends were horrified and took action to have the entrapped soul set free by having the pig killed. As the beguiled soul exited the body of the slain pig, he realized how he had been duped into believing and accepting a lie about himself. This is the story of the soul of humanity.

The subjective part of the mind colors our life today. It is like a mirror that reflects back impressions placed into it. Be vigilant with your thoughts and feelings. Make a concerted effort to develop critical thinking, pay attention to details and question everything, even divine guidance. This practice will clear the way to receive truth as self-mastery is gained. There will be fewer opportunities to be fooled by filtered information from past conditioning or outside influences. Once a greater understanding is gained as to what actually constitutes being, you will be able to differentiate between the levels of psychic and spiritual phenomena.

To question both the human and divine experience requires discernment. Although spiritual answers may be received in daily meditation and in ordinary life experiences, it is beneficial to question everything both visible and invisible and simply not accept or assume that it is absolute truth. As wisdom consciousness is established, confidence grows and you can rely on the intuitive mind and possible assistance from an invisible source.

The goal is to mold the human personality, blending it in harmony with the God part of your consciousness. When this bond is created, negative influences or messages are not as likely to occur. The ultimate goal is to allow the One Mind to be the greater influence. If a seeker experiences a temporary state of emotional imbalance, answers received more than likely will not be truth. Impulses received from the invisible vibrations are filtered down through layers of mental, emotional and physical energy. Learning to differentiate the source of the information received is extremely important. Energy is an aspect of Mind and is interchangeable with substance. It is everywhere.

In the world of matter, energy has been channeled into specific and tangible form. Mind/God is acting as energy. The layers must be clear in order to receive messages that have not been contaminated. We clear layers by developing and putting into action new patterns that are better suited to an evolving consciousness. Specific tools are given for each degree achieved in conscious spiritual evolution. Old forms are discarded when no longer useful. New forms that are capable of expanding boundaries take their place.

It is important to analyze and respond intelligently to the Laws of the Universe. Nothing happens by chance. It is foolish to take the spiritual life for granted or neglect to study and expand the mind. Learning occurs through trial and error. It is also important to sustain a spirit of gratitude. Thankfulness assists spiritual growth by understanding all creation, seen or unseen, is some aspect of God. It is prudent to question and learn from everything that appears in your life. An untrained mind can be easily deceived.

Many religions teach man to offer himself to God in love and sacrifice. Living as our true Self is an effect of surrender. Aspiring to a high consciousness provides a joy and completeness, a freedom and brilliancy that elude the unenlightened. When you live at the center of your being, the God part is given freedom to express. It is similar to being moved on a giant chessboard. All the moves can be beneficial even though the personality may disagree at the time. The higher part knows what is best at a particular moment of soul maturity. As a result of a growing and amazing bond with the Divine, an inner confidence is gained. Everything required for success from the perspective of the spirit is provided. When you draw the inner splendor outward into life, gifts surface in the form of opportunities, healings and talents.

This does not imply sitting back and waiting. Putting forth effort is required. The innate spiritual qualities already exist. The next step is developing them through deliberate use and the discarding of harmful thought patterns and habits. Change patterns and learn to express and react to life from a higher vantage point of assurance and love. Trust that life will unfold according to the soul plan and not the whims of the human personality.

Trust and belief in a higher purpose for life is a very important truth to comprehend. A higher Intelligence with its own universal laws is actually in charge, although humans would like to believe otherwise. When you disagree, resistance and pain occur. Be responsible for your share of the relationship between mind, soul and spirit. Establish a true understanding and partnership with your higher Nature. Keep trying and the God energy will honor efforts made. Although the higher Nature is in charge, it will not provide or become evident in your life unless you honor Its presence and do your share. It is not a one-sided effort.

When not divided in allegiance, the spiritual centers are protected. Burglars do not enter. The thieves are the darkness of misdirected thought and action. Every type of mischief will attempt to filter through the astral plane and mar soul progress if a working foundation is not established. Spiritual ignorance corrodes through the centers of the emotions and lower part of the mind. Learn to discriminate who or what to let in and who and what to keep out. All of life is based on two movements: opening and closing. You will be able to benefit and use power creatively in direct correspondence to your conscious connection to the One God. Our persona becomes a visible and higher form of love.

It is true that some people have developed moral character and do not experience spiritual blessings. It is also a fact that many good people live in misery and feel isolated from God. Being a good person does not mean spiritual enlightenment. Being illumined is far deeper than moral character although moral character is a prerequisite. An individual may have great knowledge but few virtues. In contrast, another person may be virtuous but have little spiritual knowledge. Both knowledge and virtues are required to be whole. Without wholeness, division still exists.

The wisdom teachings do not recognize the Supreme One as a god of fear or anger. Wisdom is a belief system that recognizes and accepts the Creator as a limitless love energy existing in all life. Remember, your body and mind exist in God. When the power of this amazing fact finally impacts the mind, the inner door to freedom opens. Revelations regarding the soul's journey are revealed and joyfully accepted. Life changes as a result of a heightened understanding and acceptance. God is right here as part of you.

At an unconscious level, all of creation desires to reflect and manifest the virtues of perfection. It is up to us to initiate the action by respecting Earth and transforming our own consciousness. Light is our benefactor. The ultimate creation is when the physical body becomes filled with light. The physical form can be regenerated by purifying and sublimating the physical, astral and lower mental body. Although our cells constantly renew themselves, a weakened condition doesn't improve because of the conditioned cellular memory. The cells are conditioned to behave in a certain way. Work consciously and deliberately with love and determination and the particles within the force fields will vibrate with a greater intensity and purity and healings will eventually take place.

Through disciplined action, memory patterns can be changed and begin to vibrate closer to Divinity. This is a law of physics. Respect for the laws are mandatory. Once a high degree of self-mastery is reached and it feels comfortable meditating, try the following. Focus your attention on the subjective/soul part of the mind. Exercising your higher Nature, request that a specific desire be impressed on the subjective level. Through passion, belief and specific direction, anything can be reprogrammed if it is for the good. It may require repeated statements and persistence to create a new mold and reflect God's perfect ideal in the area that needs reconstruction. This is a mind treatment that can be used in any area of life that could use empowerment.

Freedom eludes until the inner Light decides you are ready consciously and subconsciously to move forward into a greater sense of Self. Light is the creative power. Normally, spiritual progression moves forward gradually. It is a series of inner realizations that finally breaks through the habitual thinking process. In rare circumstances, illumination occurs overnight. The difference lies in the individual soul's past spiritual history and what lessons or challenges it has chosen to experience during the present incarnation. If a point in consciousness has been reached where change and illumination have been prepared for, nothing or no one will stand in the way of the soul's plan.

As the higher Self observes your choices and responses, more of the divine treasures will be offered to you. Nice things happen. Usually, there is a dramatic incident that works as a trigger opening the way to a spiritually-honored life. A soul decision or a change in attitude also initiates new experiences. Transformation occurs when you listen to an inner command and follow the command, willingly making necessary life changes. A new and bright person emerges. To move forward, one of the prerequisites is a willingness to change and trust in the process even though you may not yet have a clue regarding the end result.

To wipe away the tear in God's Eye, understand obedience. Mind, in Its activity as Law, is obedient. It responds to firm conviction and belief on your part. Energy responds to thought. Give the law of your life new instructions. Make your intention loving, clear, concise and positive. These qualities become patterns for action. Then when you command, there is complete cooperation. This is using the power God gave you creatively.

Creative power flows as a steady river in the lives of the willing and trusting. When we are ready, we will, without any hesitancy, use the harmonics of Universal Law for the good of all. Opportunities, patterns and challenges present themselves like clockwork. They are the initiations we pass through. Each soul has a plan to complete that will lead him to a state of perfection in form. Learning to work consciously with the subtle dimensions is part of that plan. The effort put forth will materialize results in proportion to belief and preparedness.

All is Spirit. Spirit is Mind. Mind is One. Working with the Law expands and strengthens your light and swings wide the sacred door to the Unseen and Unknown. In spirit form, you knew truth long ago. Collectively, spiritual identity has been forgotten. It is time for education, remembrance and acceptance of the One Reality and your divine birth. The energy transformation is one of vibration, power and love. Love is the real language of the universe. The whole of creation, every single creature, understands the language at a deep level. This is the only language worth knowing.

Being constantly aware of the Light and God's watchful presence will sustain an individual consciousness with a higher love that never gives up, regardless of the appearances moving across the screen of life. Without hope, energy is either destructively directed inwardly, outwardly, or both. A feeling of loss can be unbearable. Every child of God can have a personal involvement with God and with the Heavenly Hosts. God remembers, although you may temporarily experience a lapse in memory. You may think you are alone; you are not. You may be miserable and feel like a failure; you are not. For hope to sustain, embrace love. Love is the enduring power that makes all dreams a reality.

All life is connected. This is why souls who have achieved the sublime perfection return to Earth as benefactors. No one is forgotten. Ordinary life with its diverse experiences is a personal drama that has been accepted as a means to develop mastery of self and matter. The author of your book is you. Right now, it is an unfinished manuscript. The power of spirit can be used for good. Believe in perfection and invite the mind of God to think through you,

Start where you are and use what you have at the moment. The adepts and sages work with mental forces with unconditional love and unerring wisdom. This is the path of the Divine. It is both the mind and the heart working together in harmony. An awakened child of God achieves completeness through respecting creation and honoring divinity within. True vision is found by using both the heavenly and earthly eyes. When a union is established, the "Eye of God" makes an appearance.

Chapter Nineteen
Understanding

In the Bible, Genesis 5:24, it says that Enoch, the great-grandfather of Noah, walked with God and did not die, because God took him physically. Enoch experienced frequent dreams and visions and personal intuitive insights. As a scribe, his work, *The Book of Enoch,* was considered one of the most important books in early Christianity and was used widely. *The Book of Enoch* was not included as a canon in the Bible. One section attributed to him was the *Book of Dreams.* The contents referred to the truth that we could experience visions as well as otherworldly "encounters." Enoch had immensely important messages for us to learn regarding the importance of accepting and understanding words of wisdom as well as observing and walking on a path of righteousness.

There are thousands of Celtic, Babylonian and Sumerian records, as well as legends and myths that speak of the fascinating history of our world and the origin of humankind. What has been hidden is now surfacing and is revealing what humanity may finally understand. We are obliged to seek understanding not only intellectually, but for the sake of our souls as well. Many of the ancient cultures chose to examine reality through the metaphors of geometry and sound frequency. The view of today's modern force-field theory and wave mechanics agrees with past scientists. The order of the universe is an interwoven configuration of wave patterns.

Everything that exists changes and is replaced. When we search for truth, it is found amidst the constancy of change. The constancy is consistent and stable. That which is stable is consciously connected to through understanding. Understanding is a continuous unfolding of consciousness. Not all of truth has been given because understanding increases as the Light within expands. You can go only as far as your present spiritual knowledge. When we attain the understanding of a Master Teacher, the same feats as the Master can be accomplished. When an interior conviction is understood, that Spirit is the true identity, then we can better help others and self as a result of a higher understanding. When the Supreme Indescribable Spirit is correctly understood as the only Power, healing occurs.

Life is lived as a God-realized being when you understand love as the fulfilling of the perfect law. Loving who you are and using that love to bless life frees you from bondage. Love and Law go hand in hand to produce a meaningful and joyful life. To understand love and live it, you advance to the state of love that is God, the unlimited.

Increasing faith and using intuitive imagination will create directly out of the One Substance. Spiritual substance is everywhere waiting to be formed. Spiritual Law works according to your understanding. Develop the courage to advance and understanding strengthens your resolve. Build a physical body temple with Light and purity of thought, feeling and emanations. Blessings occur when you understand that the time has now arrived to be rid of all illusions and make way for truth to live consciously, creatively and lovingly as the highest Self. In thankfulness, join our physical brothers and sisters of Light, the invisible Brotherhood of Light, the Celestial beings and Masters and build a strong and beautiful inner sanctuary.

It is necessary to establish a firm foundation to be able to access spiritual understanding from the highest point of view. Consciously and continually strive to recognize and accept the One Supreme God as the most important aspect of life. Connecting consciously is through the recognition, acceptance and use of the God portion of your Mind. Spiritual discernment and true understanding will work together in protecting and illuminating your journey of rediscovery. The two qualities support the spiritual senses with surety and control.

Understanding truth is an ongoing process. It includes belief and a thorough knowledge of the hierarchal structure of the Universe and what it means to train the mind and have a developed will. A subject can be known intellectually and the magnitude of the substance and meaning in its entirety not grasped. Universal Truth, Cosmic Laws and the Hierarchy of Consciousness must eventually be understood, accepted and lived. You are what you believe. Although understanding the true spiritual individuality is mandatory, it is not always easy to convince the personality that there is the Light of God within waiting to be the power in charge.

The dragon of ignorance must be slain first.

Attaining an unlimited sense of self can become a monumental work if previous religious thought patterns have conditioned the mind, not allowing room for a greater philosophy of life. All Masters speak of the freedom of the soul as a reachable reality. Success requires disciplined reprogramming to bring forth the inner wisdom, allowing it to be an outward fullness, beauty and perfection. Change the mind and remove conditions within the soul that are false. As an example, if the infinite reality of the Supreme God's Love were fully understood, it would be realized that God has many sons and daughters and will continue to have new ones. There are no limits in God. There isn't only one Son or one epoch in the cycles of creation where a full divinity manifests in a human form. God sends exceptional beings periodically to Earth to enlighten their brothers and sisters. The beings have awakened to the power of their own eternal identity.

To be realizing God requires concentrated mind work. Many seek the darker forms of magic, believing that this is self-mastery. It is not. There are humans who misuse power to perpetuate selfish acts or, in some cases, evil. This is a form of black magic that leads to disaster. Man's lower nature, the selfish animal personality, is always ready to manifest itself and urge him to exploit others. Control used for manipulative purposes has nothing to do with spiritual understanding and soul power. The type of mind magic that controls people is not a short cut to spiritual success. It is self-aggrandizement. Because humans have not completely understood the difference between white magic and black magic, several races of mankind have already disappeared from the face of the Earth. We will meet the same fate if discernment and compassion are not practiced.

White magic consists in putting everything at the service of God. In contrast, the lower nature seeks sorcery. We live in a time where information is easily accessed and is just as quickly not understood or discerned. Man is not born to repeatedly satisfy the baser desires of the lower nature. What most people are oblivious to is the fact that we are born to consciously be active in the Light and be a benefactor of humanity.

The Buddhist principles regarding merit clarify the importance of good character. Merit-creating endeavors combined with aspirations are more than merely tools to improve one's self-image; they are major factors in attaining a compassionate nature. How can we appreciate anything if we have not developed beauty of character? Prayers, compassion, and meritorious actions are important because they propel us forward. The problem, of course, is that we live in a conditioned reality.

The creating of merit is an essential point. The tragic truth is that this aspect of understanding is sorely missing in the West. A typical human desires and expects results immediately. Spiritual evolution is a step-by-step solo effort. No one can borrow another's Light. There is One Universal Mind and each one of us uses a portion of It. Our mind is an individualization of the One Mind. Thinking mind can be improved through the process of creating positive causes and conditions. This is called merit. The merits created remain with us after we leave our bodies. All gains, whether inner or outer, result from our own character.

It can be difficult for a human to focus on the Sublime as part of himself when a poor self-image is a major influence. One of the worst hindrances to accepting truth is to identify with a lack of self worth. When a human does not understand or accept real identity and the purpose of creation, he will flounder and be lost. Spirit is the only identity. It is healing to have loving thoughts about others and self. Educate yourself about who you really are and your opinion of self will improve. The majority of people haven't the slightest idea as to why they are here or the purpose of creation. The answer to these questions and the solving of problems can be overwhelming because it hasn't dawned on them that they are already what they are seeking. The healing process begins when you turn on your spiritual light.

If you have no time for Light, there will be ample time for darkness, the ignorance that is enslaving the soul. To receive the form of help required from within or from celestial beings, it is essential to cultivate loving thoughts and actions. Lofty master teachers who have proven the universal laws as a valid means to liberate the mind from falsity have given pure truth to humankind prior to recorded history. When a soul awakens to this truth, it is as if he were born again.

Consciously connect to the celestial power line using deliberate thought. The place to start is within the mind. You are an intermediary between heaven and earth. A perfect solar symbol of this truth is the pure and graceful swan. The long neck represents the space between the regions above and the regions below. Identifying with beauty becomes as effortless as a swan gliding across a pond with confidence and grace.

BE: Embracing the Mystery

A magic wand is not required to create your ideal. Belief and willingness work toward removing doubts and corrupted patterns. Only then are you able to manifest real power in the visible world of sorrow and division. Through deliberate effort, lift the scars on your thinking and begin to reflect heaven. A prepared seeker of truth will move in one direction: simplicity, truth and love, allowing the Light of God to guide in all ways.

The majority of people live reactionary lives, all stemming from past experiences stored in the creative medium of mind. Be careful what you place inside it. The subjective is a mirror reflecting back to you exactly what is believed. It may be necessary to deliberately do reversal work by creating affirmations which are positive, claiming the opposite. Self-condemnation will destroy all efforts toward realizing a goal. Learn to be in harmony with your own spiritual identity. Make every effort to keep emotions under the guidance of clear thought.

If there is a conflict in loving and honoring either the human or divine nature, the spiritual identity remains remote and unreal. An identification crisis is in control. A deeper understanding is required. Learn to rule your own life. The body is a holy temple. It is important to be rid of impurities physically, emotionally and mentally. The physical body and current personality enables the spirit to express intelligence and divinity in matter. It is your responsibility to honor the body.

When the fullness of who you are is honored, you are accepting responsibility for the care of what the Creator has given you. A keener sense of self-worth is established as a result of purification and consciously drawing in spiritual Light. People who harm others have not learned to honor life. They are immature and undeveloped souls. They are to be pitied as well as forgiven and helped.

Bringing more light into the thinking mind will accelerate healing. An excellent practice is to impregnate the aura, energy field, with the pure white spiritual light. Light is the substance of creation. When character and the aura are strong, personal energy becomes a powerful force. Imagining a circle of white light surrounding the body is a form of protection. It is similar to a fortress and protects against most of the nonsense that bombards every living form. Imagination creates. Be conscious of the circle of Light. Create it for safety, peace of mind and health. Keep a screen of light between yourself and the darkness that is so common on

Earth today. If you forget, negativity may creep in, but it will not have the same influence as it previously did.

To receive help and protection from luminous beings, be a giver. Help others and the planet by sending forth rays of pure light. Send light to those who have been hurtful. Send thoughts of light to souls who are entrapped in the darkness of denial. Keep sending to wherever there is disorder. A good plan is to work in love, seek truth and do your part to establish order and harmony wherever you are.

Spiritual evolution is a sacred work. The higher Self is a part of God using a physical, emotional and mental form. When the higher Self is fully accepted, self-worth becomes an entirely new issue. You are not bloated with falseness, but filled with the pure light of understanding. If people young and old realized the purpose of life, they would cease abusing the body and mind with mind-altering products, which shut down the spirit and harm the body. If they thoroughly understood the higher Nature, mind power and the hierarchal structure of creation, indulging in thoughts and activities that only delay the journey to perfection would come to an abrupt halt.

When my two oldest children were in high school, they would on occasion invite troubled classmates to our home. Our guests were looking for a way to feel better about themselves and life. They did not know what constituted true being, the power of the mind or the great harm they were causing for future physical, mental and spiritual health. The young people willingly visited because they had heard through classmates about healings and the offering of nonjudgmental guidance.

A loving example of divine healing was a young girl scheduled for surgery on a growth behind her eye. I had not met her nor was I aware of the seriousness of her health at the time. The girl asked me to pray and lay on hands. Weeks later, the result came to my attention. The eye surgery was cancelled because she was healed. To be able to correct serious illnesses, one must understand the action of God's Law and apply it with love and confidence.

As a result of young people asking for guidance and healing, the devastating effects of wrongful use of mind-altering substances caught my attention. Using drugs for pleasure is one of the worst forms of self-inflicted abuse. One night, a widowed father called regarding his teenage daughter and her rebellious pursuits. The father was desperate. The daughter totally ignored his requests. I had not met the girl or the father.

Our meeting turned out to be one of challenge and surprise. We were sitting on the couch casually exchanging information when suddenly the lovely girl mentioned that she smoked marijuana. She also liked to use a psychic board game. Unbeknown to her, the invisible entities that are attracted to psychic games are usually lost souls stuck in the lowest astral plane. Many earthbound entities find pleasure in manipulating the mind of humans. They know how easy it is to control a naive human lacking discernment and psychic knowledge. At this juncture, everything I knew and felt went on red alert. I had the awareness to quickly act and help the teen obviously influenced by an unseen force.

The dark entity, a nasty parasite of the lower worlds, knew my thoughts and intent, which were to remove or exorcise its attachment and influence on the girl. At that point, something very strange happened. My body became intensely hot and uncomfortable. My mind felt clouded and concentration was difficult. The uncomfortable manifestations in my body were further evidence that a negative invisible intruder was challenging my intention. I stood up and placed my hands above the girl's head and said a "power" word demanding that the negative entity leave her body immediately.

This was my first experience with an exorcism. Months earlier, I had been given a spiritual power word to use in emergency situations. The word used was one of the many names of God. It brought an instantaneous and healing result. When the word was said, a vaporous substance left the girl's body. The neighbor stood up with a big smile on her face. She exclaimed, "She's gone, she's gone!" I asked, "Who is gone?" She told me the name of the entity attachment. Now that the lower entity had been removed, the girl's countenance was radiant and no longer troubled.

The teenager had known that there was an intruder that had manipulative power influencing her actions. This nasty interaction had been going on for months. My new and thankful friend said she felt free, a feeling she had not had since her depression began after the death of her mother. She asked that we walk into the garden and talk about the mother she loved so dearly. The girl also shared how her life had drastically changed for the worse due to experimenting with drugs and using the psychic board game.

Before the teenage girl had begun using drugs, she had been an honor student happily involved with extracurricular school activities and a source of joy to her father. All that changed when she began to abuse her body and mind. What users of mind-altering substances do not understand is that they open a door to a lower invisible dimension inviting trouble of the worst possible kind. A user is frequently in a weakened mental and emotional state, lacking in self discipline and self-worth which, combined with unhealthy habits, always spells trouble.

Earthbound souls and entity attachments are mentioned in scripture, poetry, literature, art and other avenues of expression. Lost souls exist. It is very easy to be fooled by a negative dark energy. It is intelligence separated from the Light. It is a direct manifestation of man's error thinking and feelings, when a divisive belief is held in consciousness. Outside unwanted influences, mesmeric negativity, are controlled to the degree you have developed personal awareness and Light. You can still be adversely affected, even with a developed consciousness, if the physical body is not in balance or is emotionally unstable. Humans are the authors of dark forms. Attachments are ancient and will continue to occur, causing havoc until the thinking mind is educated and whole again.

The good news was witnessing the girl instantly healed. She kept me informed of her progress through the years. Later, she studied in Germany and became a doctor. As a result of our initial meeting and healing, a heightened ministry of sharing manifested in my life. Our home became a refuge for many young people. It is very easy to hinder spiritual growth and destroy the body without knowledge of the energy systems and the powerful influence of thought and habit. Understanding the consequences of choices, life improves.

Ideally, it would be beneficial if we were taught as children that the body is to be respected. When the body and mind are harmed through debilitating physical, emotional and mental habits, the God part of us remains aloof. Spirit will not be an active influence until a connecting, correcting and awakening process begins. People experience disease, depression, disturbances and death as a result of a false belief and an unenlightened state of mind. The ultimate goal is to consciously awaken to universal laws and the truth of being, and immediately act by making better choices. The higher Self will respond and begin the process of healing as a result of an intense desire to be whole and complete. It is your responsibility to meet the inner God part at least halfway.

BE: Embracing the Mystery

In the transformation process, always be patient and trusting. If others have been illuminated and transformed, so can you. Good changes require intelligent critical thinking and healing adjustments. You have a choice to adopt teachings of a higher love and law living in harmony or continue to suffer in confusion and pain. To continue on a path of destruction through abuse on any level is to limit the spirit. Limitation enslaves the physical senses and causes sorrow. Suffering and self-imposed karma will continue through harmful choices. The law of cause and effect is an ironclad rule for the unenlightened. The subjective part of the mind creates according to belief and choices.

Since you are a creator both consciously and unconsciously, it is beneficial to receive guidance from a true Teacher. A true teacher is one with spiritual integrity who understands the journey, patterns and challenges experienced along the way toward wholeness. If a qualified teacher is not available, study the ancient wisdom teachings, the words of Christ, and the example of true mystics. They outline what all masters have achieved. Perhaps, a supportive friend has a similar spiritual ideal.

Change is not always easy and will require soul-searching in areas that are still unknown. The mystics and Masters who have "walked the Way" have proven the wisdom teachings' authenticity, so can you. With success, other seekers are given permission to follow suit. Try to realize that your destiny is to be perfection in form.

Everyone is a projection of the Supreme Spirit in matter. It is the plan of God for life to be complete and perfect. With enlightenment and the beginning degrees of self-mastery, gifts and higher powers may appear. As the eternal identity is accepted, tangible talents are given to use for the good of all. In the eastern part of the world, the gifts are commonly used as a natural part of life. Here in the western hemisphere, we tend to use spiritual gifts during times that are judged as emergency situations. From the highest perspective, the aspects, virtues, and talents of God are natural powers to be used freely as an offering of love. We are given power to bless everything and everyone. Giving is a divine habit.

As we have senses that are part of the physical makeup, there are other senses that need to be activated to fully express the invisible. To comprehend and apply Universal Laws and Principles, spiritual organs must be developed and finely tuned. They are awakened through the suggestions within these pages. With belief and discipline, the spiritual organs can be developed and be put to good use. Progress involves all levels of life. Be conscious only of order and perfection and you will, through your own mind's focus, help love fulfill the perfect law.

Imagine how a Master would live his/her life. Even if it takes a temporary pretense of mastery, disciplined efforts will eventually create a new and positive mold. During the tenth century, a scholar called Somananda wrote a Hindu text called *The Outlook of Shiva*. In it, he instructs the seeker to act as if he already embodied his goal, no matter the disparity between what he is and what he wishes to become. He is to maintain an unwavering awareness by affirming his attention with confidence and conviction. In this way, Somananda explains, he will align his being with intention, and the goal becomes manifest.

If right understanding is absent, truth eludes. Wrongful judgment of self prevents the feeling of genuine love and joy. It is the unfettered soul who creates a difference in the world. To be truly alive as a soul requires a passion for life. It is a gift that arrives with an acceptance and a greater understanding of individual identity and purpose. Heaven gifts receptive souls with sublime inner states. Regardless of appearance, background or lack of credentials by worldly standards, spiritual aliveness and oneness is your destiny.

Chapter Twenty
Fact or Fiction

What is truth? Everyone has a different view according to his level of understanding. The mind creates miracles when there is nothing to hinder the Divine from coming through. If an event is governed by the presence of a high degree of Light, it is more likely to be truth. For instance, if a window has a shade pulled straight down to the sill, the outer light normally cannot be seen. This is true regarding the subject of truth as well. If there is a shade covering the Light of God's Intelligence, how can anyone determine what is truth? Move the shade up a few centimeters and the light will filter through. The more the shade is rolled upward, the greater the intensity and visibility of the light. This is a fact that works well for both outward and inward light.

The outer life is better understood when you understand who you are. It is the intimate connection and greatness with the eternal Self that reveals what is fact and what is fiction. The more conscious you are of the inner Self, the more opportunities will materialize where you can control what humans commonly refer to as fate. Fate is a mistaken activity that is impermanent. Things of the Spirit are enduring and true.

How do you react to information that disagrees with your belief? A belief is a mental acceptance, conviction and confidence. It can change. Are you mature enough to stop, listen, analyze and think deeply regarding another possibility before making a judgment? If you do make a judgment, what is it based on? Is it based solely on what you have read or been taught to believe? Judgments are usually made by appearance. What is required is a willingness to deeply look at new thoughts, allowing them to be thoroughly digested before discarding them or making a hasty judgment.

One person's truth is another person's lie. Light returning as a direct experience is a normal evolutionary process as you awaken to being as a part of God. It is Light returning to the thinking part of the mind. Light exposes fiction, falsity and limitation. If you do not experience Light, how can you know truth? To see Light is to glimpse the very center of Reality.

A good beginning in explaining belief is the falsity regarding the mysterious organ, the brain. There has been a persistent myth that we really use only 10% of our brain. New technologies have been invented which clearly show the metabolism of the brain. Testing indicates that in any one single activity we use only a few percent of the brain. The interesting data is that over a 24-hour day, all the brain will light up on the scan. Memory is not stored in any one single place, but exists throughout the entire cortex.

A myth can be a real or a fictional story. It can be a half-truth that has been emotionally accepted. Many followers have misconstrued the teachings of the Great Initiates who have given humankind the Light they needed at the time. As a result, some souls feel divided and separated from God. If the teaching is tampered with through the centuries, a diminished version of truth, identity and purpose is taught. The teaching becomes inner law and can place a believer indefinitely in a state of bondage. Belief becomes law.

Truth has many names. You have the ability to reach in and experience the real, the light of your being. God power is a living part of you. Spirit energy is your true life. The unlimited energy is to be expanded and used. You will know God in direct relationship to your ability to accept that God is the inner life. The physical body is the result of the various areas of the mind impressing consciousness on the body. A feeling of separation only occurs in the unenlightened mind.

For a moment, imagine a sizeable piece of gold. Gold is an excellent example as energy symbolizing a Christ Mind. It is pure, durable and a treasure to own. It obviously has great value. Compare the process of hard rock mining, which produces much of the world's gold. This technique uses intense power to remove, collect, treat and process the gold and other valuable metals from the rocks. To seek deposits of gold, veins of gold are drilled and explosives are used to break up the rock.

This analogy is similar to what action must be taken if the treasure within is to be uncovered. The choice is whether effort is used to dig for the gold with a passionate energy and belief or follow the simple technique of gold panning that is used when searching in streams or dry streams. The aggressive approach brings quicker and more valuable results. Although you may already be making an effort to lift consciousness, a greater effort must be made if lasting changes are to surface for your own good and humanity's. The thinking mind must be controlled and God's Intelligence revealed.

Actual service to God in the flesh can be soul-wrenching, because you will wish to expose falsity and reverse the misuse of energy. The greater the dig into the veins of the inner gold of spirit life, the more likely you will walk the path with integrity. Human laws that have been mistakenly created and accepted can also manifest freedom when understanding surfaces and denial of the inner power stops. The mode of soul-travel is reversed and you will be equipped to fulfill destiny when you believe, accept and live your own Light, no longer divided or separated from the One.

Why is there so much fear? Fear is caused by a sense of separation and not resigning intimacy with the Whole. Once the mind ceases to be divided, Light will return to the thinking part of the mind and direct your experiences. This is what you rely on for your health, peace, love, wisdom and life. The Impersonal All-Knowing God becomes a personal experience when you understand and fully accept that there are not two, but only one. It is the will of this One Power and Presence to seek Self-expression through you.

Spiritual power is known through awareness and action. The Spirit within is your Mother-Father-God. Aliveness manifests through interaction with It. God is Impersonal yet Jesus called the Absolute his Father. Why? Because the personal Father, the higher part of your mind and spirit, is a part of the Supreme God Intelligence. The Absolute is not personal: It simply Is. Through the ability to genuinely commune with the God within, the Father and I as one consciousness becomes a reality. The Infinitely Impersonal and the divine personal merge.

Make contact with the Light to genuinely develop discernment and receive truthful answers. Otherwise, everything is secondhand knowledge. Life responds to us by the way we approach it. You may need a new belief system. Some people claim they have achieved discernment while in truth their strong belief in half-truths has actually created a bias, a prejudice, and a preference that is more judgmental than truthful. It is their belief and subjective memory. Personal belief does not necessarily arise from an enlightened mind. Judgments are usually made by appearance, and appearances can easily deceive.

In exceptional cases, the subject of character can also be misleading. All the great teachers have offered at one time or another a code, commandments, a set of rules to help struggling humans develop character. It stands to reason that if character is highly developed, it is easier to access God's Intelligence and all the riches of the Spirit. But history has shown us that nothing is black and white. There have been and always will be individuals who have personally demonstrated actions that are opposed to the teachings of Love and Wisdom and in a special moment are touched by Light and transformed.

Another half truthful myth is that God created heaven and hell. Because both religion and science have been presented in such a mysterious way, it appears that creation is separate from the Creator. Science has changed its view, but the influences are still in effect. There is a substance flowing through everyone and everything. When spiritual vision is activated, a subtle energy can be seen with physical eyes opened or closed. The substance looks like a shower of light particles and there is no place that it is not. Nothing is separated from its Source. The thinking mind through false beliefs accepts erroneous teachings. It is the belief in duality that creates a personal heaven or hell. Guilt reinforces the belief. Humankind experiences life according to what is held in the subjective part of the mind. Belief creates what is experienced in the visible as well as invisible worlds of Light.

The soul is the subjective creative medium of the higher Nature. Thoughts are reflected in it. It is the receptive feminine medium that takes thought and acts on it. It doesn't analyze or reject. It is actually a servant because it always obeys. The soul in a very real sense is the image of your conscious thinking mind. Everyone, including the universe, has a soul. The body is a manifestation of both the spirit and soul. Understanding how the cohesiveness of the energy system operates helps you effectively live as a spontaneous intelligence within a limited form.

Perceptions and lifestyles may have to be radically altered to avoid further falsity to rule. The belief that life is predetermined can be unsettling. Humans are not robots living out a predetermined destiny. The individual mindset is the creator. Everything within and without is connected not only to the past but also to the future. The present is experi-

BE: Embracing the Mystery

enced in the meditative state. Cause and effect are scientific. What you think, feel and act upon today is a direct result of past experience and conditioning. In a sense, this is similar to a robot's action because you are repeating the program by reacting from stored subconscious memories. As long as the same pattern continues, the influences spill over into the future.

The subconscious mimics the animal world through which the spirit passed for millions of years. Action and reaction must rise above that realm. There is no good or bad luck or even miracles. When you view life as a natural and orderly procession of effects unfolding as a result of causes, interpreting the reality of fate, destiny and karmic possibilities is better understood. In other words, the subjective soul is Law. It receives, reacts and creates what happens to us according to the state of our thought.

There are both universal laws of mind and laws of nature. The ideal choice is to evolve into conscious self-mastery where you can control old conditioning. Learn to think deeply and access the knowledge and patterns of the personality to learn why struggle is a frequent experience. The goal is to be a conscious spirit thinker who dissects and asks the right questions and deliberately chooses the correct steps. By becoming a conscious thinker, positive action creates new causes that will later manifest and not harm your higher purpose or the purpose of others. The Sacred is reached through thought and feeling. Think independently and correctly. Thoughts must rise above the difficulties in the lower worlds of physical, emotional and mental vibrations.

I have already mentioned that there is a hierarchy of consciousness both in the visible and invisible dimensions. When help is asked from an invisible being, receivership is in direct relation to preparedness. I have never encouraged channeling because the typical human lacks clear judgment as to the source of the material. There is a tendency to become dependent on information being received from an invisible entity. If an individual does not develop his own soul connection, he remains separated from his Source. On the bright side, many of the transmissions that have been received, such as commandments, codes and rules of life, have been given to humanity by highly evolved souls who understand universal laws.

Another false myth is that God dictates what we are or are not to do. Suggestions are given by beings both visible and invisible who have

Fact or Fiction

walked the Way and understand what works and does not work. The Infinite Impersonal Creator God has left you to your own devices to discover who you really are. Remember, created intelligence has self-will. The finite mind is part of the Supreme Infinite Mind. The more you accept and hold on to this proven truth, the more likely you will have a direct relationship with the One Mind. Awakening, you become a conscious living God Intelligence in form. God, the Impersonal, becomes personal through the individual spiritual force being activated. Otherwise, half-truths and subjective memories are controlling the thought process. The majority of people are reactionaries. They live from memories both positive and negative.

Is punishment for a sin fact or fiction? When a mistake is made, it may appear afterwards that some unseen force meted out punishment. What has actually happened is that making a harmful choice creates a consequence. It is the law of cause and effect. No one is punishing you except your belief of what is true and not true and the intensity of your emotional guilt.

Is personal responsibility for our behavior fact or fiction? You are responsible for setting something into motion whether it is a positive or negative reaction. When a dependence on chance is given power, it may not work according to your highest good. Normally, cause and effect will bring forth a perfect balance. By being responsible and endeavoring to uncover truth, you work with the Universal Law. It is a team effort between the conscious mind and the inner divine intelligence. The higher the shade is pulled up inviting the light to shine, the easier it is for you to come out of the shade into the sunlight.

In the presence of Light, it is understood that souls are ruled by fate only when that is their truth. Fate becomes a creation when you don't stop, listen, think deeply and act from the inner Self. It is a false state of mind that takes on an activity of its own. Destiny on the other hand, is when you fulfill the purpose of your creation by liberating the inner Light. It is your conscious choice.

Although we are free to live according to our own desires, there remain universal laws of life that cannot be trampled upon. The laws are in place because they make the journey more beneficial to soul growth. In truth, we can do as we please. If in the doing, we harm self or others, the unruly winds of fate take charge. It is never too late. Falsity and division can be reversed. Appearances may be dire but in truth they are temporary creations and can be transformed. What you need to do is be at attention, think deeply before you judge or act. Do nothing to tarnish the gold of your inner mind. This means not engaging in useless conversations and activities. It means giving priority to the journey of the soul and not be swayed by any life situation.

Learning the difference between what is true and what is false is about awakening to a higher love for the eternal inner Self and for the entire creative process. It is your understanding manifesting as your reality. It is the destiny of every soul to know truth, be free, harmonious and joyful. Love the journey and do not allow it to slip away. If you allow it to diminish, life is lackluster and tarnished and is no longer a luminous gold essence. The inner treasure is temporarily lost through ignorance and negligence.

Sometimes, an invisible and caring being will help, such as a relative, angel or celestial being. Together, you work with the Substance, the energy behind all forms. The world needs intimate spiritual experience. You attract to yourself that which is like your thought. The connection begins on the personal level. The goal is to hear the inner Voice of All Truth. Eventually, your eye becomes single and everything is perceived in its entirety, as a Whole with no divisions.

To stop being a prisoner of the past, transcend the lower dimensions and reach inward to the Causal mind intelligence. This is your link to God Intelligence. By seeking expansion of the God mind within, a higher power is accessed that will bring forth good action and results. It is a lifesaver to understand and control causes. Resonance with truth is not reached through a "slave" consciousness. Being stuck in an identification crisis where life is lived as a result of former conditioning is the greatest threat to permanent healing. The battle is with the human personality, who is resistant to change. The eternal part of you must take control or the battle is lost.

A change of perspective may be demanded of you. By learning to shift into a new perception, you are able to transform whatever needs to be changed in a belief system that is not productive. In this instance, mind work must begin at the top. Thoughts must be lifted to a higher plane than the mundane human level. Study the personality and confront the weaknesses by turning them around so the energy being emitted works for enlightenment and not against it. This is the beauty in creating an expanded energy field. Thoroughly understand and respect the Universal law of action and reaction. By changing the mental and emotional patterns, life experiences change.

The first pollution was on the mental plane where laws were broken. The transformation filters downward from the mental, through emotional desires and eventually manifests in the physical body. If God's Intelligence within you is allowed to be free, the physical responses will be a welcome surprise. Look squarely at a weak or negative condition and heal it through a deliberate change in consciousness.

Understanding the continuity of life is one of the central points of healing. Trials come and go and it is hoped that growth occurs. The trials actually are useful in molding character and drawing forth spirituality. You have an inner power that will stop chronic suffering and spiritual deprivation. It is far kinder to begin now than to delay spiritual awakening. Immortality as a soul is a fact whether a personality agrees or not. Help is available.

A perfect state of health is not required to make positive changes nor is material wealth a factor. It is not necessary to fly to the Himalayan Mountains to meditate. Transformation is achieved in one's own space. Transformation work is mental. Imagination is a powerful force. Use it with trust and determination. Whatever the need, create a vivid image of perfection and harmony in the mind. Build a mental equivalent. Feel the image with intensity and as a definite possibility. Cells are affected through thought. Mind manifests what is accepted in faith. You can make your ideal come alive through you. Stop frequently during the day and nourish the perfect image with love and admiration. Allow faith to take action and it will work. Give your desire constant attention and eventually faith is grounded in certainty. Affirmative thinking and love create. The inner power will make your goal come alive in the realm of Cause.

As a direct result of the level and integrity of your belief, you are either bound in chains or liberated. You can remove all self-created limitations. A belief that will prove successful is to develop a genuine love for the Creator of All, God Intelligence. It is also important to accept and love your own spirit and do likewise towards others. Study and understand Universal Mental Law. Search out what is proven truth. Share Light, understanding and kindness toward others. To be successful requires remembering, discipline and loving the growth process. The result is self-mastery.

It is wisdom to realize that that both the invisible and visible parts of the self influence and impact health as well as the energy charging the surrounding environment. Keep in mind that desires use the emotional astral matter, a close vibration to Earth. Energies not only create future experiences, they also magnetically create a new physical body. Everyone and everything in your current life is basically present through former thoughts and desire. This truth alone is enough to make some people desire change.

Belief and desire mold the present body and experience, as well as the future experience. As long as there are desires, incarnation continues. Desire is an outgoing energy. It always seeks a means to gratify feelings. Desire usually determines the place of rebirth and the souls who are to participate in the next drama. Desire is the connecting link, and the effect can either be positive or negative depending on past mental longings. Although it may seem at times that you do not deserve unfortunate experiences or relationships, they were very likely initiated in the past. Memory is hidden and will eventually reveal itself with or without conscious permission. Creating new and positive mental forms will create a brighter future.

Power works on its own level whether it is physical, emotional, mental or spiritual. Motives are a power in themselves that create effects. Eventually, in another cycle, a new time and space, a soul reaches a point in consciousness where there is no motive left except to be active in divine service for the good of all life. There is more than one choice available to the soul. Eventually, souls are free not to return to Earth and serve. Choice continues regardless of the spiritual level attained.

There are souls who have reached illumination and are perfect transparencies of purity. These souls desire to continue as emissaries of Light, benefactors for the good of all in a physical world. Their heart desire is a call for a return visit to planet Earth. Many enlightened ones choose the path of service and will not experience rest until they have done whatever they can to benefit life and lift world-consciousness. Earth is an experimental school with daily lessons. Negative effects will continue to torment until a student has grasped truth and intelligently works with Universal law. There are rules governing the universe. If there were not, everything would be in a state of chaos. A personality is liberated from the myth of fate and falsity through the right use of mind and an intense love of God and the living of that love.

Man has not evolved into a complete understanding of himself. To cease being blown by the winds of chance, stop making an idol of any form, whether it is of heaven or earth. In truth, you can see only that which you are like. Truth is known by allowing God Intelligence to expand and be visibly active in your life. As the mind expands, your efforts will provide a mold for the inner Law to work. The sacred lineage is for all those who dare to be the Divine Intelligence. The belief in duality acts as a torment, which follows a divided soul. Destiny is to be whole again. An example of wholeness was Jesus. He was a man who knew himself and his direct relationship to the Whole. Strive to be whole again and you will realize that the treasure is in the rediscovery of who you eternally are. Be open and invite the indwelling Presence to be the power in your life.

Chapter Twenty-One
Character

Truth is understood when spiritual evolution is viewed from the point of inner knowing versus outer teaching. Religion is the outer teaching that man has created for the personality. Mysticism is the inner teaching directly from God. Creativity occurs in the highest part of the mind working in cooperation with the Invisible Worlds. The same golden thread of love runs through all outer religions and yet it is not comprehended or fully embraced until a firsthand direct connection with the Divine is experienced. There are certain fundamental truths common to all spiritual movements. Major religions advocate character values of compassion and wisdom, ethics and awareness, grace and charity, and surrender and mercy. Religions serve man's belief about his relationship to God. As the Koran says, "There is no God which is not all Gods."

Robert Browning wrote, "All is love, yet all is law." To understand love and law, it is necessary to have an advanced knowledge of the One Mind behind manifestation. When it is understood that the universe is organized intelligence, it is easier to base life on Law. It is also beneficial to learn how to use Universal Principles of Mind. The idea is to live according to natural law and cosmic order. With acquired maturity, you become a mouthpiece, or personification of the Infinite in form. To make use of Universal Mind, understand that it is an aspect of the One Indescribable God. To work effectively with the One Mind, a personal relationship with the inner God part is a prerequisite. True identity requires free passage. To be a conscious creator, a healthy physical, emotional and mental atmosphere is necessary. The development of character transforms energy and the individual into a transparency without blockages.

Many people haven't the slightest idea of what it means to have moral or ethical strength. History and brilliant messengers have given us endless tools of love and wisdom. If the guidelines had been adopted in daily activities, negative crimes against life would not continue to be collectively and individually experienced everywhere. Soul evolution occurs in a race of men and women of noble character. The individual God-Realized beings who have graced the planet have given humanity keys that will allow the soul to live fully. The keys are not effective unless there is a foundation of integrity.

Belonging to an outer religious organization is not necessarily the way to reach God-realization. The answer to wholeness and perfection lies within. Before the inner treasure can be claimed, the way must be prepared to receive it. A thief is not given the jewels. He may steal them, but he will lose what he takes that is not rightfully his. The inner jewels become visible when a strong moral character has been established as well as a genuine respect and use of Mind. A seeker must be convinced of his natural perfection and that spirit can manifest in the tangible affairs of daily life. To consciously change life, change yourself. Consciousness expands when there is a deep love for God, truth and the ability to approach the subject of spiritual evolution scientifically. By following a proven procedure, success follows.

Individual Spirit is gravitationally trapped light. The spirit will release itself in every aspect and fulfill the purpose of life when the mind is open to relearning truth. Learn and apply the laws of Infinite Mind and you will be richly repaid on all levels. Application allows the spirit to rise. Conscious connectedness is actually a scientific process of revelation and healing. It is ongoing. You become humanly what you are spiritually. The mind thinking correctly becomes spiritualized and is filled with Light. A true seeker is an artist of the highest degree, one who is constantly at work transforming the matter of his own being.

Transformation occurs as a result of studying and applying the suggestions of the great prophets and teachers, mystics and healers whose lives have been inspiring examples of conscious choice and application of Universal Law. Strength of character is required in the quest for enlightenment. As mentioned earlier, there are rare exceptions. Enlightenment is a series of revelations, which bring forth inner beauty and wisdom that is enhanced by unconditional love. You become a god-like being. With attunement to The Great Spirit, the Impersonal becomes personal. A well-developed character creates a happy person. When you are sincerely interested in improving consciousness, the ability to reflect the attributes of God increases.

BE: Embracing the Mystery

A path is a personal choice from one point to another. Any path begins with relative ease and becomes progressively more difficult as souls ascend the Tree of Life. Ascension is similar to a ladder. Each rung presents physical, emotional, mental and soul issues to be mastered. The ascent is the result of empowerment through love for self, God and all life. Nothing worth attaining comes to us without a wholehearted commitment. Effort, perseverance, patience, devotion and a passion to be whole are necessary character aspects that will directly lead to your goal. Attitude, integrity and belief in your inner worth will awaken every level of your being, revealing the hidden and the good. Illumination is earned.

There is no such thing as instant mastery of self and matter. It may appear as if some individuals are gifted and have mastery without effort. These souls have done their homework in previous life experiences. They have gained knowledge of the Sacred Wisdom Science discovering all the subtle currents that flow within and without. By entering into the inner realm of mind and spirit, they aligned themselves with the vastness and power of the higher worlds of thought.

To the extent to which love and wisdom and mental science is mastered, you dwell in truth. Truth actually has two sides: pure and impure, light and dark and true knowledge must embrace both. Duality continues to exist as you move forward. It continues to the Summit. There are definite patterns leading to perfection and they are to be followed. It is a science of living. Even with an illustrious past soul history, a wise one gently awakens into his or her mastery for the safety of the nervous system and eventual role in society. In some cases, it may appear as if a good soul is drinking from a bitter cup while in a physical body. The appearance of a bitter cup is temporary and veils the reason behind the experience.

Advanced souls incarnate in chaotic periods of world history because of their great love for the downtrodden. They arrive during times of utmost disorder anchoring the laws of thought into the visible universe. Souls who already are clear transparencies of God assist through the power of heightened energy. The high beings frequently serve secretly and silently, anchoring light into the Earth's aura and vibration. The illumined ones are perfect examples of St. Paul's words, "It is no longer I that lives but Christ that lives in me." It is the Christ Principle that lives within.

I have observed that self-condemnation and personal distrust is the worst mental offender against healing and truth. The belief of unworthiness prevents an individual from achieving an intimacy with the Divine. It works against love to indulge in thinking that is self-destructive. Guilt makes the individual feel unworthy. Understanding truth principles and our potential for conscious oneness with God opens the door to a dramatic change in self-evaluation. It becomes obvious that wrongdoing would not happen if a personality were not ignorant of his/her true nature. Education regarding the inner, eternal identity changes everything.

Remember, God does not condemn. Only personalities that are unenlightened condemn. God is love. God is not conscious of evil. Evil is a false state of mind. The personality will need understanding of the infinite and all-embracing nature of God. Knowledge of what constitutes intimacy with the Divine must be introduced and acknowledged within personal consciousness to be able to return to the Source of joy and peace. When an individual is reconciled with the inner Divine Nature, understanding releases the mind and soul and healing begins. We can only experience what we believe and act upon.

How can a soul live in peace and certainty, joy and love if a damaged sense of self rules the consciousness? It is a form of malpractice. Fear is usually the companion as well as doubt because division is the belief that creates and controls experience. Knowledge, realization and acceptance of the inner Teacher are the healer.

The idea of our intrinsic value as goodness is beautifully illustrated in the experience of a new acquaintance who felt suicidal. In spite of being physically attractive, intelligent and blessed with many friends, she firmly believed herself to be unworthy. Deep within she felt remorse over her character, the habits which controlled her life. Depressed and feeling worthless, she was contemplating ending her life. When we met, I gave her an intuitive message, which offered her disheartened personality renewed hope. The emphasis was on her inner identity as goodness temporarily using a physical form.

The distraught woman was a victim of amnesia like everyone else who has failed to establish a conscious and enduring connection with God. I reminded her as to what constitutes real identity and how, by holding on to that belief, behavior is transformed. Exposing an erroneous belief system, she was able to dramatically change her life. Hope, truth and acceptance awakened her soul. The young woman made a decision to claim her inner spark, an emanation of the Great Flame. A light switch had been turned on. As quickly as understanding is aroused, transformation begins.

Our culture is not a happy one. Souls are disconnected from their Source. Happiness is hidden under the veil of spiritual knowledge. It is a matter of feeling connectedness. Ignorance, greed, growing populations and diminishing resources lead to annihilation. People must awaken to the inner intelligence, beauty and love. Energy must be changed from a material-based philosophy to one where knowledge of who we are and where we need to be going is self-evident. To be happy, knowledge of the spirit, mind and body, the relationship of the spirit to the body, and the relationship of the body to the spirit are necessary. Knowing what we desire and how to attain it, what to pursue and what to renounce requires intense study. Humanity is in dire need of a true insight into human nature and our relationship to the whole of creation. What we create, we are. To change the world, we must change the mind. We must deeply care to do this.

We are all spirit in form regardless of appearance. If God is Spirit and is good, it follows that an individualized spirit is also good. To tell anyone that he is not good is only seeing a part and not the whole. The personality may need maturity and healing, but the spirit providing life is good. There are no chosen or elect people. We are recognized by what is in our consciousness, the developed light energy. If people could comprehend on a conscious level the reality of the threefold self: body, mind and spirit, character would reflect kindness towards themselves and others. Harsh judgments would diminish and a genuine caring interaction would be the norm.

Wisdom has been given to evolving humankind since ancient times. The principles and laws of the universe must be applied. When Jesus said, "I am the way, the truth, and the life," He was identifying with the path, the way to regain freedom from spiritual ignorance, suffering, lack and limitation. He walked on the path and he was the path. And those who follow the example of an illumined being also become the path. In this way, identification is love in action, a Christ teaching. When we love, we are a whole being. We discover our own divine nature. It is through the revelation of knowing the love of God that we are able to truly love ourselves. When we understand the science of thought and allow the Spirit to love us, it is easier to love others.

It serves a higher purpose to fully integrate the holy teachings, which lead to inner and lasting peace. Jesus achieved the point in consciousness where he could say with integrity and confidence: "My Father and I are one." He had evolved his consciousness where his humanity and spirituality were in perfect harmony and he thoroughly identified with the One Source.

As mankind spiritually evolves, a universal teaching of Love and Light will arise and all the purity and goodness of each great spiritual teaching will be incorporated as one unitive action, a new culture, where humans will recognize and live the sacredness and oneness of all life. Awakened humanity will finally understand who he is and his role in the creative plan. The burden of feeling separated from our Spiritual Parent will be removed. It is a self-inflicted illusion that creates division. God never leaves us; we leave God. Any separation that is felt is caused and fed through spiritual ignorance. By changing thinking and accepting the eternal nature, we personally experience the assurance that God is here right now and has never left us.

The chaotic collective world energy teeters on the edge of the precipice. Individuals who study life and the nature of the laws of thought and how they impact life remain, relatively speaking, untouched. Through a higher understanding, they remain centered. An invisible protective energy shields them from the onslaught of darkness. The Divine provides ample evidence of its Power and Holy Presence. Being fooled by collective mesmerism ceases. Aliveness flows, encouraging others to awaken as well.

Our convictions determine what happens to us. When a soul arrives in the Invisible World, it will have to face the reality of its character regardless of the path it has taken. Practice self-examination and review your progress periodically. Look at each new day as an opportunity for spiritual growth. Has the mind behaved like a monkey or is it controlled? If you are serious about being whole and free from suffering, love the idea of reorienting the mind and desires toward the goodness within. Everything that happens leaves a trace. Humanity is responsible for the consequences of wrongful thinking. It is up to us to stop being subjected to blind forces.

We are watched by an Invisible Cosmic Intelligence, which automatically records whatever has happened in the history of the universe. This record is called the Akashic Record. The record contains information about every created form. Any event that takes place reflects and leaves traces on all the objects in its vicinity. Sensitive souls know intuitively the truth about people, places, things and events. The traces can never be wiped out, whether they are major or minor events. Reflect back on personal and world events and understand that the vibrations still exist and always will. Everything that occurs in the environment leaves an imprint, an image, a photograph, which is like a negative.

Advancement is limited if you rely solely on personal strength and abilities. Take charge of your own character and develop luminous, pure and generous thoughts and you will receive the blessings of the Law of Affinity. Whenever you assert spiritual strength, it is realized that something greater is at work in consciousness. In embracing the Divine, the mind and soul is expanded and will naturally help elevate others. Merits remain with the soul. Merit and virtue accrued through effort relieve the suffering and spiritual ignorance of those who seek the Light. Virtue is harmony. It brings a true happiness.

Understand the malaise felt around the world. The feeling can be changed and further destruction stopped. Spirit is the secret. It will lead us into the Light, helping not only humanity, but also Earth and her life. The majority would like to experience a world of peace, hearts filled with love and gladness, and an Earth where the air and water are clean and the environment healthy. Through changing perception of self and cleansing the inner environment of selfishness and arrogance, energy can be used for the good of all. We transform ourselves and our culture. Redefine life both personally and impersonally. Believe in yourself; be a mover of energy. Since the material world is nothing more than a construction of the consciousness, why not assist and be a master builder?

The goal is to be directly programmed, guided and protected by God's Intelligence, the spiritual part of us that never dies. When this process becomes active, something quite amazing occurs. The physical body gradually escapes from the bondage of biochemical slavery within a three-dimensional consciousness. Because character is refined and ready, you can consciously move back and forth between the original blueprint of your eternal higher Self and the pattern of the human form. You will claim the priceless treasure that was lost long ago. A heightened awareness and the subsequent regeneration and expansiveness of love will gently move you into frontiers not yet explored. As you attain a higher integrity and allow unconditional love to fill you with vibrations of God's power, your light will be a beacon to others. The final result is freedom from mental, emotional and physical pollution, and the joy of interacting as a soul who is loved and in love with the Living Light.

Chapter Twenty-Two
Love Energy

A seeker of truth will understand Divine Love when there are no longer contradictions in his life. There is no separation or interruption in consciousness; it simply expands as a result of thought and takes charge of life. The way of love is morality, sacrifice and challenges, which we pass through willingly. Challenges test and strengthen our perseverance and faith. Fear no longer exists when we allow Divine Love to rule. Although circumstances can be outrageous, we trust that Spirit knows best. A love of truth increases oneness and harmony in both the seen and unseen. The current of Love purifies, uplifts, heals and inspires. Spiritual love does not betray; it simply Is. As wisdom expands, peace is stabilized. The spark can only be a flame by fanning the fire of devotion. Genuine love is an outpouring freely given without thought of reward. We live for a lofty dream that is the measure of a God-realized life. Love is realization.

The Divine manifests when we know with a certainty that the universe is within. Everything operates through us as a result of the infinite Creative Mind. The ideal is that we learn at an early age of a spiritual power that is available and how to access our good. Those who understand this as their truth are in the minority. The few must become the many. Thoughts create cause. They bring results both good and bad. Understanding the purpose of creation and living our understanding, we are able to evolve into conductors of light, warmth, a transmitter of a higher energy, used for the good of all. Love is the name of the energy.

Everything can be explained as energy. You are a conduit. When you are open to the powers of the higher Nature, a shift occurs. All is energy and it is fluid. Every person and every thing is linked together. The energy I speak of is Spirit. We are all one. Earlier, I mentioned a hierarchy of energy existing both in the visible and invisible worlds. In truth, regardless of the intelligence or form, the same Energy gives all creative expression its life. It is a real power and all-pervading substance. Use it to energize and verbalize your ideal daily.

True happiness is experienced when personal energy is purified. Purification brings more Light into the aura. The more you have, the greater your evolution. The Presence, Power and Wisdom are felt and you actively participate in the Cosmos. The mind is free of doubt and fear and knows that you are an integral part of the Whole. Although you live in a physical body, you learn to understand how everything is done unto you according to belief. It is possible to create freedom as well as awareness that all space is inhabited, one world, one family, and a living part of God. God becomes visible as Light through belief and living truth. The All-embracing Oneness is experienced in transcendent personal moments because the sacred is awakened.

It is your higher Self who blesses you with an awakened inner sight. Spiritual vision is the favored organ of divine perception. The physical world is real and illusory because it is held in mind. The illusion of separation exists and endures because of man's lack of spiritual knowledge and misplaced desires. As the soul awakens to its own divinity and the higher vibratory worlds, it begins to experience freedom from the idea of pain, division and evil. The soul slowly detaches itself from the base desires, ignorance and bondage of the human condition. The more the soul loves the Light, the more personal energy changes. When identification is with the higher light body, true joy manifests.

Scattered throughout history and the present world are people who have extraordinary abilities. This does not mean that they are necessarily illumined or completely whole. They are examples of endless possibilities that all souls can attain. There are always some students who only seek development of occult powers as a means of control. While other seekers are born with supernatural gifts as a result of the soul's previous spiritual endeavors. Powers have always existed and will continue to manifest more noticeably as Earth and individual intelligence gradually becomes spiritually energized.

When spiritual vision is awakened, guard against psychic excitation when confronted with phenomena. Humans may psychically witness phenomena from the various levels of the lower worlds and the vibrations of fallen energies. There are some unfortunate humans whose consciousness holds them to the chaotic realms of the lowest astral plane. To experience darkness is to be challenged on every level. There are also psychically aware people who are able to see neutral extraterrestrial appearances.

In direct contrast, healing assistance and guidance may come from either the higher astral planes or the causal mental plane. The Language of Light, the sublime visions of the diamond brilliancy of Spirit pulsating and offering symbols, beatific visions and pure teachings emanate from the highest celestial realms. The Holy Spirit provides the light transmissions, the codes to those who have pure intent and have prepared themselves.

This is a simplistic explanation. For now, it is enough to comprehend that there are endless levels of consciousness and orders of higher intelligence, whether they be seen or unseen. What is most important is to understand that the consciousness, ideal and intent of an individual attracts the knowledge or assistance needed.

For a human to perceive energy from any plane, the subtle senses for that particular plane must be developed. In other words, besides the physical senses, we have latent subtle senses for the emotional, mental and higher celestial vibratory planes. It is through our love for beauty, truth and longing to regain the divine image that these subtle senses are quickened.

It is best not to become attached to miraculous abilities. Powers do not belong to the lower nature. Powers are to be used to benefit life. They serve a definite purpose as they perfectly demonstrate a reality that is true, harmonious and scientific. Powers are real and range from a simple manifestation in correcting matter to a stunning, indescribable appearance of brilliancy and magnificence that lifts the soul into the realm of the transcendent. The goal is to experience Divine Light and Divine Power from within as well as without. When the Creator is deeply loved and purity reigns in the heart, the blessing of intimacy is experienced in God and with the celestial beings.

In reading and hearing of sacred moments, you receive a shining glimpse as to what is waiting for souls who love the Supreme Light. Words fail when we attempt to describe something so poetically overwhelming and otherworldly. Sublime revelation is experienced as vibrational energy that transcends time and non-time. It is humbling to have personal proof of a loftier intimacy and ever-present holiness.

The following personal experiences are stunning in their scope, clearly demonstrating moments of connectedness where time and space did not exist. Keep in mind that in the higher spheres, matter is so subtle that it is instantly obedient to the commands of thought, imagination and will. Beings in the finer dimensions can do what they like with it. This fact also holds true for humans whose souls have established the Kingdom of Light within them.

One of my sons and I decided to unite our spiritual intention, an ideal that we both fully believed in. We had discussed the possibility and knew within our hearts that what we desired was harmonious with the path of spirit evolution. To live fully in the magical presence of the Divine, we had reached an agreement regarding intention. One late afternoon, we decided to meditate together. As the sunset completed its cycle, the room darkened and the peace that comes with stillness and is experienced in communion with the Cosmic Radiance settled in. Suddenly, we witnessed an immense transcendent purple Light as glorious vibrating energy.

It is unusual for two people to experience a superconscious experience simultaneously. In gratitude, we continued with our meditation. Something very extraordinary occurred. We experienced a state of being where only love and light existed. The feeling of reverence that enveloped us swept away the illusion of division and materiality and brought forth the splendor and the beatific majesty of a higher life. Together, we witnessed great beings of wondrous light who lovingly gave approval to our mutual goal. We were conscious and alert.

In vision, the walls in the living room dissolved. The earthly surroundings became invisible and the Invisible Celestial became our conscious reality. We were lifted in consciousness to another dimension. We stood in the center of an arena. Surrounding us were hundreds of radiant beings who had come to support our intention. The startling scene manifested as dazzling white Light. The individual intelligent forms looked like living white flames. They were pure energy, God's holy representatives. We experienced a mystical blissful pulse projecting from a vibratory dimension that far transcended the lower dimensional worlds of matter. The gift of wonder and overwhelming love of the sacred emanating from the heavenly visitors linked our hearts in such a way that we understood our part in the Whole. Beauty came to us as a garment of truth.

Transcendent glimpses of the Divine belong to the Universal mystical tradition. The poetry of life lasted for several minutes, which actually felt like an eternity, as the glorious beings confirmed the rightness of our spiritual quest. We were mightily blessed. The limitless love and splendor felt like a great sea of power. When individual will is in harmony with Divine Love and Divine Wisdom, it is as solid as a pure diamond. We were not alone in our ideal nor will we ever be. Neither are you. The ultimate kindness is God's magnificent generosity and blessings bestowed upon His children. No one else can prove God's existence for us. It is perfection revealed. To be graced with celestial visions is to witness with the higher causal part of the mind. This is called the nous. Noble Mind, God's Intelligence, is an intermediary between heaven and earth. It is a dimension beyond space-time. The nous is the realm of creative action, the Holy Spirit.

Angels and other forms of higher intelligent beings vibrating as evolved consciousness willingly offer love and assistance to souls who believe and persistently put forth effort. To receive their beneficence is a breathtaking experience lifting the beholder to a loftier realm of lightness and supremacy. Many worlds interface one another. Vibration determines the visibility, tangibility and the potential of direct spiritual experience. Conscious contacts with the higher dimensional worlds, realms that transcend the astral and lower mental planes, manifest when hearts and minds are pure and open to infinite possibilities and the truth of being.

Angels are from the highest astral plane and are very close to humans. In future time, humans will be similar to the angels who live to serve God. The topic of Angels is usually a favorite subject on the lecture circuit. There is always a gentle soul in the audience who is willing to share a personal angel encounter. A typical example of helpfulness was the story of an aged woman who was walking across an ice-laced street. She was late for mass and in her rush fell. Everyone was already in the church and the service had started. All of a sudden, the woman felt strong arms behind her gently lifting her frail body upright. She turned around to thank the person. No one was there.

The grateful woman shared her angel experience after the service bringing hope and inspiration to those who stayed to listen. Experiences of this nature commonly occur all over the world. Although it was not a human who lifted the woman off the ice, we, too, in the physical body can act as angels. In essence, we are made of the same cosmic substance, which is Light. By increasing the power of our current, we can generate the same goodness and luminosity.

The magic of celestial assistance occurs in the more mundane experiences of material life as well. The Invisible ones can easily manipulate inanimate objects and so can we if we realize our word is law. The invisible field of creativity is plastic and receptive. Heightened consciousness knows that the slightest thought makes an impression in the subjective part of the mind. Mind creates for us whatever we believe. Spirit energy is fully capable of transforming anything. The following story is a good example of humor from a celestial point of view.

The dining room ceiling fixture in our home needed a new pull chain. A neighbor offered to fix it, assuring me that it would be a simple task. The neighbor took the fixture apart without marking the wires for future reconnection. Realizing he had made a serious mistake, he said he would return the next day with a friend who claimed to have more expertise in this area. As soon as the friend began to work with the fixture, sparks began to fly and there was an explosion. The electricity went out in half of our home. The two men decided to dismantle the circuit breaker box. They then went to a hardware store to purchase new parts. When they returned and placed the new part in the electrical box, it failed to work.

In the meantime, it was becoming cold and the available light diminishing. I could hear the two frustrated men whispering. It was obvious that they were embarrassed and at a loss as to what the next step should be. Originally, all that was required was a chain replacement. Instead, our home was now without light or heat and the fixture was still not repaired. The men decided to contact an electrician friend. Since the electrician could not come for at least an hour, the two stymied men decided to go out and get something to eat.

Physically alone in the darkened living room and feeling the cold, I walked over to the fuse box and talked to it. There is a higher law that comes into action when we understand and use it. Beliefs are energy. Energy moves when mind directs it. The "word" is the activity of our spirit speaking. The One Mind is our own mind and it has creative power. When we believe, it creates or provides whatever is given to it. In speaking to the electrical unit, I was in essence talking to the intelligence of the subtle energy field and calling for higher dimensional assistance. Mind cannot act unless intelligence sets it in motion. The last thing desired was to spend a night in a cold house without electricity. We must have an overwhelming confidence in our prayer request. The furnace and lights suddenly came on. It is done unto all of us, as we believe.

Fifteen minutes later, the men arrived at the door walking into a warm and brightly lit home. What happened next was worth all the nonsense and delay experienced. They were stunned beyond belief and said it was impossible. Still shaking their heads in fear, the electrician arrived. The electrician said it was impossible for the lights and furnace to be working. The three men kept repeating, "You must have ghosts in your house." They were obviously shaken.

The volunteers cleaned up the mess and the electrician replaced the broken chain. Man breaks things; Spirit breaks all records. It is a delight to personally experience the practical side of subtle love energy. Invisible helpers know that they are welcome in our home. All the rooms and belongings are at their disposal. Divine love is the materialization of the Creator's Light in the physical world. We are here to make the Earth vibrate in harmony with heaven, to bring perfection visibly on Earth.

My first book was written on a typewriter. Today, we have the convenience and ease of a computer. Computers, being material objects, present challenges as well. Recently while typing one of the chapters, an important letter on the keyboard would not work correctly. To make it worse, I could not type in lower case letters and part of the keyboard refused to function. The left button when touched would delete everything on the page. When I would highlight one document in my manuscript folder, all documents would be highlighted. To my horror, the files automatically scrolled fast-forward and not one of the documents could be opened. The system tool restore function would not work. In the computer's Word program, I could not type in a file name. The Word program was totally disassembled, incorrect. The manufacturer's technician could not offer any help.

Since technical assistance could not correct the problem, I called on Creative Mind. Placing my hands over the computer I demanded that everything be corrected. In less than a minute, all functions were normal. I mentioned the experience to my daughter on the east coast. Her reply was interesting. She said. "My computer at work experienced problems similar to yours and the computer technicians had a hard time fixing it. It took numerous tries over several weeks to get it fixed. It would work and then revert back to the old ways. It was a failure in the software." In my situation, real Power permanently fixed the computer.

Religions and philosophies speak of a subtle and universal force, etheric in nature, active everywhere. The high Initiates attract it and concentrate and project it. Moses used it dramatically and is only one of many examples. The Brahmins call this force Akasa, it was called the fire element by the Magi of Chaldea, and the great magic agent by the Kabbalists of the Middle Ages. Many Christians call subtle power the Holy Spirit. This phenomenon is governed by changeless laws, which are always proportioned to the intellectual, moral and magnetic strength of the user. The Force also works for good when invisible friends and trusting human beings consciously connect and use the White Light selflessly. According to the teachings of ancient masters, the Supreme Spirit is Love. As our love for our spiritual Source expands, virtues and abilities are given to us.

All actions are an interchange between energies, regardless of form, because whoever gives love is in truth giving his love to God. Whether our need to be filled is for practical and convenience purposes, inspirational guidance, protection or healing, love acts when we realize all creation and Spirit are one. This state of mind becomes a living reality for the sincere, the faithful, and the lover of truth and knowledge. To know in confidence that we are all in Spirit and that Spirit as Mind is always creating for us as we think, is liberating. One day each soul will be able to say with conviction the words of a Christ: "I live in God and God lives in me." To behold a Christ, a Buddha or the Limitless Light, we must identify with the Christ Mind, the Buddha Nature and the reality of our own evolving individual Light.

As personal love energy is understood and expands, the soul's purpose is fulfilled. The following quote from Master Omraam Mikhael Aivanhov perfectly expresses the message of this chapter. "We may have penetrated a mystery, but this does not mean we understand it. Only when we succeed in manifesting what we claim to have understood, do we truly understand."

Chapter Twenty-Three
The Emptying

Everything that takes place in the world reflects what takes place in a human being. Humanity is in need of a change. The laws are the same whether they are within or without. Good change will come when we ask for Light. Returning of Light brings knowledge, love and freedom. To receive uncontaminated truth, souls must reach higher. True knowledge is received through Spirit and Law and an active intuition where the indwelling Presence knows itself. Duality and the sense of division lessen when the soul dares to think in universal terms.

Our greatest enemy is the lower nature. Weakness keeps us from our higher Nature. Disorder and duality thrive in the physical world. Evolving consciousness is constantly being challenged. We must walk boldly to develop strength and expansion of the inner light. We need to understand the false self, the personality. Develop peace within and you will gain the needed strength for the struggle without. The soul's fire is gradually rekindled through effort. If you do choose to seek outside of the intimacy of prayer and meditation for answers, make certain that the contact, visible or invisible, has attained stability in mind and heart and is not mesmerized by a duality consciousness. The last thing desired is to become involved in someone else's shadow perceptive.

It is time to stop indulging in false dreams. Perceptions can play tricks in the mind. Wisdom is to search inside the depths of your own sacred, secret Self. Working with a spiritual ideal will help you. It determines the way life is lived. Select an ideal from the depths of your soul that you would like to manifest as reality. Energize it daily through choices and the words you speak. Affirmations vitalize faith. With a bounding confidence, state your ideal as a desire already realized. Think and speak with confidence and understanding, knowing that the subjective part of the mind will act on it.

Be expectant. Living in a limited body is specifically for the purpose

The Emptying

of discovering and manifesting a higher or superconscious existence within the finite. You have the power to do this.

Everyone has a mountaintop; it is the Causal Mind, God's Intelligence. We reach the mountaintop as a result of faith, discipline and shifting our energies to meet the needs of the moment, meditations, focused thoughts and prayers. Imagine that you are sure-footed. As the splendor of the mountaintop reveals itself, build your life upon its wonders. Besides using imagination, lock in the visualization and keep the image of victory in the front of the mind. If this is not done, it will fade and the knowledge that arrives with freedom will take longer than needed. A higher focus must be consistent as well as intense or it will lose its life energy. All aspects of the mind must work together as a team.

Right identification, focusing on your inner wise being and learning the correct way of using the creative part of Mind, will lead you into the mysteries and the knowledge of the universes. God comes alive as you return to Wholeness and enter into the Great Work. A pure heart and a respect and love for life are required. Life is meant to be an adventure and fully lived. The power and responsibility to put the inner world in order is yours. The spirit energy is already a part of your system. Using God power for good is the key in transforming thought and attracting more of the Celestial Light into your force fields. The ancients said that the journey is a long one, perhaps a million years. It is not as if you are only beginning the journey; the past has simply been forgotten.

I will not tell you everything I know, but I can share what has worked successfully and then it is up to you to evaluate what is offered and take action. The advantages of the spiritual life far exceed the human imagination. Spiritual understanding is a belief in goodness. This is why it is of the utmost importance that a seeker learns to look behind the appearance. Suffering occurs when you are not in both conscious and subjective communication with the affirmative side of the universe. Spiritual ignorance influences humanity and the effects are far from pleasant. Today, the majority does not understand or live unconditional love.

In the far distant future, the collectivity will be enlightened. People will understand and live the truth of the inner being and create harmony with purpose and confidence. This will not happen all at once. Evolution manifests over a long period of time and change. It works through man's imagination and will.

Change happens in a few at first and gradually expands to embrace the whole. The same pattern will occur as humanity evolves and is prepared to receive what could be best described as the Supramind. As souls are ready and prepared, the superconscious state, another term for God's Intelligence, will be more evident and function as a normal part of man. This means that the essence, your personal portion of God Intelligence, expands. The Divine does not operate through impurity and corruption. Analyzing the current cycle of history, it appears as if the majority no longer believes in the beauty of life. More souls must respond and choose a path, which leads to the sunlight of truth, their own glorious mountaintop. The world is as we dream it.

What can be done now to transform consciousness and bring in the new is to empty the mind and heart of that which does not work. Begin by eliminating the thorns and poisons that disintegrate wholeness and freedom. Do not dwell in the past. Eradicate hate and pride. Avoid all appearances of evil. Remove all fear and situations that tempt. Learn to control thoughts, words and actions. Forgive and forget. Greed must stop. Why persist in anger, hatred and fighting? If not healed, the energy will follow you after physical death.

Stop playing the blame game. Everything an individual does arises from feelings and thought. When the mind and body are undisciplined, nothing in life can be accomplished. To access that power and succeed in life, learn self-control. Develop concentration and a peaceful attitude. Pay attention. Think before you speak or act. As a result of new choices, you avoid the risk of losing equilibrium causing a strain upon the soul. Understand the importance of your chosen ideal and a grander energy is generated. Your faith will grow through knowledge and experience. For some of you, the thought of making so many changes will be overwhelming. Take one step at a time.

Exaggerated enthusiasm may cause you to become ensnared in the glamour of visions, lucid dreams, symbols or the kundalini energy rising up the spine. The purpose of phenomena needs to be understood. Phenomena in its first appearances are a wake-up call from the inner Self to the personality attempting to arouse it from the lower nature. There are people all over the world experiencing the subtle dimensions and receiving assistance from invisible beings, but this does not mean they are enlightened. Experiencing fourth dimensional phenomena or higher are memory and teaching tools given to help awaken the soul and personality to the spirit identity.

Glimpses of the Divine are not intended as lovely interludes in a hectic life. They are messages reminding the evolving soul that it is caught in duality and must evolve into a higher awareness. Pay attention. Observation is a matter of training. What must be understood is that the human personality is the experiencer and usually does not yet realize the great truth that from a celestial perspective there is no division, no duality, only the false human perception of separation. As an example, the beauty and wonder of the celestial realms of White Light are experienced as glimpses into the perfection and harmony existing in the higher worlds of creation. They serve to expand the mind's view of a beauty, truth and love that transcend mortal consciousness. Miracles and Invisible assistance are reminders of the connectiveness and power of personal mind to the Impersonal Mind and the fact that we do not walk alone.

When the soul is prepared and willing to go beyond the psychic glamour and even the mystical experiences, it will suddenly awaken from the imaginary character called the lesser self. In some cases, the seeker is so immersed in the phenomena that he cannot move past it. If truth is actively sought through Divine Love and not phenomena, the goal of God Realization is reached more quickly. Through the ages, we continually change chemical bodies and personalities. The goal is not to solely identify with the form, the temporary self. The ideal is to penetrate the eternal reality and grasp the truth that we are already what we seek and eternity is ours. We have to step away from self-imposed limitation. The self returns to the Self. We are consciously enlightened when we are spiritually aware in every moment.

From the highest perspective of Mind, conscious enlightenment occurs when the personality makes a deliberate choice through intention to turn the shadow world into the reality of Light. You step out of the darkness of ignorance into the revelations of the Sun. The psychic and mystical experiences occur to shake the soul out of its slumber. The goal is to be awake, no longer deluded or feeling separated from God. Once division no longer exists, it is your responsibility to apply the truth about the indwelling Presence. What is grasped at last is the true nature of being. The sense of imprisonment will leave and in its stead rests joy and freedom.

The closer you are to a full enlightenment, the less duality rears its ugly head. The clutter and confusion is observed with a fresh and unconditional love and knowingness. Enlightenment feels like a satisfying form of emptiness. Yet, this emptiness embraces the invisible immensity of the Fullness; it also views the surrounding environment. Listen and feel and know as your truth that the inner essence of you is already an integral part of the Supreme Reality. Wakefulness is truth, a fact, and not a temporary experience; it is ongoing. The more active the higher part of the mind, the more fully the Light of God leads you to a state free from the clutter of delusion.

A spiritual transformation is possible. To accelerate spiritual evolution, exercise greater knowledge and effort. Until you are psychologically ready to be fully alive and knowingly accept consciousness awakening to Itself, it is wise to help the process along through serious study. Knowledge leads to wisdom. Hand in hand with knowledge is discernment. Discernment is one of the most important virtues required by a soul who has chosen spiritual evolution. I cannot emphasize this fact enough. Many of us learn discernment the hard way. An unsuspecting seeker can fall into the hands of people with ill intent if this important virtue is lacking.

As a young adult, I learned the lesson the hard way. A man came into my life posing as a mystic and teacher of truth. I believed him. As a result of naivety and lack of discernment, serious suffering occurred. It never entered my trusting heart that he was a manipulative actor with negative intentions.

The higher spiritual teachings encourage us to look past the physical appearance and to trust, love and see only the good in all that we perceive. The higher perspective cannot be successfully practiced if discernment is lacking. To be discerning can be a lifesaver. The innocent and uninformed are open to abuse. When a seeker is not mature in the discernment area, it is easy to become involved with a black magician. Black magicians promote untruths, are manipulative and selfish, and their intent is driven by the lower nature and astral desires.

A simple description of a physical black magician is one who may have achieved psychic powers and is using them selfishly. Or, he could simply be a pretender. A deceiver usually has extensive book knowledge and self-interest is the motivator. Pleasure is gained by controlling other souls. If you become caught in the web of falsity, horrific problems may arise such as losing physical and mental health and even safety.

Devastation, trickery and feeling deeply wounded were the outcome of my encounter. Looking back, it is difficult to believe that I could have been so gullible. Innocence does not entertain the thought nor understand that another person would choose to manipulate truth for a selfish purpose. When we are mesmerized and trusting and obviously not exercising common sense, negative situations can easily occur. What happened to me was an initiation into the influence and power of a shadow world of soulless humans without hearts who are motivated by self-aggrandizement. If discernment and focused thinking had been strong, the wounds and sorrow would not have been life threatening or so devastating.

There are few accidents and no excuses. What I thought was a blessing was a misplaced trust which created a harsh and lengthy learning experience. When my mind was finally open to the falsity of his persuasive character and manipulative intent, the veil lifted and denial stopped. It was an experience that clearly demonstrated the glamour of false teachers and hidden intentions. It is altogether too common to be enamored with the charm and power of someone who appears to have a greater "inside" connection to the Invisible worlds. Be on guard.

To have any degree of power and remain pure in heart and behavior is a challenge few can handle. There must first be a firm foundation, a steady conviction and a high degree of character refinement attained to escape temptation. Unkindness, deceit and deliberate manipulation of another soul to satisfy uncontrolled desires are unthinkable. The fact is, deception on many levels happens to thousands of trusting and innocent seekers. Always ask the Divine for truth, be vigilant and look for integrity in another, not allowing anyone to mislead you. Examine the life and accomplishments of the one who claims to be a spiritual master. Be wary of glamorous appearances. They may fool you.

Life externalizes at the level of thought. As your mind and heart open to infinite possibilities, you can innocently make enemies. As energy and habits change, friends and family may not like the new you. They may become upset. If possible, try not to preach or abandon them. Being an example is the best teacher. Unexpected things do happen when you change. If this occurs, do your best to understand and love those who are temporarily criticizing your transformation. Opposing forces often help achieve liberation. It is to be hoped that one day, friends and loved ones will understand how you have been blessed and they, too, will seek to break away from limitation and division. Real love must be allowed to flow freely.

Many teachers, gurus and saints warn their students not to become involved with the gifts and powers of spirit. Fear for the student's safety may be influencing the admonitions. The leaders could also have a personal memory of an experience where they became entrapped by the gifts of the Spirit. Listen to the whispering of your heart and not the lower nature. It is the Voice of God. It will hold you in safekeeping. Develop pure intent, allow the intuitive part of the mind to guide and be of service to others.

When intent is pure and discernment strong, the chances of falling victim to self-aggrandizement are less likely to happen. If an inflated ego is in charge, powers are misused. In some cases, people have earned the powers in past incarnations and the powers remain in the present personality. If the current human personality is weak and has not acquired the strength of character to rightly handle psychic and spiritual powers, misuse and self-interest may tragically occur.

Spiritual gifts are inspiring and give hope, but they also are a means to lead us to a deeper spiritual process. Do not fear gifts or shun them. They are to be understood for what they are. Spiritual gifts will work towards Truth Realization if you understand that they are a process that encourages the removal of division within self, others and God. The powers are independent of the personality; they are of Spirit. There is no cause to fear.

It is done unto us, as we believe. The God Nature is the true teacher, the White Light that will guide the soul homeward. The process of awakening is to reclaim spiritual identity and dissolve all inner conflict. You do not have to be an extraordinary person to spiritually evolve; it happens to anyone, anywhere. What occurs is that you finally see with clarity. Learn to look through the appearance and realize that you are a part of God and all life. The pieces of the puzzle finally come together and inner peace returns.

The most important subject to study in life is the wise inner nature. As you begin to analyze the workings of the mind, you become aware of where thought and feeling as well as certain actions have not been productive. The next step is to retrain the personality. The mind is the composer of an inner music. The goal is to make the music grow more harmonious. The soul is either elevated or damaged by the power of thought and the words that come out of the mouth.

In helping others, learn not to be attached to people, places and things. It is the bondage of attachment which divides the mind and heart and causes separation from the sacred. Life is very much like water. Some people cannot swim and may drown. Another swims beautifully and with ease reaches the other shore. While the few, learn to walk on water. Mistakes manifest as a result of spiritual ignorance. Now you know how to stop ignorance from impacting your life.

Reasoning and the judging faculty create opinions. Opinions clash when two people of different stages of spiritual evolution express themselves. Changing points of view are the outcome of the evolution of a soul. Every evolutionary step taken changes perspective. As the old patterns fall apart and clear the way for a heightened energy, there may be a friend who cannot resist judging your progress. A soul has its own principles best suited for its level of consciousness. It is a waste of energy to argue spiritual topics with anyone. The spiritual evolution of one differs from that of the other. If a friend or relative is always complaining about everything and everyone, perhaps they need a new path.

Human beings are brothers and sisters by way of the divine life, which flows in them. Each lives the divine life according to understanding and awareness. Think about these things and apply them as well to your own inner knowledge. At every step in soul evolution, belief changes until you arrive at a sublime belief, which mere words cannot explain.

The secret of soul evolution is to rid self of everything that impedes growth. Rather than function from a mundane mental attitude, the goal is to achieve a super mental attitude. Create an atmosphere of thinking that works for you. To overcome a downward pull into a lesser consciousness, seek a higher wisdom and ask only for truth. Self-aggrandizement is not an issue because intent is pure. The inner gifts received are to be used for the good of all, not as a sensational magic show. Use them understanding that the gifts and the giver are one and the same essence. The truth of who you are is the reality and not the experience.

When wisdom is the goal, you become a warrior who consciously defends his own spiritual integrity. It is best not to accept something as

BE: Embracing the Mystery

absolute truth unless you have tested the validity for yourself. The stronger the individual light, the greater the attempts that are made by those who are still wallowing in spirit ignorance to deter you from a foundation of strength. Those who live in the shadow of duality, separation, fear and hate shun the White Light. Fear in many is a negative use of faith. The White Light is used exclusively to restore and enhance life and to spread authentic love, peace, beauty and truth throughout the world. Life externalizes at the level of thought.

To see clearly the intent of another as well as establishing an assurance of your own relationship to God is to achieve a gift that will serve you well. To attain the goal, you cannot afford inattention. Fixed attention must keep pace with intention. The old ways are obsolete. Don't limit your life by that which has already occurred. The Eternal is incarnated in you and limitation is not part of eternity. Develop the practice of monitoring thoughts and feelings and question all responses.

Choosing regular and honest self-examination of intent and responses will create new energy patterns, which will work to free you from false judgments. To move forward spiritually, it requires flexibility and being responsible at all times. Responsibility is a state of being many people find difficult. To be in control is a new way of viewing life. Strive to see things as they really are. A soul in love with truth must keep the sacred fire from going out. One life is like a moment in evolution. Use it allowing truth to impress the soul.

Pure White Light is universal. It is the energy of the three highest heavens known to man. White Light is the original subtle matter created before the visible universe, as we know it. As a divine creation, it contains all the qualities and virtues of the Sublime Intelligence. We cannot live without the Light, whether it manifests as our Sun or the individual sun within. God is known through the Light both visible and invisible. The greater your love of celestial Light, the more you will attract and absorb it.

Begin regeneration by befriending and building an intimacy with the Great Light behind all creation. There are also students who benefit in meditating on the rising Sun, a magnificent symbol of the invisible Light. The morning hours are the best time to receive its powerful rays. Focus and meditate at that time and the pulse of the life force will help switch on your personal light. Light is a gift to life.

The Emptying

Think of light as God in manifestation. Concentrate on the image of light; imagine the Earth and yourself bathed in light. Do this discipline when alone and with groups of likeminded people. Perhaps, you have had the stunning experience of suddenly observing a physical landscape dramatically change to a subtle landscape composed of light. Matter disappears and the etheric blueprint of Light behind form remains. This is not imagination; it is a glimpse of the pure substance behind form. In my current embodiment, I have never experienced darkness. Meaning, if I am in a room devoid of light at night or any enclosure, I always see the etheric light as well as light manifestations from higher realms. Physical eyes are so used to observing matter that they have forgotten the light behind all materialization.

If you already psychically or spiritually see with physical eyes closed or have experienced flashes of activity from subtle realms, you know the truth of which I speak. The ideal of an awakening mind is to visibly and tangibly resemble Light. Personal awareness expands when others are helped who have less Light. The greater the attachment to the things of the world, the less you are able to love with intensity and vibrate in union with the Light. Connect and you will verify the truth of Light for yourself. Live your intent with intensity and the inner life will gain in strength and beauty. You will become radiant and intuitively recognize truth and be able to calmly handle it.

During ancient times, divine Osiris, Sovereign Intelligence, capable of unveiling everything, said when speaking to Hermes that as we cling to pure Spirit, we belong to the resurrected living. Research the great Initiates and Master Teachers and in so doing you will be delighted with the revealing accounts of the power and beauty of the Perfect Light. As you seek, you cannot ignore the material dimension. It is through the material dimension that you bring forth the invisible dimensions of Light. Action happens here in visible form. The ultimate goal is to be fully human and fully divine, united as one.

Manifestations of the spirit are determined by the degree of spiritual evolution. You evolve into an alchemist. By taking time transforming, purifying, and sublimating matter, you create a more pliant receptacle for Divine Light. Creative Mind requires a willing intelligence to accept and work with it. What must be transformed are the dense body, the emotions and lower mind. Become a scientist who allows the divine individuality to live freely rather than the little ego personality of the human nature. This is a proven way to be free from the world of limitation and yet live in it. The process prepares the soul to receive the gifts and enlightenment that is the nature of the higher Self. The higher Self will overshadow the lesser fields and personality, making its presence known in a powerful way.

The faculties and powers needed in order to transform conditions already exist as part of your makeup. All that remains is to believe and act. It is time to honor who you really are and not squander energy. Too much rushing and scattering of energy works against the brain and the soul. Life Force is precious. Stop using it on non-essential activities or people. It is possible to create a new and powerful identity by keeping an ideal always in mind. Put resolutions into practice. Persist in the right attitude. To be a whole human being, anthropos, cultivate the following: One, focus on a spiritual ideal. Two, be vigilant and learn to control negative emotions and past conditioning so they will not interfere with spiritual work. Three, gain knowledge, which equates to understanding of Universal Laws. Four, listen to the intuitive voice within. As the four areas are developed, you are cleansed of prejudice, old grudges, delusion and selfish desires.

As a result of personal spiritual evolution, many benefits manifest. As an example, the soul will eventually reach that special place in superconsciousness where a genetic weakness can actually be removed. Many of us have done this with ease. It is the Holy Spirit, Creative Mind in action, answering the call that corrects and heals when you passionately believe and use the science of thinking and cultivate a knowing mind. It is a good desire to benefit life. Opportunities will arise to help you be consciously aware of the power of the "Word." When you allow Spirit to give to you, it is like breathing pure air and drinking in Divine Light. Challenges present an opportunity to bring the holy part of the fabric of being into manifestation.

To bring in the new, remove the old. Anything can be reversed. Spirit will correct and assist. With willingness and readiness to receive, there is finally peace and a genuine happiness. God is known through love, receiving and giving. Once a commitment is made toward union of matter and spirit, the Kingdom of God employs you. The Kingdom of God is a state of mind that is harmony, a state of perfection, of absolute plentitude that contains everything good. Learn the power of the "Word" and Universal Law. In prayer ask for the Kingdom of God for all people. Everybody possesses a kingdom, but he has to find it. There is only one truth. It is hidden under every religion. As you journey towards perfection, the mind and heart is lifted above limitation and embraces the whole world.

If you study these words with both your mind and heart, you will detect the truth that humanity has been confused in many areas of life. Since the beginning, misinterpretation of pure teachings has been persistently planted within the mind and soul by people who did not fully understand the truth given to them. To tear through the veils of the ongoing deception that has entrapped the spirit, openness is demanded. Be willing to not only survive, but to persistently seek and be a living truth.

It is up to those who think deeply and sincerely care about life to empty themselves of all darkness and falsity. We must be wide awake and do everything possible that will expose truth, allowing the revealing Light of the higher dimensions to bring forth a healing of Mother Earth and all Her life. When we are knowledgeable, we see ourselves in all and all in us. We are forever free when we have broken out of the ego cage of I and mine and swept away the deceptive veils. When that luminous moment occurs, we are stunned by the hidden knowledge.

Chapter Twenty-Four
The Filling

According to legends, Earth has experienced worldwide destruction four times. Being a material planet, we are in our fifth creation. Will the past become our future? Civilizations have come and gone. As long as an individual expects salvation from the glamour often associated with an outside source instead of connecting to the Divine within, fulfillment will not be a reality. Souls on this planet have had a long history to realize truth and connect with the Divine. Because a genuine understanding, heartfelt love and respect for God and each other has been displaced, the world is again undergoing extreme changes. Not only is it mandatory that we make a serious personal assessment of the chaos that has been created, we need to take immediate action.

Collective humanity will lose what freedom it does have if the Source of our creation is forgotten. To be blessed, we must honor and understand what the Creator actually is. There are too many gaps. The gaps must be filled with truth. Humankind is in an advanced state of decadence between the lack of moral values, worship of money and obsession with material things. All are false gods. Humanity as a whole is deeply flawed. If we are to survive and change the outcome of the present cycle, we must embody the divine nature at the center of our being.

To be an enlightened civilization, it is necessary to be balanced spiritually as well as technologically. It is time we be people who are good and capable of love and compassion. The Feminine Energy, which is nurturing and creative, also needs to be recognized. Gratefully allow the compassionate energy to move into your consciousness. It is through the medium of Light and the power of the holy Creative Spirit that consciousness evolves. Survival is assured when we knowingly embrace Light, trust it, be it and use it. When we are filled with Light, we are a conscious living spirit. We have the power to reverse negative conditions and activity by bringing in and working with the fullness of the creative force. It is a communal movement of real love and inherent wisdom in action. When we are conscious of the Light, allowing it to penetrate and participate in our life, all the dark and oppressive clouds will disperse.

The secret is to think deeply, allowing the mind to be open to the Presence, Power and Activity of a higher Power. The Infinite can only be comprehended to the degree that It expresses through you. The message herein will hopefully impact in such a way that worldwide action will be taken to help pull us together before it is too late. A culture must always aspire to greater heights. We can experience heaven on earth if mass consciousness decides to empty itself of all that has worked against love, truth, beauty and harmony. A hole has been created and now we must fill it with knowledge and love. A higher help will come when we take responsibility for our thoughts, words and actions.

A soul is healed through belief and trust proving Divine Law. To create a transformation, deliberately choose and mold all thoughts and desires. A changed attitude towards Impersonal Law works in such a way that a new order is established. A new order is to declare the truth of the higher identity and live the connection. Only then can you develop and prove that Universal Law governs life. As an active conscious alchemist, you are then capable of being a center of divine attraction, reversing and creating a true and powerful design.

In each stage of matter, in each stage of life, spiritual intuition operates and acts from behind the veil. The intuition within develops according to the consciousness of the seeker. Intuition is a higher state where one goes beyond the thinking realm into the spiritual domain. The thinking mind must be kept flexible and controlled for the workings of a higher knowledge to come through unimpeded.

Physical form and the lesser mind have been manipulated by fallen mind energies separating man consciously from Divinity and full potential. Through individual effort, a heightened consciousness is gradually emerging. It is through a conscious awareness that the Divine is personally experienced and the lost inheritance regained. Religion as taught today offers only a glimpse of the immensity of the Infinite God and the Cosmic hierarchy. Now that people are asking for answers, more can be given.

If you are ready to mold your mind in line with the purpose of Spirit and universal understanding, you will discover that there is no disparity between worldly life and spiritual aspiration. Train yourself to look behind the appearance and see the blueprint of the Sacred. Discipline your thoughts to remain focused on Light, as you feel, speak and act from an expanded perspective. Seriously make an effort to believe and rely on the Cosmic Plan. Acquire the habit of scrutinizing and removing the falsity. The spirit Self is the eternal and real identity and not the familiar human personality, who is mesmerized by falsity and divided. All good progress is stored in the soul memory and will be put to a positive use, and not against Itself, in future incarnations. It is earned spiritual wealth.

There are proven methods that fill us with the power of God. Expanding the mind and dropping the undesired from our thoughts, forgiving and starting over will create a new causation. Embrace the universe, the stars, the soil, and the different kingdoms of creation and activate your cosmic self. Allow yourself to entertain the idea that perhaps your evolution began on some distant star. Allow your mind to willingly look at any creative possibility.

It doesn't help to cling to robotic thinking. Imagine how different life would have been if we had been taught as children about the Law of Causation and our role in the cosmos. The cellular memory of the universe is encoded in the cells of the body. We attract Light into our cells when we think and love deeply, take positive action and are consciously connected to our divinity. It is then that we have the companionship of celestial beings and experience the grace of the Holy Spirit.

Everything that appears in life is created by the mind. Everything is done by agreement. The requirements necessary in order to create a heightened energy, a being that is free from suffering and limitation, disease and yes, even the ultimate victory, conquering of physical death as it is commonly experienced, is an intense desire to return to original perfection. A right attitude and firm belief will set in motion the beneficial forces. A soul returns to completeness through its own nature. The gateway is the mind, which opens the door to illumination, realization, inspiration, intuitive perception and healing.

As hindrances are removed and belief strengthened, the inner presence begins to rule the mind. It is then that you have access to a higher vibration. The higher vibration will bring the hidden to the surface. To consciously cooperate in giving birth visibly and tangibly to the inner Self, investigate and see clearly all parts of the lower nature and heal them.

Be courageous and use curiosity and expose unknown facets of your self. Success is commonly called the second birth. To do so, the seeker must provide the right conditions.

The inner Light contains the blueprint and plan for perfection. Work in harmony with it. The process attracts forces and elements that help to move energy toward the ideal of perfection. The spirit is waiting for the changeable soul/mind to be receptive to its presence. The greatest gift is to move into a more complete expression of divinity. Understanding the history of the evolving soul produces clarity and liberation. Purity is essential for soul growth. Impurities create ongoing obstacles within the circulation of energy whether that energy is visible or invisible. Light does not make its home in impurities.

The world is called to express the Divine. The initial step is the acceptance that you will experience a conscious intimacy with the Source once you are fully awakened. This is a Universal fact. Next, take action to transform the human nature and remove any flaws. Evolution takes place on the Earth for the souls who are incarnating and therefore, the Earth is the proper field for soul progression. The goal is to establish the principle of a supermind consciousness in the Earth evolution. Plant truth in consciousness and deliberately nourish the divine thought until it bears fruit. The thinking mind cannot understand the supermind until it seeks and allows its Power to expand and express.

Do what represents who you are. The ideal is to bring the divine outward and establish a higher consciousness in the midst of disorder. If souls focus on this divine thought possibility, the supermind will support an increase of personal spiritual Light. The Law of Attraction will bring forth your ideal. The ultimate goal is to bring the higher consciousness into substance. This is the beginning of the Kingdom of God as a reality in matter. Your mind can help change the whole balance of the earth nature for the better. It is in your power to prove the Great Power behind Universal Law.

Superconsciousness is from the transcendent. It is a dynamic truth consciousness. With the inner spirit active, life will reshape itself. A different energy will emerge. Complete truth has not been openly manifesting on Earth. What humanity is experiencing collectively is a corrupted energy, which is fragmented and not full knowledge. Because it is not All-Knowledge, the mind today is ruled by limitation, conflict, confusion and error. We are obliged to reach higher. It is the superconsciousness that must rule. There is but one Mind. The conscious thinking part of Mind has the potential to evolve into a state of super consciousness. One must put aside resistance and the transformation will not be painful.

What occurs is a movement from the ordinary to the extraordinary, from happiness to an indescribable joy. With purpose a focus, you will experience a slow and beautiful efflorescence. Spiritual visions of gold may bless you. You will discover that one of the greatest moments of life are visions of mystic grandeur. The pure particles of gold shower you with gentle dust magic. In receiving, you are free to give the purity away. The supply is always replenished.

In your heart and mind, join us in the ever-expanding circle of light. We have chosen to establish the ancient science of wisdom and love not because of fear, but to fulfill our longing and passion for truth and freedom in the material world. It is time to gain possession of the lost dignity originally experienced eons ago. By shifting perspective, a new form is created that is ruled by the highest part of the Mind. The key is to sustain the field and watch the inner activity of the mind. Link yourself with souls who are similar in consciousness.

Ironically, with the expansion of inner light, you remain exposed to the darkness of the unawakened. This is in reference to the darkness of selfishness and indifference common in fallen mind energies/entities. The unenlightened are thieves. Once the Light is chosen, a soul may find itself involved in an invisible battle. The darkness in others, whether visible, invisible or negative thought forms, may try to exert an unhealthy influence. Be vigilant. Keep focused on truth and a lesser mentality cannot influence or take control.

My assignment is to encourage and educate people so they may understand and use God Intelligence. What we share, we must live. Light is a protection. Our ultimate aim is to produce light in everything we do. Spiritual light is tangible. It is universal. Light rises above individual spiritual beliefs and the teachings of the familiar religious traditions. When a strong moral code of conduct is developed and the heart is opened to subtle energies that are nondual, infinite possibilities manifest. Grab this opportunity to prove and live a direct relationship to the Whole. Believe in God living within you as power and reality. When you do believe in

The Filling

God within, you are compelled to believe in yourself. By deliberately educating the mind with a new awareness and power, a race of superconscious beings is created. It begins with a few individuals and then becomes part of the earth consciousness.

To remain impartial and not judge is a tremendous gift that works towards inner peace and the ability to live in an appearance world where collectively the two-legged creatures frequently appear to be insensible to the divine currents. Patience and trust in the unfolding process are strong allies. The view becomes a totally different perspective than the norm. Heightened awareness places everything and everybody in a revealing light. In the religion of the Hindus, Shiva, God, reveals in the *Divine Play of Consciousness* that the state in which one experiences God in everything and in everyone is the highest state of consciousness. Everything is a play of Divine Consciousness emanating from inside.

Storytelling is part of the shape-shifter's tradition. It is all about belief, intent, imagination, energy and faith. It is an excellent way to easily offer a message. The following is an amusing example, which clearly demonstrates a connection with the invisible realms, and one of my favorite "rescue" stories. In sharing stories, it does not diminish their power; a glimpse is given where the visible and invisible blend as one. The supernormal events are evidence of a higher Law and Presence. It is also a reminder that the Divine is right at hand, waiting, ready and willing to do for us all that we can believe.

A friend and I had been sailing. We had just finished a lovely afternoon in the sun. Once the boat was securely anchored, the next move was to step into the dinghy and row back to shore. While my friend was busy dismantling the sails, I gingerly stepped off the sailboat only to find that my foot could not reach the dinghy. Leg outstretched in a split position, it was obvious that in the next second I would drop into the choppy waters of Lake Michigan. Not only was I unable to swim, I was not dressed appropriately for a watery grave. Inwardly a call for help was sent.

A stunning turn of events immediately produced a rescue. My body was actually lifted into the air by an invisible power, carried faster than light to the dinghy, and comfortably deposited on the wooden seat. In shock and gratitude, I sat trembling from head to toe, relieved and stunned by the speed of the rescue and the disaster that could have been. Overwhelming feelings of gratitude and love enveloped my being.

BE: Embracing the Mystery

When a deep trust in the Divine is developed, we are privy to a very loving and cooperative relationship with Invisible helpers. When we accept and love them, they are eager to assist. If we have done our soul work, invisible, higher powers and sublime beings that can be trusted walk with us. When we have a deep yearning to fulfill God's Idea of perfection in matter, every individual interest is subordinated to the desire of bringing the Kingdom of Heaven to Earth. Our will and intention is comfortably expressing whatever is required of us. In the meantime, guardian angels and celestial friends truly care about our well-being. They also rejoice in human victories. I was deeply touched and grateful for their concern and immediate response.

Unity exists in the Higher Unseen Worlds as well as in the nature of our seen world. Understanding that the finite is a projection of the Infinite, we gracefully blend with the wisdom of nature and the wisdom of the Cosmos. Nothing of matter holds us, nor does clinging to life in a form. We free ourselves and see everything equally. Limitation of form slips away and we know who we are as an expanding higher mind and light. We are transformed. The Beloved and the lover unite as one and balance is achieved. God Realization as perfection is our inheritance, a treasure we have the right to claim.

As these words are being written, a dazzling, limitless celestial light is touching and surrounding my form. For many years, this particular visitation has periodically manifested. It appears as an infinite mystical stream of luminosity connecting my energy to the Celestial regions. The intimacy of the vision is a link that leads directly to the One Limitless Light, the Center. It also signifies change. Good in some form will manifest in a new way. The vision lasts for approximately thirty minutes. It is an intense and colorful pulsating chain of triangles vibrating as living Light. The power display mimics an umbilical cord connecting personal energy to the Impersonal Energy. The union reveals unearthly colors of vivid and luminous beauty, which permeate consciousness. Gold and white are the central colors. As the stream of intelligence increases in its majesty, I no longer am the observer. My being is filled. Light is the language of God and is used to lead us to wholeness and liberation.

A vast body of science exists concerning our relationship with the Earth and the attitude we should have towards her. Research this important truth and it will help transform your needs and benefit all the kingdoms of life. You will not only create personal changes and improvements, you will bring light wherever you go and to whomever you contact. Take time to go near moving water and see the image of the feeling source of life that flows through you. Attend to flowers and plants and ask them their secrets and listen carefully. Go to the Sun, the giver of life, and contemplate the symbolism of the Greater Light that invisibly sustains it. Open your aura to its warmth and pure particles. Everything in creation speaks. Start listening.

Evolution, whether it is physical or spiritual, remains a science. Love is an interaction between the two. Love is creating, being, unfolding and filling. This is real love. This is not an invention; it is reality. I wish for you a physical body, a mind and soul that are balanced and luminous, an energy that is wide awake and ready for action. Ask for Light and good will follow. You have chosen the best and most perfect activity. Your ideal is like a rope attaching you to heaven.

Chapter Twenty-Five
Truth

Let's talk about you. What is your truth? Have you forgotten it or are you allowing people, events or environment to prevent you from living your truth? Has this most important subject been given the thought it deserves? No one can afford to be negligent regarding the meaning of life and the destiny of the soul. Authentic freedom occurs when spiritual identity is understood and lived.

It is time to take a stand for the rights of your true Self. You have the choice to rebel against anything or anyone who is preventing you from realizing and living Principle. To evolve and be the wonder that you are, I urge you to go beyond your frame and see the vastness of the divine beloved within. It is through the union of the body, mind and soul that you are eventually able to remove the veil of illusion. Pythagoras taught that the experience of life in a finite, limited body was specifically for the purpose of discovering and manifesting supernatural existence within the finite. Your responsibility, dear friend, is to discover how the finite can express the power of the Infinite.

Truth is who you are. Do something greater, blow upon that inner spark until the flame arises. Learn to say no to everything that clouds your good. Honor the spirit within and come alive. An inner power will emerge. You will find that truth was never absent. Most people have no idea as to who they really are and what is to be accomplished in the flesh. Be different. Be in charge. Only you can live your truth and be your truth. If you desire happiness, completeness and love, do something about it. Trust, act and treasure the perfect Self within and ask for help from a higher Source.

Once you feel the inner power, there is no stopping you. The journey is about remembering, hope and sharing. The limited personality is like a huge wall creating separation from the Self of God. Let us together break down the wall. God speaks to everyone, not only the messengers and teachers we have read about. Remove the wall and identify with Spirit, which lives in light and eternity. You can still have the good things in life, but now there is a difference. They do not blind you. Your eyes are wide open.

A common madness in the world has dominated for thousands of years. It is selfishness and spiritual blindness. All the things that man desires and thinks beautiful must be sought and developed within instead of looking for them outside of self. Although recorded religions speak of loving God and respecting one's neighbor, the pain continues. Humanity doesn't fully understand the meaning of life. The physical world exists in the bosom of the world of Spirit. To explore finer vibrations, learn how to bring thoughts and perspective back to original identity. Generally speaking, people have lost an understanding of religion's origin, its spirit and its significance. Spiritually alive intelligence has a reverence for life and is genuinely concerned regarding the subject of mind and soul evolution and the care of the planet.

There is a shift occurring, an awakening to the true teachings that have been flaunted by the masses throughout the known ages. There are souls awakening to the fact that there is an abyss separating truth from fiction. The great Initiates have provided a bridge that is similar to the morning sun dissipating the mist. The Illumined insist that man must unfold his capacities for knowledge and understand his origin both physical and spiritual before any true peace and union can be attained.

There are souls on the planet who patiently wait for the collective consciousness to awaken from its slumber. The knowing and trust of those who care are a form of madness as well. Except, it is a holy madness, an inner drive that keeps life moving forward although the world appears as if it is self-destructing. It is a conviction that is in alignment with the Cosmos both visible and invisible. It is naturally understood that all life has the right to live in dignity and peace. The foundation of understanding is built on a pure healing balm of divine love. Souls, regardless of spiritual leaning, who have chosen a disciplined life, keep an open mind and listen to the intuitive voice. They are the "chosen ones."

It is the certainty of the immortal life that can form a solid basis for earthly life. Souls who have chosen self-mastery and are driven by a genuine kindness and concern for life follow a pattern. They achieve transformation through focused thought, listening and love. They choose to improve their ability to listen to the inner Voice of the Spirit in every moment. They use all their senses and remember what they learn. They understand that when harm is done to others or the lesser kingdoms destroyed, humanity is harmed.

The typical human is so absorbed in his personal drama that he forgets that he alone, through responses, has created his life and has the power to change it. It is time to wake up to the possibility of reaching beyond linear time. Truth is not the exclusive property of creed, caste or race. We are all the children of God. Develop a feeling of brotherhood and share helpful thoughts with one another. Also, align your mind and heart with our higher Brothers and Sisters of Light. When you do, a sense of intimacy with the Creative Spirit is gained.

Everyone, consciously or unconsciously, is striving toward spiritual attainment. The means is not always the same, due to past soul history and desires. A spiritual ideal is beyond religion because beliefs change as we spiritually evolve. Every forward step we take in both physical and spiritual evolution initiates a new chain of causation.

It is vital that a seeker properly understands and expresses intuitive knowledge. This is an art in itself. With a feeling of aliveness and hope, more souls are ready to receive and live the promise of a new cooperative life that is also shared with the angelic/higher Invisible beings for the advancement of creation. To choose to make contact and hold on to the highest part of our Self, we participate in a community of life both visible and invisible.

We become one with the All. Spiritual knowledge is practical and universal. It is available to those who are listening and ready to act. Earth is ravaged. As suffering continues, more humans will be forced to move from a materialistic worldview to a heightened spiritual view.

A being that elevates consciousness benefits all the created kingdoms. He is immersed in universality. He deliberately shapes his vibrations and in so doing has a positive effect on life and the environment. It is not only a personal act of love; it is an unconditional attitude embracing all of creation. We are moving into a period of evolution that revolves around the power of Light. We are slowly leaving a long cycle of darkness where the intensity of spiritual light has been at its lowest. We are living in a time of adjustment. This is a no-nonsense period when restitution and conscious awareness leading to a heightened spiritual growth is mandatory if souls are to survive, as vibrations descending to Earth increase in their intensity.

During a shift from one cyclic age to another, anything can happen. There usually is a series of disorders. Ancient secret knowledge is revealed and more spiritual Light and subtle energy is available on Earth as well as within individual intelligence, making the future quite different from the previous 6500 years. An amazing event happens, and triggers what occurs in the ages that follow.

God-realization is experienced through direct spiritual vision, communion with the Divine and intuitive cognition. In religious terminology, the Holy Spirit is the link between matter and pure consciousness. There exists a prophetic science describing a celestial energy cosmically timed to engulf Earth and her life at the end of the current Piscean Zodiacal Age. This teaching states that creation evolves according to a pre-set schedule and that a new cycle of Light will eventually be upon us. The coming Golden Age is an Age of heightened spirituality. There are many enlightened seers of the Biblical, Egyptian, Vedic, Taoist and Native American traditions who agree with this cosmic revelation.

When the energy changes without, it is also experienced within. We adjust on an internal cellular level. The external change includes our Earth and its solar system. What globally occurs will manifest regardless of what we personally do. How we are personally impacted is directly related to the level of individual consciousness and whether we have faith and a deep sustaining love for the Divine. All life will be affected on a subtle level. The spiritually unprepared may also experience unpleasant sensations in the physical body.

It is time for collective humanity to move forward and consciously receive more celestial Light into their force fields. The greater the power of compassion and unconditional love, the stronger individual light is. Any negative effects of global change will be absorbed because of preparation and knowledge and the deliberate integrating of the Divine light with matter. From both a scientific and spiritual point of view, a greater influx of pure energy will be in Earth's atmosphere, influencing all life. The new cycle of heightened energy opens the way for the balancing of the Masculine and Feminine Principles. More light and intensity means more creative power and creative power is feminine and manifests Light.

On a human level, the image of the creative power of the feminine has been distorted for thousands of years as the result of a patriarchal ideology. Historic negativity toward women has created gender conflict, ignorance, suffering and lies, both reducing the importance of the feminine and demeaning the reality that a woman has the sameness of a man within her. This sameness is found in the qualities of character that need to be openly lived so everyone can develop into fully enlightened beings. The idea is for women to become male and for men to become female. This means that we develop the strengths from each gender. In victory, we return to our original state of consciousness. The origin and home of perfection is transcendent.

The character of the Master Teacher Jesus is a perfect example of a complete human being. He fully expressed the positive feminine virtues when he nurtured those in need, was concerned for children, comforted others and struggled against oppression. Jesus fed the hungry, washed the feet of his disciples, openly wept and was confident in expressing intimacy. His behavior is particularly impressive because of the patriarchal time period.

What Jesus did was be an example destabilizing the boundaries between male and female. His teachings encourage gentleness, understanding and forgiveness as well as the male virtues of courage, strength and mental reasoning. Because the souls who lived during that time did not understand him, he suffered. His respect and love for the women disciples served to expose the falsity of gender identity and differences as not fixed.

Whatever gender we happen to be is fully capable of authority, responsibility, courage, strength, intelligence as well as love, compassion, perception and creativity. This sameness is for all of us. Whoever is gifted with the light of understanding must stand forward and speak. Regardless of gender, that individual has the right to act as a spiritual and intellectual authority. Women are fully capable of walking with God. The ultimate goal is to be fully human. We can accomplish anything if we fully understood what thought could do. Our present world can change into a kingdom of heaven as soon as the collective point of view has changed.

Both men and women need to develop character and nobility and be absorbed in the wisdom of the Absolute. Each of us is a unique soul who is required to go beyond the limited ego of the lower nature. We must remove the mask of personality and cease being caught in the shallow interplay of appearance. No one else will rescue us, whether it is a Master returned, an outpouring of the Cosmic Light, or a glorious Golden Age. God realization and enlightenment is not a giveaway program. It is an earned soul journey. Victory is realized through effort. The beauty of the divine drama is that in spending our lives focused on loving God first, honoring and expressing our inner Light and respecting all life, we are finally liberated.

Why not create a new human, a divine one? We are obliged to cultivate the truth that we are divinity. Life is inseparably linked to the past and the future. As we expand and elevate the vibration of personal consciousness, the result will provide positive programming for fresh experiences. Instead of remaining immersed in a psychic ocean, we build a shining future. Think about the immortal Self, visualize, communicate, and eventually the hidden will become a living tangible reality.

Whatever effort is put forth will remain with the soul and spirit regardless if we are in this body, the in-between worlds or a future incarnation. When we deliberately write our own book of splendor, we become the dance and the art and the poetry. Nurture the ideal and it will deliver the soul from duality and suffering. Whether it is a dream or an ideal imagined in the subtle worlds of thought, desire appears in the invisible worlds first and is destined to eventually materialize in the worlds of matter. The desire has been planted in the soil of Creative Mind.

Don't worry about the outcome or length of time it may take for union with the Divine to become a conscious actuality. Simply honor and love the journey. Realize the great truth that in desiring perfection in the human scene you are accepting spiritual identity. We must love who we are and what we are forming into existence. The ideal we create will determine every aspect of the new life. Knowledge, will power and belief will bring what already exists in the Divine dimensions visibly into the physical plane. We each become a light stream who is free to ascend, access and explore higher dimensions of thought and wonder.

Generally speaking, the purpose of creation is collectively ignored, laughed at, or totally disbelieved. The masses have been fixated on matter. They are not aware of our amazing potential and how we can evolve and access higher paranormal powers, mentally interact with subtle realms and receive higher knowledge regarding the many other dimensions of thought and light. Neither does the common man understand how all

BE: Embracing the Mystery

life is interconnected, whether that life is visible or invisible.

Consciousness will never rise to the heights as a collective energy if humanity continues to accept the ordinary philosophy of the masses. This truth has echoed throughout the centuries. The Greek philosopher Plato urged his students to transcend physical desire and move toward the purely spiritual or ideal. What he said then applies to now. "Strange times are these in which we live, when the old and the young are taught falsehoods in the schools of learning and the one man that dares to tell the truth is called at once a lunatic and a fool."

Earth is changing. We need in our hearts to understand and join the growing network of people who are doing something positive about the global crises of environment and culture. Education on how to respect and restore balance to our common foundation—the Earth—is needed. The bioelectric energy of the Earth is being profoundly scrambled and disturbed by modern technology. War is barbaric and creates toxins that kill on every level. Not only are careless and selfish thoughts and behavior destroying the balance of the planet, they are contributing to an invisible subtle energy field that must be cleansed and healed. If not, a good part of what we call civilization and its toys will be destroyed. Respecting and caring for the Earth is something all people can hold in common without dispute, thus providing a healthy survival for future generations.

Throughout the chapters, I refer to the Creative Power of truth as the Holy Spirit, a "Mother" symbol. Our inner spirit, when aligned with the Holy Spirit, is capable of offering wonderful works. In the coming cycle of heightened spiritual energy, the Feminine aspect of creation will be experienced as increased vibrations of Light. Remarkable gifts of the Spirit are given to those of pure heart and mind. Spirit and Light represent the Masculine and Feminine Principles of the One Mind. The two principles balanced within are referred to as the sacred marriage of the polarities. The symbolism of the Masculine and Feminine Principles is beyond the anthropomorphic forms of physical male and female. The infusion of power can either be an individual experience or a collective one.

It is destiny to become a finely tuned instrument capable of experiencing the Immensity, the Light and the depths of our own being. This is a scientific mental work that is nurtured through a feeling heart. We must be passionate, confident in reaching higher and merging matter with Spirit. Spirit speaks and acts through intelligence and form. The incoming impulse of the Creative Energy is the perfect power through which matter is spiritualized.

Joyfully accept your role as a part of a Divine family and take action. There is a new direction of spiritual and scientific studies quietly blossoming all over the planet. It is with a great sigh of relief that humanity is emerging from the darkness and regaining a firm foothold in the Light. Celebrate divinity. Join those who are seriously exploring and rediscovering both the history of evolution and the harmony of the spirit that have been lost from conscious mind far too long.

We deserve to understand the infinite possibilities of the mind and soul and comprehend our origin as spirit. Discovery will accelerate soul memory and give renewed hope and the missing peace that many long for. In so doing, the thinking mind is educated regarding the Universal Self and how intelligent vibrations shape us all. Unite the heart and intellect and we are capable to act as wisdom and goodness.

Eventually, humankind will realize that there is a harmony of wisdom and love pulsating throughout the eastern and western teachings. Soul theology will shift into high gear as we open the library of the ancients and finally reclaim our own cosmic citizenship. What is now being experienced on Earth is only one of many physical cycles of an evolving experiment. Life takes on a richer as well as a scientific understanding when attention is not only on the local scene but embraces the Limitless Light of unending creativity. A desire for truth is surfacing again in consciousness. Individually, we have a choice to regress or to move ahead and reclaim our position in the grand scheme of creative thought.

Use mind to create perfection, beauty and peace. Believe and be an artist at living. Create the life that you were meant to live. Use the Light of the Divine as a medium of expression. Be an artist of a higher Reality, a spiritual perspective. Wherever needed, mentally draw the Light around every living thing and object. Mentally paint an environment and self with the healing energy of Light. See the sun blazing in the breast of everyone. Look at others as souls hidden behind the flesh. This is a discipline that will create a harmonious and truthful reality. In gratitude and joy, work toward bringing forth a heightened energy.

Individually, we can transcend physical entrapment. We can become power and perfection, an offspring of God. Through a heightened understanding of science, unconditional love and wisdom, the Divine manifests in matter. Remember, the whole of creation is a result of order, harmony, and mathematical precision, a science that is available to everyone. It is our destiny to use the science of thought and unconditional love to return to an original state of spiritual perfection. Every advance we make in evolution makes life more valuable.

To create perfection is one of the reasons we are in the flesh. We are obliged to rebuild and spiritualize what we ignorantly diminished. The ancient wisdom teachers have always encouraged students to bring heaven to earth. When the spirit of truth is alive within, genuine joy is experienced, a joy that is sorely missing in the world of matter. Individually, we transform ourselves into the Christ energy, and the illumined energy will make lasting changes for the good of all life. Humankind will finally seek and obey universal laws of order, beauty and truth. Boundaries become a thing of the past as we become unlimited and live as Light.

Humanity is called to awaken. The ugly patterns of destruction existing for thousands of years must stop. Instead of selfishly focusing solely on physical and material needs, consciousness must expand and include the needs of all people everywhere. When we become universal in the mind and heart, we are healed of old wounds and false thinking. Knowledge and application of truth dissipate falsity. People need to learn why physical life was originally created, our purpose on Earth, the continuity of life, cause and effect, the moral code, and the variety of intelligences existing throughout the universes and hierarchal invisible realms.

To create harmony, return to the Cause and awaken to a higher form of thinking. What is truth? Answers will come in the days ahead. The real book of truth is found within the soul as it opens the door to hidden memories. Truth is the energy combination of wisdom and love balancing both sides of the brain and the masculine and feminine polarities as one unit of light, will and intelligence. The real and unlimited is waiting patiently to be revealed and lived. People are crying for the authentic freedom that only Spirit and its power can offer.

There are levels and degrees of enlightenment leading to full illumination. When we understand the movement of consciousness from simple to self to cosmic, we also understand that there is a vast unknown knowledge waiting for our discovery. We become a perpetual student. The journey will never be boring. People must have sufficient emotional maturity and understanding to hear and respond to a spiritual evolutionary call. Desire manifests according to the soul's awareness. Hold the thought of the world's people united as a family. It is time to remove all resistance and remove the chains that bind. Life can do for us only what it does through us.

To be finally at peace, assume a new role as a full participant in the unfolding drama of the cosmos. If this divine idea is ignored, an ongoing experience of separation and suffering will result. There will be disastrous events, gigantic upheavals, turmoil and many changes before a positive world is experienced as a sanctuary. The collective view must dramatically change. How can a sanctuary exist if reverence for life is lacking? The human race must have courage to evolve and experience the cosmos as a whole. Purification is required on all levels. The mind must be retrained, falsity unlearned.

Hearts must be tuned to a vibration where a feeling of oneness with all life is the foundation. Together let us be educated and awakened so we may do what is right and serve and succor humanity. Be gentle and strong, loving and yet powerful. Understand the science of mind creating and be the spirit giving. To know truth is an inner experience. True peace does not depend on conditions outside our selves. What we need to learn is how to become a pupil. The greatest teachers of the world have been the greatest pupils. Learning never stops. This is my truth.

Chapter Twenty-Six
Magical Moments

To put into words what is in my heart, the Indefinable, is not an easy task. My love for that which we call God is overwhelming in its scope. In peace and joy, I live with visions and healings, wonders and grace. That which I have grown to experience as my reality is offered below in the hopes that the examples will help clarify some of the questions you may have.

No human can teach spirituality. We can be an example and share our own experiences. There is only one teacher and that is God. Those who have a strong connection and hear the words within are pupils and revelators. One of the ways we reveal God is through the power of healing. Through healing, the soul and God are brought together.

A feeling of joy, gratitude and intimacy fills the minds and hearts of the healed. Their lives are changed for the better. There is also another aspect of healing that is revealing. It is the individual who decides that he or she would be better off if the healing was refused. People have their own agendas. If the old patterns no longer exist and some of these patterns had strong comfort or convenience levels, the one who is healed may decide the old way is better.

The love of family members for your health may be the trigger point for recovery. Sometimes their love is not enough because you must also have a fervent desire to be whole. If not, you will sabotage the healing energy that is offered although your words and actions appear otherwise. If you accept and act upon the wisdom knowledge through the direct experiences that are being shared with you, I have succeeded. You are your own healer. Keep this always in mind. This is one of the reasons that I have "moved" away from a ministry where physical healings played a major part. A patient must heal in consciousness first. Time is ripe for individuals to be responsible.

We have many options available to help us heal physically, emotionally and mentally. When we combine the offerings from earth with the offerings from heaven, a true healing occurs within that purifies the body, mind and the soul.

Fear Filled Choices:

I have already mentioned the young woman with cerebral palsy who did not sustain her healing because of a deep sense of guilt. There was another woman, a mother, who was healed of multiple sclerosis several weeks later and decided on her own that healing was not for her. Why? She was receiving a monthly disability check that was deposited toward her young daughter's future college tuition. Ironically, the husband could easily provide for the daughter's education but fear of lack prevailed. The mother chose illness and a disability check rather than wholeness and a pain free life. Although her healing was very dramatic while it was in power, she chose financial security over wellness. The woman was bowling, enjoying sex and doing all the normal things that had been missing in her life for years. Because of her choice, she gradually returned to her former crippled state.

Healing in the Unseen:

There have been occasions while involved with exorcisms when a departed soul has come forth and requested a healing. This has been true for suicides. One such soul asked if I would create a service with music, candles and incense for him because his body and soul were denied the experience. The more I observe, the more I am convinced that we are creating what happens to us, whether we are in a physical body or the subtle body.

Influence of Unseen Entities:

A soul vibrating in an invisible dimension can also cause a human to become sick or die. A young woman was brought to our home that smelled of death. She was anorexic. My friend held on to her very carefully as she gently helped her settle down into a comfortable chair. As I stood over her, I became aware of an entity, her sister, who had died last year. I intuitively knew that the deceased sister had also been anorexic. The "dead" sister was attempting to influence the living sister to stop eating and join her on the other side. Until that moment, the plan was working. I lectured the departed sister about moral issues and that it was time for her to leave the sister alone and move onward into a new life for herself. I also called reinforcements, angels, to come and remove the lingering earthbound soul.

The Holy Spirit stepped in and everything was corrected. Once the young woman became free of the attachment and the influence of her deceased sister, her health rapidly improved. The debilitating experience changed her consciousness. She decided to help herself and others. The young woman enrolled in courses of study that would provide education and treatment for ongoing health, diet and enhancing one's sense of self-esteem.

Spirit Knows Our Needs:

The Holy Spirit knows what is to be corrected. There have been occasions when the patient does not share information regarding the issue in question. I frequently learn of the results much later. A teenager came to me with a diagnosed growth inside her head. After we met, surgery was cancelled. Another woman asked that my hands be placed on her hands/wrists. Later, she casually informed me that her carpal tunnel surgery was cancelled. Recipients can be very nonchalant. They frequently assume the practitioner knows everything about them. The healing channel simply serves as a conscious transmitter or transparency of the sacred energy available anytime or anywhere. The only power that the "healer" has is his/her confidence, love, understanding and gratitude toward a Sublime Power that can be directed and received through unconditional love.

Healing is a Partnership:

A stranger came to a healing session in our home, never informing me of any of his concerns. He sat quietly in the chair. Months passed and one day a mutual friend casually mentioned that the gentleman's hearing had been corrected since the healing session. In his case, it was a gradual improvement over several weeks. With faith and confidence on his part, he kept offering gratitude for his perfect healing. Remember, a soul healing occurs first. Sometimes it takes cooperation from the patient for the physical healing to manifest.

Look for Cause:

There are teachings that state that specific parts of the physical body represent emotions attached to people, events and experiences that have occurred in the past. If there is a weakness in a body part, it can be corrected by looking for the cause, whether it is a thought, feeling, person, place or thing. This teaching has proven to be true. It could be something simple like a painful shoulder and arm being triggered by carrying too many real or imagined burdens.

There are causes for everything that happens to us. Once we are aware of the cause of the imbalances, it is up to us to decide whether we want the suffering to continue or not. Use self-analysis, prayer, contemplation and meditation and you may uncover the origin of the problem. Develop confidence in your Beloved higher Self and answers will be revealed.

Mind Over Matter:

There are always a few courageous people who decide to heal themselves when informed of any form of imbalance in the mind or body. They don't have the time for illness or inconvenience. They deliberately change attitude and lifestyle and with persistence, knowledge and a strong belief, many succeed. They reprogram thought, belief, feelings and actions. The emotions are intricately related to the health of the body. Strong and believing minds offer gratitude every step of the way, recognizing that God desires for us to be perfect.

Enabling a Critic:

In contrast, there are other people such as the elderly woman whose arm was damaged as a result of a stroke. After treatment, the arm became strong and useful. A couple weeks later, she called and said that she had decided not to keep the healing because her husband kept ridiculing and making life miserable for her. The ongoing criticism wasn't worth the healing. She felt he would be nicer if she was disabled and he had control of her life. Unbelievable, but true! Yes, there are people who allow themselves to be weakened and limited because they desire attention or release from responsibilities or simply wish to soften a miserable situation. The personality is in control.

Reverse Energy:

If you have someone close to you who frequently bombards you with negative words and actions, remain alert and do not accept the fear-filled energy. When a person feels happy and secure, loved and good about himself, he does not abuse self or another. The abuser is obviously miserable and is projecting his misery on whoever is near by. In this case, I am referring to a frequent misuse of energy and you being the target. It is also wise to examine criticism and determine whether it is valid or not.

Control Reactions:
If you allow an imbalanced person to convince you that you are less than you are, whose fault is it? Stress destroys on every level. It is best not to respond outwardly. Inwardly, do your own mental work and refute the negativity, stating firmly in your mind the truth of your own being. Think deeply. Ask what is really happening and don't allow anyone else to undermine your truth or energy. The choice is yours to play the blame game or not. Be in charge of your own mental atmosphere.

Reason to Live:
On another occasion while visiting a stranger in the hospital, I observed the woman carefully as she lay in bed with the family gathered around her. She had pneumonia, was on oxygen and also had cancer. I asked her if she wanted to live. She quickly replied yes, because she had an adopted daughter who needed her. The Holy Spirit gave me a vision of the woman in a black print dress quickly moving through her activities. I described the dress to her and she acknowledged that she owned a dress that fit the description. Then, I told her that she would be well; I had seen the future. The husband called the next day and said that her temperature had returned to normal and she was taken off of oxygen immediately after I left. She went home soon afterwards.

Choose Departure Time:
To a great extent, we determine both consciously and unconsciously what happens to us. Choices are constantly made on every level of our being. We appear to have a choice regarding the timing of physical death as well. We all know people close to passing who wait until after a holiday or special occasion to leave their body behind. Not everyone desires to be healed physically. There are those who feel they would have a better opportunity to offer help to others or simply be themselves if they were free of a body or mind that is handicapped. I have felt the joy of a departed

soul when it is finally free of a dysfunctional body or mind. The truth is that we are not meant to be imperfect and deep within us we know this eternal truth.

A Mother's Love:

There are times when a patient is not conscious or aware of a serious threat to his life. A young man had been in a very serious automobile accident and was not expected to live. When I arrived at the door of his hospital room, I waited. A priest was administering last rites. The young man's mother and friend were at the bedside. When the priest left, I entered the room. The two women later told me that they had to leave the room when I walked towards the patient because the energy that walked with me was very powerful. They both felt an electrical energy in their arms and hands, a vibration. The energy was the Holy Spirit. I don't recall touching the patient, only praying. The young man recovered.

Absentee Healing:

Absent healings are just as effective as being in the presence of the patient. There was a time in my life when I used Tibetan bells during a healing session. Some people feel something more is being accomplished when symbols or tools are part of the healing process. I received a call from a mother about an hour's distance away from my home regarding the serious illness of her young boy. The father was also by the child's bedside. The mother asked if I would call on the Holy Spirit to ring the bells. She already knew that my personality did not ring them. The Holy Spirit is the mover and healings would occur as a result of the bells clanging together.

The bells look like discs and are connected by approximately a foot-long thin leather cord. I hold them in front of me. Immediately, the Power comes and moves the bells and the healing begins. What was interesting was the fact that the father who knew nothing about the bells said to his wife, "I hear bells ringing off in the distance," during the time I was focusing on their son. The boy was healed.

The Innocent:

Animals are easily healed. They are innocent and do not judge. My first experience with an animal happened when our cat behaved so strangely that we brought him to a veterinarian for a thorough examination. He was always acting as if he was startled. The doctor included a hearing test. The sweet animal was deaf. We brought Rama home and offered his hearing to the Holy Spirit. He was instantly healed. On our own, we devised tests to verify the wonderful change that Spirit had brought about.

Use What is Available:

Whether you normally use traditional medicine or alternative healing products and techniques, your state of mind determines the outcome. Common sense is also vital. If you combine the power of love through directed thought and the faith of a heightened spiritual sense, you will heal more quickly than using traditional or alternative methods alone. Both the reasoning mind and intuitive awareness will work beautifully together when you combine them. Use whatever is available, but use it knowing that there is a grander power behind whatever method you use.

Healing Service:

Earlier in life, our family went to see a famous healer. Thousands of people came. Many were on stretchers or in wheelchairs. They came with hope in their hearts. Only a few dozen were healed. With flowing tears, I watched the disappointment and sadness throughout the audience. I am certain that the dear people who came, and some from great distances, questioned why they were not healed.

I have never forgotten that poignant scene and will address it from my point of view. If you are not physically healed through prayer or in an emotionally charged spiritual situation, do not condemn yourself. The action of healing is very mysterious and rarely understood by the thinking mind or the emotions. A profound healing of the soul could have silently and secretly taken place. Hardship is sometimes a tool used by the soul to awaken the personality to truth.

Mystery:

God loves you unconditionally. Clearly understand that your situation is not a judgment against you by God, but could possibly be an effect of an old cause. The cause has absolutely nothing to do with God or your spirituality; it may have to do with old memories, genetic tendencies, neglect, mistaken thinking or feeling. Our Creator never desires pain and imperfection for the offspring. There are many answers. We do not always know why something negative happens.

If you could look within your consciousness and turn back time, old stories and belief systems hidden in the subjective part of the mind may reveal the cause of current suffering. This does not mean the cause is either good or bad. It means that a condition was created in the past as a result of misunderstanding and the purpose has long been forgotten.

Understanding:

You may or may not be healed through prayer. This is a decision that is made at a very deep level. There is no purpose in blaming the past; it is over. There is always the possibility that what was created before can be removed today. It is not necessary to know the cause although it does bring more light and understanding to the situation. Perhaps, you do not honor your physical body. Perhaps, you need to love this moment of revelation in which you can finally forgive yourself completely for not being as great humanly as you judge you should be. Allow yourself to love totally and you can move closer to the perfection you seek. As the journey unfolds and is understood, you make yourself whole again.

Acceptance:

Sometimes, you must give yourself permission to heal. You may need to remove roadblocks that are hindering your path to living the best life that you can. When you refuse to love yourself, it is a form of abandonment. We all make mistakes, but that doesn't mean we must experience an ongoing punishment. Perhaps, you wish you had done things differently in the care of your body, career or in a relationship. Accept yourself just as you were at the time of the mistake and forgive. It benefits us when we learn from past mistakes and make better choices in present time.

Think Things Through:

It is important to think things through. When you do, you are more likely to make constructive choices. If you have high hopes for the grace of God to heal you, look deeply at the hidden corners of your life. Honest self-examination will reveal emotional issues. Emotional imbalances eventually create health issues. Understand the emotions; heal them and in many cases the body will respond.

BE: *Embracing the Mystery*

Learn from the Past:

When you forgive by accepting the person you are, it is easier to celebrate your own uniqueness. It is not healthy to punish yourself for a life that is less than you dreamed. Nor is it a crime to stumble and fall. You are who you are. Honor and respect your journey and forgive the mistakes made. This is how you mature. It doesn't help peace of mind or health to dwell on the life that might have been. Be thankful for the miraculous gift of life that you have right now. It is difficult for the soul or the body to heal if you have not sincerely forgiven self. This also holds true regarding not forgiving others. Your inner Self knows what is required for you to be whole again. Sometimes, it takes a health issue to reveal hidden parts that need to be healed. Embrace all options and do not judge yourself harshly.

There are No Failures:

If a physical healing does not occur, you have not failed. The efforts you make are never wasted. When your soul journey is viewed from the perspective of the Immortal Self, it is the healing of the consciousness that is of prime importance. Be grateful for understanding. Be grateful for love. Know that you are a wondrous, splendid, glorious being and it is a remarkable move toward wholeness when you shift your perception to a greater image of your self. When you begin to comprehend the journey of the soul, you finally know what a true healing is. Understanding is a magnificent blessing. It is a blessing that is eternally yours.

A Grander Perspective:

Why not be balanced in the mind and in the body? Great teachers have told us that we can experience Heaven on Earth. They tell us that we can be as perfect as our Creator is perfect. They are undoubtedly referring to perfection as consciousness. It is proven that through disciplines we can evolve our consciousness and attain self-mastery. Why not also be master of the cells of the body? Why not live for as long as we desire in good health and youthfulness?

Must the physical body deteriorate? What causes decay? Isn't it neglect and false programming? Neglect happens first in consciousness. If we change consciousness, would not the body eventually change as well? I believe we can be limitless. Of course, to achieve perfection would have been an easier journey if we were conscious of this possibility in the cradle. To discover an infinite possibility later in life makes the transformation a greater challenge. It can be done. Regardless of timing, why not try? Even if you do not reach your goal, a seed has been planted that will come into full bloom in another time and place. Think deeply about this. Why degenerate? Start changing your mind and you will change your destiny.

There are well-known spirituality teachers who have dismissed the importance of the physical body. Some barely tolerate it. I disagree. If we truly love the body and the Divine Intelligence that runs it, we experience our own personal paradise. The physical body reflects consciousness. Evolve consciousness and the body will eventually evolve. The physical body is meant to be beautiful, strong and enduring. The soul is given a greater opportunity to evolve when the body is healthy and fit. Isn't it time to expand thought and scrutinize other possibilities? If the mind and heart are pure, it follows that the body will be likewise. Perhaps, if more people would change their belief systems they would experience a perfect vehicle here on Earth. Why restrict the Self? Why not experience each day as magical?

Chapter Twenty-Seven
A Healer

Thirty-seven years of healing opportunities has provided the knowledge and experience to share these words. The examples described have occurred over the larger part of my life. Healing began in my own mind and body. A passionate desire to be free of any form of bondage and live as wholeness and truth became the measure for my life. My desire was to fully remember who I spiritually am and consciously reflect the Light. I have never known fear; the Power is from on High. I was and still am determined to live by the One Power and Presence and allow no thought, person or experience to deter me. I knew that with my healing I could help others heal themselves. Success attracts other souls.

You can be a healer not only of yourself, but a remarkable healer helping other people as well. Do not be intimidated by someone else who appears to have a greater spirituality or power flowing through him/her than you. They obviously have in the past accomplished serious study and application of universal principles and now their efforts are bearing fruit. You have the same spirit essence. The secret ingredient to your success is to fall in love with God. I cannot give you this gift. You have to seek it. Once you have attained the right attitude towards God and experienced the intimacy of your inner spirit, understanding is yours, power is regained, joy is infectious and you know what real love is all about.

Mental Tool:
There is a mental tool that will create a powerful healing. It is the tool of detachment. Learn detachment and you will be able to heal yourself and help others to be healed. Detachment from the influence of emotional energies will set you free. Yes, I have mentioned that our emotions serve us in myriad ways, but they can also hinder our goals when we become so embroiled in their influence that we can no longer be objective.

Negative Emotions:

Negative emotions can stagnate the soul. They can block any movement forward. If you live with someone who is constantly creating dramas that work against peace, God bless you. You have chosen an environment and family that will force you to take charge of your own emotional and mental nature. If you do not, you may possibly falter, be miserable and temporarily leave the path of the soul.

Damage Control:

To heal yourself, you must step out of your own "story." To help assist in the healings of others, you must not include your feeling nature in their story. Your true identity is spiritual. The dramas of life are created to force you to look at your eternal identity and do something about it. The soul makes a choice to live in a garment of flesh to experience itself as divinity in form. There is a pattern that goes with this choice. The average soul forgets its spiritual identity once it enters matter. Eventually, it awakens to its true sense of Self, but much damage may have already taken place prior to its awakening. The damage is conditioning, false judgments and belief systems that work against the soul's ideal.

Soul's Ideal:

The soul's ideal is to be a perfect being while it is here in the flesh. To be a perfect being, it must remember who it is, use its God given talents and not fall prey to falsity and delusion. That is a huge package to unpack and live. We are given reminders to help us regain our balance. The ideal can more easily materialize if a harmonious environment and spiritually active parents are chosen. This is seldom the case because the soul feels free before it enters matter and often judges it can meet any challenge.

Stabilize:

Although a healing has occurred, new issues may arise in the body, mind or soul if there is not a thorough cleansing of the subjective part of the mind. To stabilize a healing, a change in attitude supported by a strong understanding of the Universal Law of Mind is necessary. Meditation, contemplation and prayer will assist in discovering, facing and releasing false memories. You must consciously make the effort and probe for the hidden conditioning that is holding you back from conquering yourself.

Emotions:

Many diseases are the result of suppressed emotions. The feelings keep magnifying until disease is created in the body. What is interesting is the observation that strongly expressed emotions will also cause instability in the body. This is particularly true if the individual is sensitive to changes in energy. Obviously, strongly suppressed or strongly expressed emotions have a powerful impact on the health of the body mentally and physically. The condition of the body is an effect of the inner state of the mind.

Be Still:

Heartfelt grief over the plight of a loved one, friend or stranger, as well as the imbalanced state of the world consciousness and the abuse of our planet, can also cause serious imbalances in a sensitive individual's state of health. Be at peace within your self and then the surrounding energies will not harm your own sense of well-being. It behooves you to remember that every one is creating and living his personal drama. If you do your best to remain in a state of calmness, your energy will not veer off the path of balance and equanimity.

Learn When You are Well:

The time to expand consciousness and learn about the infinite possibilities available is when you feel well. Of course, few people think of this while they are healthy and life is pleasant. Thoughts, deep thoughts, usually arise when everything goes awry. When imbalances occur, it is best to review the truth of who you are and your purpose on the planet. All weakness, all ignorance keeps you from the truth of your being. In a simple prayer request, ask the highest part of you, the spirit, to take charge and direct your thoughts and feelings so you will act in the best interest of your own health and happiness.

Ask for Help:

There are beings in the Unseen vibrations that enjoy helping and they will if you are earnest, persistent, grateful and patient. They lead you to a book, an Internet connection, or an individual who can shed light on your challenge in a way that is beneficial. There are intelligences that will also send healing energy, a form of love that many desire to share with

Earth beings. Although help from the other side is wonderful, don't solely depend on it. You may fall into the habit where you become so immersed in relying on other entities/personalities assisting, that disempowerment of your own spiritual strength and talents may occur. The One Power will flow through you if you have prepared the way for Its love.

The Right Connection:

The being to consciously connect with is your own higher Self. Be intimate with it. Your higher Self is the real you. It wishes only good for you. Learn to trust its wisdom and love and follow the intuitive thoughts it sends you. You are destined to develop a working partnership with the eternal spiritual part of your Self. Use every opportunity that arises to strengthen the relationship. It is a friendship you can always trust. It will never leave and loves you unconditionally.

Allow Spirit to Be in Charge:

There is no spiritual law that supports disease, which is a form of falsity. What must be healed are erroneous beliefs. When you see and accept the truth of how you cause your own pain, lack and separation, the spirit of Life is able to help renew and rebuild your energy fields. You evolve into a harmonious person spreading vibrations of wholeness which fine tune the atmosphere to the pitch of your soul. The spirit within will create a healing in the mind and body if you allow it to take control, and not the limited sense of the personality. Remember, the physical body is a reflection of the subjective state of thought which is the vault of all belief systems. Your assignment is to illuminate thinking and not let the heightened awareness slip back into chaos and confusion. Adhere to constructive thoughts.

Understanding is Vital:

Before you can permanently establish completeness or perfection in the physical body, mind and life, understanding is required. You must learn how transformation actually works. There are attitudes and habits that require changing, such as fear, unforgiveness and doubt. What I share is not only my song but also the song of every soul, whether it is in a dense or finer form. If you stay with the understanding, nothing can keep healing from you except your limited sense of self. God is the life that keeps you in the body. If you forget the truth of whom you really are, your life energy is weakened.

Love Your Higher Identity:

Healing is about loving Self, the truth of your being. It is one of many ways to demonstrate understanding of what God is. You awaken to the joy of loving the truth of your own spiritual identity and the identities of others. Loving the unpleasant as well as the pleasant is another way of understanding, truth revealing itself. You are like a scroll unfolding memory of a beauty and magnificence that is beyond words or finite understanding. You are love rediscovering itself.

Personal versus Impersonal:

Some humans serving as healing channels shortchange power by believing that they are only transferring their own energy to the patient. If that is the belief, exhaustion may be experienced afterwards. True healing is an objective and impersonal attitude when the practitioner steps aside from his own personality and energy and calls on a higher power. When the Holy Spirit is active, both the transmitter of power and the receiver are energized and exhilarated. A true healing is more likely to occur.

Build a Strong Foundation:

Healing is a two-way exchange. Spirit offers love and perfection through the transmitting of the healing power. It is then the recipient's part to accept and hold an attitude of patience, trust and gratitude. This is why it is best to remain silent regarding issues of a personal nature because someone else can undermine your faith if personal faith is not built on a strong foundation. If you share thoughts and dreams or fears and doubts with another, the likelihood of corrupted thought from the other party might begin a process of erosion of your confidence. If you choose to share, only share with those of like mind.

Monitor Thought:

I suggest you make a promise of your intentions to the highest part of your consciousness. Remind your personality daily what is wholeness and what is not. When you deliberately allow no thought of depression, fear, or suggestion of imperfection to flow through the mind, you are well on the way of creating a new pattern of perfection for your own health and happiness. God's Nature is perfection. There are virtues and perfection hidden within. Man has abused his real identity. Monitor the patterns of thinking and you will be surprised by the positive changes in your life. Of course, to monitor thought takes discipline, but it is well worth the effort.

The Power of Words:

A serene, expectant, grateful and trusting attitude will mentally attack any appearance of imperfection. If you are called upon to help another, first make certain your mind is at peace. Begin your prayer or treatment with confidence and understanding and mentally state that all falsity is not of God. Acknowledge that your words are the Law of God being expressed through you. They have power to correct, transform, uplift, offer hope and give new life. Visualize the energy of the pure and perfect Holy Spirit cleansing your own energy first and then visualize and claim likewise for the recipient.

The Power of Visualization:

Clearly understand the power of imagination and thought. Visualize the love, light and life of the sacred substance of God permeating every atom of your force fields as well as the patient's. Know the highest truth of your own spiritual identity and the true identity of the individual you are helping. Offer joyful gratitude towards the Ever-present Power that has already done its job with ease and perfection. Remember to offer your love to the true nature of all intelligence, which is Divine. Then, with a sense of knowing that all is well, accept the patient's healing, trusting that the patient will accept the gift as well.

Answered Prayer:

When the Holy Spirit is involved, only a onetime healing session may be necessary. This will vary according to consciousness. The part of both the healer and the recipient is to keep the thinking mind focused on the healing as already accomplished. Don't question or doubt. Release the results. An attentive attitude of being blessed with the One Power must be the focus, otherwise other people who are not in the same harmonious vibration will cast doubt on the beauty and wonder that is taking place.

Exchange of Love:

Healing is natural. It is an act of love. It is an exchange between the inner Spirit, the conscious part of the mind, the subjective (soul) part of the mind and the physical body. Healing demonstrates unity, balance and our true nature. One must be like a trusting child to receive the full benefit of its grace. It is our Creator Parent giving to its offspring. It is a natural and total love when we are receptive to the idea that we are worthy to receive Good. Sustain a silent conviction; it is a perfect power.

Accept Identity:

To live and sustain a consciousness of healing in the midst of disorder and separation, one must be at attention and know with all his mind and heart who his true identity is and accept the truth of a living Christ within. Yes, Christ, the perfect being, lives within us and we live within It. Allow the perfect image to emerge in your mind and body.

Proving God is Love:

A healing challenge when embraced through love and the command for perfection will expand individual spiritual evolution. You are the doorkeeper to the mind and body temple. Constantly monitor thoughts. Do not allow false thoughts or unenlightened souls to interfere with your sense of what is and what is not. God is love. You can prove it through your own consciousness. It is time more of us accept this great truth and participate in joy and aliveness. One by one we awaken. In our awakening, we help others to do likewise. This is how we save ourselves and all life, including our precious planet.

Choose a Script:

When you understand that there are multiple parts to what is called the self, greater choices for good can be made. Each part has a script of attitudes and beliefs. When someone triggers an old part of you that is negative, you move back in time to a conditioned part of your mind that is dual in its nature. In other words, you tap into an emotional experience from the past. You can move backward or choose to change the reaction and move forward to a nondual place of light and freedom, the energy of the greater part called the higher Self. When you relocate to the highest part, you discover a different set of attitudes and beliefs that reflect a true spiritual identity.

Make a Choice:

If you really believe in the old scripts, you are held there playing out the old roles. The goal is to be aware at all times as to whether you are reliving a part of the past or activating a higher awareness that will serve you in grander ways. Emotional energy defines consciousness. The point of perception from which you view it creates reality. In every moment, we have a choice as to whether we live in duality or a higher field that is not polarized. You can deliberately remove yourself from the polarized field. Old scripts are movable. Healing helps you relocate into the higher Self where you may be fully conscious of your spiritual identity and power.

No Rules or Procedures:

I prefer simplicity. There are times during a healing session when sacred music is played and candles and incense lit. Some people expect ritual. Ritual is not necessary, although it creates a sense of familiar ambiance. Healings can occur at the strangest places or in the most unexpected moments. For instance, a male friend of mine was experiencing excruciating back pain and could not sit or barely move. He was lying in his car next to his wife. Climbing into the back seat, I told him that the spine would be corrected and laid my hands on him. The Holy Spirit knew exactly what to do. He was healed faster than it is taking for me to describe the situation. He was so startled by the speed of the healing that had crippled him off and on for many years that he assumed I had hypnotized him.

Everyone is Not Physically Healed:

Healing is required in the mind and soul as well as the body. The cause of a problem may be healed, but the physical counterpart may remain unhealed. Physical healing does not always manifest. There have been occasions where I feel an intense love and desire to help another to no avail. The patient's soul or subjective part of the mind has its own agenda, although outwardly the individual is pleading for help. Perhaps, the soul feels the personality needs further maturity or to love self more or cease feeling guilty. Only God knows the cause. This does not mean that that same person may not be healed at a later time. If there is any residue of guilt, resentment, condemnation or lack of self-worth within the consciousness of the patient, it becomes a challenge because resistance and fear of change can be in charge of the situation.

Remove Judgments:

For instance, if an individual has a set idea as to how he thinks a healing should occur, he could possibly block the natural healing flow by placing conditions on the healing process. Preconceived ideas of how healing should or should not work can hinder positive transformation. If you want to be healed by Friday at noon for instance, don't count on it. There is a higher power in control. If the higher power agrees with the conscious mind, your deadline will be reached. If not, you may have to wait longer. Whatever happens, Spirit provides greater results than you can visualize or imagine.

Release Results:

The soul can also use a weakened state or limitation of any type as a tool for drawing the personality closer to God. I've also observed that whether a person is religious or not has no influence on the outcome. I have been an instrument for wonderful healing results with people who others would judge as low life. It doesn't matter; God is All Knowing and All Loving. Results have a great deal to do with how we see ourselves and what we desire to manifest in our lives.

Be Wary of Making Predictions:

Thoughts are powerful. As an example, there are people who earlier in life actually make judgments on what their future will be, and later, when they reach the age that they have decided life should end for them, everything deteriorates and the prophecy is fulfilled. The self-fulfilled judgment can be reversed, but not everyone knows this truth. Our choices determine the future. Change the program and evolve by creating and sending opposing desires of health, joy and prosperity. There are universal laws of life that will help transform patterns. Become educated, act, and eventually you will function from a level that reflects the highest part of you.

Most people take the backdoor method regarding their health and spirituality. At one time, I offered classes that would help the participants face subconscious hindrances and fears. The classes were very successful but time consuming. I soon realized that if people really wanted to remove the blockages and falsity of old scripts and conditioning, there is a better way. The shortcut is the front door approach where you deliberately create as your primary focus an intimacy with your eternal immortal divine personality. Yes, it means that you are responsible for your own healing work. The results are revealing, lasting, exciting and very rewarding. When you understand that your current personality is only a very small aspect of what you really are and form a solid connection with your own Beloved, healing takes place and spills over upon others. Life will be a celebration.

Strive for Equanimity:

Everyone can serve as an instrument of love and compassion. My attitude is to remain objective, placing the personality aside. I observe and view every individual as a child of God, a spirit in form, who deserves to be whole, loved and happy. When we serve as a channel for the Holy Power, stability in mind and emotions is vital. Compassion and love are in force, but it is a higher Power that is making the "crooked places" straight. Silently reviewing in my mind the truth of my own spiritual identity and the patient's spiritual identity, I acknowledge the eternal Life that flows through us. Visualization is used declaring the completeness manifesting as perfection in the objective form.

Goal of the Soul:

We begin to understand the Power and Presence of God through healing. The Invisible becomes visible. Our inner nature is that same Power and that is where we are equal in substance in God's sight. Realizing, accepting and using the Power for good are up to us. God Realization in the body is the goal of the soul. Healing, whether it is physical, emotional or mental, is part of the process of our remembering spiritual identity and becoming visibly, tangibly who we are in the objective world of the senses.

When we heal, we feel a higher love. We gain the intimacy of God. Love is our power source. We attract to us what we believe. Freedom is the result of healing our soul, mind and body. All healing begins within and if the soul chooses, the healing will naturally work its way outward. We can be healed in a moment. The Spirit of you desires a stable home. It requires harmony to be Its Self. God does not favor suffering, lack and limitation. These are conditions created by the personality who has temporarily forgotten the true inner Nature.

Love Unconditionally:

It is God's good pleasure to give to you. Allow Spirit perfection to manifest as physical and mental perfection. Change the way you look at things and reflect your higher Nature. You must do this for yourself. In your prayers, contemplations and meditations, see the God part in others manifesting wholeness as well. This is the most loving gift you can offer another. See them joyful and complete. Although they may not resonate to your vision of them, the thoughts you are sending will not be wasted. Love is received on many levels. Hold that image and you will help raise not only your consciousness but also others' to a higher vibration of a light-filled life. Be confident and love unconditionally and wholeness manifests. Remember who you are and become a blessing to the world.

Be Conscious of Perfection:

Healing merges the individual spirit with matter, transforming the appearance through the conscious direction of the power of thought. I firmly believe the more stable and healthy we are in mind and body, the greater our ability to freely serve life. Anyone playing the role of the transmitter of the One Power and One Presence must be in a state of balance to be truly effective. The human personality is best forgotten during the treatment and the spiritual identity remembered in all involved. Healing occurs when we are conscious of perfection and unconscious of imperfection.

Do not make imperfection your focus. See balance and beauty, strength and wholeness. When you focus on flaws, negative energy increases. It is not a form of denial to see wholeness and beauty in its stead; it is looking at a grander possibility. When the focus is on what you don't like or want, the Law of Attraction brings more of the same to you. Focus on what you deserve and what you feel is good. If persistent and believing enough, the intelligence within the cells will eventually take you seriously and obey the thoughts sent by creating a new mold.

Beauty:

True beauty is not measured by the flesh's appearance. Beauty is the inner spark that illumines the body temple. Haven't you at one time or another observed what normally is judged as physical beauty, but the appearance, although seemingly perfect, was dull because the inner light was not shining? In contrast, you probably have seen individuals who at first glance appear almost plain, and when they smile, an unexpected beauty blesses you. The purpose of your being in the flesh is to remember your spiritual identity as a part of God and consciously live it in the world of matter. The more you remember, the greater the evidence of health and beauty.

Know Who You Are:

Spirit must be expressed if you are to be truly alive. There is no greater joy than to participate in cleansing and bringing forth healing and renewal. Do what needs to be done with a calm and unfaltering trust. When the truth of your spiritual divinity is firmly established in your mind, you know it. When you know it as your very own, you can heal yourself and others and bring balance to most situations that surface. The only Substance that is constant is Spirit. Everything else is fluid. Strong beliefs and words of power transform matter. Perfection is a natural law that man has temporarily forgotten.

Perception:

A practical demonstration of a belief in God is easily made manifest when fear and doubt are set aside. Petty things that poison consciousness limit the potential of your thought. With a heightened understanding, you become very careful of thoughts and the patterns they create. Learn to control what happens and life will benefit you and all those who come into your loving and peaceful vibration. Be gentle with yourself while learning to move your mind from old destructive scripts to a new script of giving birth to change. You give yourself hope when you have an awareness of the experience of God and the fullness of God's riches. The point of perception is your reality.

Love:

The Holy Spirit becomes a reliable source of power and renewal. Its Presence will go with you everywhere. I am urging you to allow the Power of God to work through and in you. When you are asked to pray for another or need help for yourself, why not ask yourself the following question? What would Love do? Believe in the intuitive thoughts that arise and be aware of the power of emotional energy. Emotional energy really defines what is going on in your mind.

Release Desires:

Be willing to allow your affairs to be controlled by Divine Intelligence. Maintain an unconditional belief that Spirit heals and all the false images stored in the subconscious part of the mind can be neutralized. When you move your point of perception, a psychological change takes place in the inner creative thought. The higher perception changes your entire life. Trust and let go. Your spirit life is forever. Enjoy it!

Suggested Healing Approach:

Acknowledge spiritual identity (self and patient).
Create and feel an intimacy with God.
Visualize and state prayer request.
Trust and surrender results.
Accept the healing as already accomplished.
Offer love and gratitude for the healing.

Chapter Twenty-Eight
To Be

Years ago, I read that approximately four-fifths of the world population feels that life on planet Earth is a trial, a time of testing and suffering. What does this indicate? A severe lack of true spiritual knowledge coupled with a strong identity crisis is holding the majority in a self-imposed prison. Collective thought demonstrates pain, separation, lack and abject misery. Many believe that joy only becomes a reality when they depart to the afterworld. You can help change collective thought by transforming yourself. If you don't like suffering, stop it! You are made of the same "stuff" as saints, mystics and saviors.

Since the majority of people focus on survival, spiritual evolution is basically ignored. Those who do focus attention on the Law of Attraction develop an advantage because they quickly learn how the mind works. Some use the power to amass great fortunes and easily control those who are either indifferent or too lazy to think for themselves. If a person does not think for himself and simply accepts conditions as they arise, he lives either by other people's rules or through his own past emotional and subjective conditioning, which can be nonproductive.

In direct contrast, we have always had great minds among us to lead the way. The problem lies with the followers. If a person struggles each day at a tedious job, supports a family, experiences health or relationship issues, it isn't easy to find time to ponder about what is true and what is not. Anyone in a confining situation benefits from mindfulness and not mindlessness.

Not everyone can make the choice I did. I literally stepped away from a day job, a social life and many activities that were an integral part of my life. As a result, I went into material debt, but the material debt cannot compare in importance to the inner riches I gained through available hours spent in deep contemplation, meditation and prayer. The way a soul can survive is to take charge and question everything and everybody

BE: Embracing the Mystery

and search for what is true and what is not. To not take some form of action is to kill the spirit.

When the facts of life finally strike emotionally and soul-wise, you may become upset with yourself. The shock is felt because you start looking back at the time wasted on nonessentials. It is one thing to read about a genuine closeness with God and another thing altogether to experience it. When you begin to penetrate the veils, it can be upsetting. Now is an opportunity to take control and change what has not been productive. You may think deeply, feel strongly, but it is up to you to change the patterns and do something about living from a higher perspective.

When you awaken to the fact that you have been fooled by minds with their own agendas, whether it is in the church, government, business, medical field, education or anywhere else, you may be sickened with disbelief. If you have already realized this, you know exactly what I am talking about. Please use your awakened grasp of reality and forgive yourself for being fooled. Every step towards the Light is enhanced when we forgive ourselves for past weaknesses. Each day is a day to give to your self the best life ever. Consciously acquire the habit of gratitude. You will find that you carry a magic wand capable of transforming everything by saying "thank you."

Everyone has his own set of challenges. The rich are not at peace, nor are the poor. Material possessions are not the answer. Be intimate with the Light that gives life. Feel and live the awe inspiring Love that sustains all creation. Truth and satisfaction are found in a happy soul. Realistically, everyone cannot take time out of life for a specific period as I did to find answers that are beyond linear time. What can be done now is to take quality moments, asking the inner spirit to help you evolve.

Take action. The personality can monitor what is allowed in the mind and what is sent forth. This sounds almost too simple but it will serve you well. Become a conscious thinking being, a soul who is in control of the inflow and outflow of energy on all levels of being. You become your own watcher. Analyze and do not accept something as truth until you have investigated all angles of it. Nothing is real unless you make it your own experience.

Some people are naturally deep thinkers and yet they may be missing the point of what I am trying to convey. Intellectual knowledge is only a partial answer and may through time be proven inaccurate. There is a higher knowledge that transcends worldly knowledge. To access the transcendent wisdom, you must also be able to transcend the human misinformation data that has been absorbed by the subjective mind throughout the ages. The source of knowledge is not only from the educated with strong scholastic credentials. One must be expansive and invite the intuitive part of the higher Mind to reveal Universal knowledge.

The human experience is a means for the inner Self to express in matter. For most souls, the journey has been a hard one. It doesn't have to be. A new road can be chosen when we become a deep spiritual thinker and ask the Universal Mind for answers. To be successful, develop pure intentions and a loving heart. Again, responsibility comes right back to you. There is a great deal to work out in the mind. This is the assignment of every soul. When you are willing to look at the journey in a new light, it becomes easier and very satisfying.

If you are ready to make the choice to cooperate with the higher Self, you will live as a conscious being rather than one who remains in the throes of subconscious emotional influences. You will no longer be led astray by falsity. You will understand that duality is simply a manifestation of unity. You will be capable of distinguishing between what is true and what is false. Because you have stopped clinging to dualism, peace is eventually yours.

Hell is a state of mind that is caused by stagnation, division and confusion. It is an emotional trap for those who refuse to think or to change. To know identity as light and then be in control of your life rather than being controlled is the outcome of choosing to be what you really are.

I have learned through pain that you cannot be at peace if you judge yourself short. This is a form of expectation. Simply be yourself, but be it naturally and with love. Pay attention to feelings and the words you speak and you will observe how every once in a while you undermine who you really are. Be gentle with yourself. When you live in matter the challenge of opposing forces is always present. Why add to these forces, which work against love and joy?

Love self as well as love others. We are all on the same journey. Be true to your own innate goodness. There are no rules that state that an aware or spiritually motivated individual should be a certain way, either in appearance or behavior, except that we not harm life.

Be true to your higher Nature. The truer you are, the happier you become. It is not necessary to accept other people's opinions and programs. Follow the Light and listen to the guidance of a higher love and you will delight in who you are with no regrets. Regrets come from unrealistic expectations. Do the best that you can at the moment. In trust, offer your hopes to God. Surrender creates results that exceed imagination.

It is not for you to fill someone else's mold, but to create your own mold of beauty and harmony that joyfully demonstrates your special uniqueness. Whatever you do, do with a feeling of lightness. Changes will come simply and effectively because what you do will have a joyful energy and not a heaviness. Be lighter and appreciate the ride because you are ready to enjoy the infinite possibilities waiting for you. Follow your heart and give whatever you feel is right to others knowing that you are giving back to God. In essence, you are giving to yourself. Be at peace for you are awake!

As you gradually purify and stabilize consciousness, Divine Energy is comfortably received. The power is transmitted from the higher star regions descending through the invisible higher parts of your being into the lower vehicles of matter. It is through alignment with higher energy that a human is educated and made whole. When you have established a direct connection with the eternal life force, you have also made a connection with brothers and sisters of Light in the higher worlds of divinity.

You may not be in a position to materially or physically stop a drought, world pollution, earthquakes, volcanoes, rising water levels, solar activities or celestial objects impacting Earth, but there is something you can do. You can simply be your higher Self. The result is regeneration and wisdom. To become wise, open your heart and embrace the great mysteries. As you awaken to the truth behind life, you join all those who have become stepping-stones for the whole Earth.

We transform darkness with the power of intention, attention, and the workings of the heart. Social regeneration is accomplished in the mind. We are moved to action through right motivation and right use. To survive, we cannot remain in denial pretending that there is nothing that we can do. The mind with a high ideal will accomplish the heart's desire. Demand truth and work in harmony. If we are to exist on a healthy planet and live together in peace, we must unite our energies. This is true empowerment.

We live in a time of partial truths. This is partly the fault of the majority because they have become lax and inattentive. Those who have a greater amount of freedom have become lazy, allowing the freedom experienced to insidiously degenerate. Suffering is the consequence because not enough people have cared to remedy the situation. There is power in dreams, visions and ideals. When we cultivate them, the wounds will heal and we can make a difference. As we heal, we become self-governing and equally informed regarding our spiritual, mental and physical nature.

We are the mystery. As it is embraced, life is good. We have a Tree of Life within that will grow, flower and bear fruit if we nurture it. We nurture the inner tree by being alive to infinite possibilities and a willingness to evolve. The divine part of us offers the personality life experiences where we can attain stability, integration and harmony. The spirit places the seal of eternity on everything. This is a workable map of consciousness that has been successfully proven by those who have chosen to evolve. The map may appear as a difficult assignment, but it is not the personality who fulfills it. When we are willing and allow our higher Self to be in charge, it smoothly runs the program.

To perfectly describe the Sublime is beyond my capabilities. What I have done is report firsthand experiences that expand the soul and make a spirit soar into regions humanly unknown. Angelic experiences, celestial visitations, departed friends and relatives, slipping through different dimensions and other hyperphenomena are rapidly manifesting all over the globe. Interaction has increased due to the times we are living in. Advanced Intelligence desires to help us, but only will through our permission and acceptance of multiple realities.

Look behind the words and allow yourself to feel the universal energy. Soul evolution is the greatest love story ever written. As you journey homeward, be calm and confident that there is a Supreme God and a hierarchy of invisible beings who genuinely care about you. Come to the realization of who you are and acknowledge your relationship with the Great Power behind All. You can be just as much of the Divine as you are prepared to be. You create your own drama, direct and act in it either willingly or unwillingly. Once you make a conscious decision to remove the old order and reestablish a new one, you seriously begin to transform your life.

There is One Self in the universe and that Self is looking through our eyes. Learn to appreciate the One Self as an extension of an indescribable Supreme and Infinite Spirit living as each one of us. A human being is unique and sacred. The mind is a stargate opening consciousness to infinite possibilities. The Mind of the universe is our mind. The identity of the Creator is our identity. Truth is realized as we learn to respect and trust the inner life and light. The inner essence is greater than anything of the world.

The world is tired of unsolved mysteries. Humanity is moving into an evolutionary cycle where there are no secrets. There is a thin veil between matter and spirit. When we consciously commune with the Divine, we penetrate that veil. A simple example happened as I was contemplating God's Ever Presence and love for us. I became aware of something hovering above my head. Looking up, I saw a huge hand with palm facing downward.

When we love God first and put our lives into the hand of the Divine, we are never alone. Metaphysically, the hand represents man's ability to grasp ideas and uphold sacred convictions. When we reach out and ask, God responds and we become a partaker of the Divine Benefits. Good always comes out of God's assistance. We are secure. Whether you witness the Divine or not, it is more alive and present than any other energy in the universe.

It is our responsibility to demonstrate supremacy of spiritual thought force over apparent material resistance. The Law of Spirit will find an outlet through our trust and understanding. It is an invisible actor. We get out of life what we put into it through trust and belief. Another opportunity is upon us to receive the scepter and ascend the steps to a loftier view. The ideal will manifest if we allow a sublime opening to flower within and exercise enough commitment, courage and strength to follow both the heart and the head.

Why prolong the journey? It is to everyone's advantage to evolve. No one can afford not to. Together, we can reshape patterns and create new horizons that complement life and do not destroy it. We can rule matter with love, integrity and belief if we place our intellectual doubts and conditioning aside. Together, we will walk on a pathway of Self-discovery. Destiny is what we are making. Divine inspiration and powerful revelations thrust us consciously into a direct contact with our interior reservoir, the sacred space between the mind and spirit. The inward authority dissolves the shadows.

God's Kingdom will exist on Earth in our personal experience if we understand God's Will. To understand Divine Will is to recognize that at no time can there be a sense of separation from the Supreme One. God is approachable and is creator of our spirit. God is a living Presence within us. The Aramaic word for "thy will" in the Lord's Prayer means "thy desire," "thy wish," "thy delight," or "thy pleasure." Our Source is similar to a good parent who desires the absolute best for the offspring. When personal will is in harmony with God's Will, the way is made clear.

To grasp the fullness of what I am sharing, allow yourself to fall in love. What you fall in love with is the Source behind All that has created both the seen and unseen. An intimate bond accompanies this amazing feeling with the wise inner Self. The love bond connects you to the pure and sacred energy existing everywhere in the universe. It gratefully embraces the hierarchies of beings who serve God and all life. A conscious connection has set you free.

Honor the truth of who you are and the truth of others and the Kingdom of Light is a constant companion. Renewal arrives daily. You experience a co-citizenship with higher evolution and give forth pure and unmixed Light. Strength and compassion surface as a result of a conscious God connection. The heart's desire is to live what is within and assist others in realizing their own spiritual identity as Light. What you bring forth is life.

To be victorious, unabashedly love truth and enjoy the play of the virtues. A point arrives in consciousness where spiritual integrity comes first. The tools are love, purity and gratefulness. Anyone can commune with holiness. Everyone has his place in truth. The All-Knowing One can be approached directly without intermediaries. Make your approach simple. Results depend on receptivity and understanding. Ask for more of everything good. Spirit only gives what we can take. The experience of a higher love that is imbued with Light must be nurtured.

When you make a choice to be who you really are, you make a covenant with God. As a result of the covenant, you are a strong living Light in tangible form. You emerge from the shadows into the sunlight. Spiritual senses and their gifts are used for the good of all life. You have the power to restore what has been shattered. Reach higher and live a more universalistic view where you actively participate in the repairing not only of your life, but help in the protecting and healing of the entire world.

There is a difference between the past and now. An increasing percent of souls are receptive, willing and intuitively ready to demonstrate a spiritual perspective. New choices are being made. Self-mastery is up to us. As intelligence with a spirit, we can develop to the degree where we have power over sin, sickness and death. It is only then that we can deliberately go behind the appearance form and manipulate flesh, creating a new mold that represents the culmination of our journey. A human has the possibilities within to conquer and be triumphant over any cross. We cease being helpless when consciousness is awakened. We are magnificent beings when we give ourselves a chance.

When truth is understood, accepted and lived, it diminishes ignorance, selfishness and fear, opening the door to eventual freedom from suffering. The revealing energy of a higher understanding is one of love, an unconditional love that does not leave room or entertain the thought of the need to suffer or to harm life, whether that life be our own or another's. In the light of truth and a pure love, it is finally understood that negative karma is a mental law and can be nullified through increasing personal light and mastery of mind. In living the Christ Principle, we realize that nothing is hindering us from the past or in the present that was or is real. What is mistakenly created in mind can be uncreated. When we have that conviction, we are free.

There is a Law which responds to every man's level of belief. If there is an accepted belief in a selfhood apart from God, this belief will produce suffering. Lift yourself into a new dimension of consciousness where limitations do not exist. In seeking truth, the principles are revealed. The One Supreme Indescribable Creator is the only Power in the universe. When there is only the One Power operating in your mind, pretenders will not be an influence. Understanding removes ignorance and fear. It is to your advantage to learn to do this.

We are in the midst of global change and no one can afford to be idle. Transformation is coming whether we are ready or not. A major turning point in history is in process. Open your mind and heart and receive higher knowledge. It will serve evolution for each of us to mentally transcend third dimensional limitations. When achieved, we become a keeper of the Light. With united effort, the human race will manifest an elevated state of mind and soul development. The soul must be nourished with the Sacred Fire. Give yourself permission to enjoy the journey into Self-discovery.

The pouring down from Heaven of the Holy Energy is already occurring. It is a fire of pure consciousness. It can be spiritually seen as White Fire, unpolarized energy. I have also witnessed the energy as a white pillar of dazzling Celestial Light with a pattern that resembles a string of triangles reaching from Infinite space to here below symbolizing the Knower and the known. This is our destiny. We can be a direct receiver and giver of divine energy.

We are here for the purpose of raising life to a higher level of expression. Spirituality is natural goodness. We experience the goodness when we fully recognize that God is personified as spirit in us, not a person. We are obliged to raise the conception of the Unseen All Pervading Presence from the anthropomorphic to the Spiritual. Our assignment is to joyfully transform the darkness into the Light. This is God's Plan ... divine humanity. Accepting the plan as our truth makes one feel like a bright balloon gracing a cloudless sky.

Some of you have already achieved self-mastery. Nonrecognition of what one has achieved may occur because mastery is usually equated with control over matter, not only victory over mind, emotions and actions. The truth of self-mastery must be recognized by the human personality. The personality will continue to hinder growth if knowledge and achievement is not accepted.

The sweetest personal moments are in the quiet stillness of communion. To rest with eyes closed, comfortably knowing that God is an immediate Presence and immediate experience is truly being alive. When the mind asks, "Why did the Supreme Spirit create me?" and accepts the answer, "So that the lover and the Beloved become One," the mystery is revealed. The intimate touch of the Beloved is always present, singing an eternal melody, pulsating in creative response, beckoning lovers to Its bosom.

I strongly believe in who you are. I know from my own journey that anything is possible. The sublime is waiting to bless you in ways far beyond hope or imagination. I believe in your inherent goodness. Accept the goodness and be free of restrictions.

Many of the acts in the visible world are outrageous. Simultaneously, there is a radiant beauty and hope behind the scenes. To understand that

BE: Embracing the Mystery

the old must be destroyed before the new can be fully experienced is wisdom. Be what you are. Yes, you are beautiful. Accept this truth and allow your mind and body to feel and express the wonder completely and joyfully.

To be one's true self is to be alive in the deepest meaning of the word. It is a gift. The more we gift others with what we have embraced, the less life will be a mystery. To fall in love is to be who you are. To be who you are is beyond words. It is an energy that heals and inspires. You are the mystery. Unveil yourself and the riddle is solved. The mysterious power of the inner Self is unraveled and the grace and glorious gift of Spirit is finally alive. You are aglow with the fire of immortality. Rejoice and be filled with gratitude. Stand tall, go forth, heal and bless humanity. Speak of their divine birthright!

I offer you my love,

Shirlee

Afterword

An Affirmation of Faith

I am being humanly what I am spiritually
My body is a temple for my soul
It is my church, perfect in its wholeness
I am the priest and my heart is the altar
My life will be one of love and service to my fellow creatures.

I am being humanly what I am spiritually
I recognize that it is I who transforms my human hood into spiritual hood
Through my thoughts and desires
I recognize that there is a universal harmony and I am an integral part
Of the whole
I accept God's loving grace and compassion and thus my body becomes
A sacred temple for the spirit of love to dwell
In humble thankfulness I look upon my mind and body as it becomes perfect
and energized in truth.

I am being humanly what I am spiritually
In faith I live knowing that God loves me
As I walk in newness and life, I offer my soul, mind and body to a life
Of spiritual awareness
As I grow stronger each day basking in the love of God, I give humble
Thanks for my many blessings
For I truly know that God loves me and thus I am humanly
What I am spiritually.

S.